COMMENTARY ON FILANGIERI'S WORK

BENJAMIN CONSTANT

# *Commentary on Filangieri's Work*

BENJAMIN CONSTANT

Translated, Edited, and with an Introduction by Alan S. Kahan

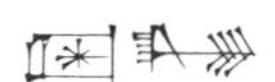

Liberty Fund

INDIANAPOLIS

This book is published by Liberty Fund, Inc., a foundation established to encourage study of the ideal of a society of free and responsible individuals.

The cuneiform inscription that serves as our logo and as the design motif for our endpapers is the earliest-known written appearance of the word "freedom" (*amagi*), or "liberty." It is taken from a clay document written about 2300 B.C. in the Sumerian city-state of Lagash.



Frontispiece: Portrait of Benjamin Constant by Lina Vallier (fl. 1836–52), from the Musée du Château de Versailles. Photo credit: Gianni Dagli Orti/ The Art Archive at Art Resource, NY.


Printed in the United States of America

C 10 9 8 7 6 5 4 3 2 1
P 10 9 8 7 6 5 4 3 2 1

Library of Congress Cataloging-in-Publication Data

Kahan, Alan S.
[Commentaire sur l'ouvrage de Filangieri. English]
Commetary on Filangieri's work/Benjamin Constant; translated, edited, and with an introduction by Alan S. Kahan.
pages cm
Previously published: Paris: Belles lettres, c2004, under title, Commentaire sur l'ouvrage de Filangieri, with the series Bibliothèque classique de la liberté, no. 2.
Includes bibliographical references and index.
ISBN 978-0-86597-882-9 (hardcover: acid-free paper)
ISBN 978-0-86597-883-6 (paperback: acid-free paper)
1. Filangieri, Gaetano, 1752–1788. 2. Filangieri, Gaetano, 1752–1788. Scienza della legislazione. 3. Political science—Philosophy—History—18th century. I. Constant, Benjamin, 1767–1830. Commentaire sur l'ouvrage de Filangieri. II. Title.
JC183.F4C66 2015
320.01—dc23 2014049745

Liberty Fund, Inc.
8335 Allison Pointe Trail, Suite 300
Indianapolis, Indiana 46250-1684
www.libertyfund.org

# Contents

## *Part Two*



## *Part Three*

# Introduction

Benjamin Constant's *Commentary on Filangieri's Work* (1822–24) discusses almost every important political and social question that Constant, one of the most important liberal thinkers of the nineteenth century, ever discussed. It bears on politics, economics, religion, and criminology. It contains extensive commentary on Montesquieu, Malthus, Turgot, and Adam Smith. It summarizes the mature views of an important writer who often changed his mind—and yet all this has not preserved the work from being out of print in French from 1824 until 2004, nor prompted anyone to translate it into English before now. While the *Commentary* has not been ignored by scholars, it has never received the attention given Constant's *Principles of Politics*, his writings on religion, or his novel *Adolphe*. Why? The reasons owe something both to the character of the book and of its putative subject, the work of Constant's not-quite-contemporary Gaetano Filangieri.

Filangieri published the first volume of *The Science of Legislation* in 1780, when he was only 28. The fifth volume (of a projected seven) was unfinished when the author died of tuberculosis, in 1788. All the volumes were translated and acclaimed throughout Europe and even the Thirteen Colonies. Benjamin Franklin read Filangieri and corresponded with him. Today, however, Filangieri is of interest to relatively few. This is not only because Filangieri was, as Constant puts it in this *Commentary*, a man of "uncritical erudition, and a mediocre intelligence."[1] Those traits were no bar to his international success in the late eighteenth century. Constant's *Commentary on Filangieri's Work* helps us understand why Constant is remembered and Filangieri forgotten.

1. See p. 228.

Filangieri's *Science of Legislation* was a compendium of Enlightenment commonplaces. Constant by no means rejects the Enlightenment, and he often lauds Filangieri's intentions, but the *Commentary* is a litany of corrections of the means Filangieri and many of his eighteenth-century contemporaries chose to attain their ends, informed by bitter experience, yet retaining hope and faith in human perfectibility and social progress. Constant's critique of Filangieri is a young Liberal critique of a well-meaning but ignorant and bumbling Enlightened parent. What separates Filangieri from Constant is the abyss of the French Revolution, and we are on the same side of that abyss as Constant. The presence of Filangieri in the title and to some extent in the structure of the work has done much to limit the attention given to it.

Why did Constant choose to comment on Filangieri? We do not know, exactly, but history and circumstances give some hints. Constant had been aware of Filangieri's work for some time before he published the first volume of the *Commentary* in 1822. Constant had served briefly as a member of the Tribunate, one of the Napoleonic legislative chambers. The president of the Tribunate, Gauvin Gallois, was Filangieri's translator. He, or simply the wide renown of Filangieri's work, may have introduced it to the young Constant. But Constant's acquaintance with Filangieri went beyond the superficial. From 1806 he refers to it in the manuscripts of the *Principles of Politics Applicable to All Governments* and with particular frequency in *On Religion*, where he takes Filangieri to task for his understanding of Greek religion, a theme he returns to in the *Commentary*. However, familiarity with the work does not explain the decision to write about it. That decision may have been encouraged by Filangieri's resurgent popularity. *The Science of Legislation* was seen by many as a blueprint for a moderate constitutionalism, and in the Restoration era of the 1820s, this led to three Spanish and three Italian editions being published between 1820 and 1822, culminating in a new French edition by Constant's publisher in 1822. After the second part of the *Commentary* was published in 1824, it was bound and printed together with this edition. At the time Constant wrote it, a commentary on Filangieri might reasonably have seemed both a timely subject and a good means of creating a summary of his own views, in contrast to those of the Enlightenment represented by Filangieri.[2]

2. See Antonio Trampus, "Introduction" to the critical edition of the *Commentaire sur l'oeuvre de Filangieri,* in Benjamin Constant, *Œuvres complètes,* vol. 26, *Commentaire sur l'ouvrage de Filangieri,* edited by Kurt Klocke and Antonio Trampus (Berlin: De Gruyter, 2012).

The *Commentary* is indeed a summary of the conclusions of a lifetime of reflection. In his book on Constant, Stephen Holmes writes that "throughout this study I have taken the *Commentaire* as a yardstick by which to gauge Constant's mature views." But it is noteworthy that this remark appears in a footnote. Other leading commentators have referred to the *Commentary* as the "most complete and bold statement" of Constant's economic views, and his "*ultima verba*" in political philosophy. Nevertheless, while scholars have always been aware of the work, from the time of its publication onwards it has been the subject of little or no sustained discussion in its own right.[3]

This is despite the fact that the *Commentary* treats subjects, such as poverty, immigration, and the slave trade, that drew a great deal of attention as the nineteenth century went on. Like his fellow French liberal, Alexis de Tocqueville, Constant fell into a certain mitigated obscurity in the decades after his death, and for somewhat analogous reasons. Both Tocqueville and Constant suffered in the public imagination for what was perceived to be their lack of interest in social questions, particularly poverty and class struggle, during a period when those questions increasingly preoccupied French society. Speaking of Constant, Helena Rosenblatt writes that "indeed, there is very little about poverty or class antagonism in Constant's writings, which gives him the appearance of having been relatively unaware of or unaffected by working-class misery and industrial unrest." The *Commentary* is counter-evidence to this statement. Had the work been better known in its time, Constant might have retained more interest. Like Tocqueville, Constant was preserved from complete oblivion by the enduring reputation of a single work. What *Democracy in America* did for Tocqueville, *Adolphe*, his romantic novel, did for Constant. But *Adolphe* did nothing for Constant as a social and political theorist.[4]

3. Stephen Holmes, *Benjamin Constant and the Making of Modern Liberalism* (New Haven: Yale University Press, 1984), p. 269, n89; Kurt Kloocke, cited in Alain Laurent, "Préface" in Benjamin Constant, *Commentaire sur l'ouvrage de Filangieri* (Paris: Les belles letters, 2004), p. 8; Laurent, "Préface," p. 8. An exception to the lack of sustained discussion is found in Jeremy Jennings, "Constant's Idea of Modern Liberty," in *The Cambridge Companion to Constant,* ed. Helena Rosenblatt (Cambridge: Cambridge University Press, 2009), pp. 69–91. The *Cambridge Companion* should be regarded as the first place to look for anyone interested in the current state of Constant scholarship.

4. Rosenblatt, "Eclipses and Revivals: Constant's Reception in France and America, 1830–2007," in *The Cambridge Companion to Constant,* pp. 354–55. For the texts of the handful of reviews of the *Commentary* that did appear, in French and Italian journals, see Antonio Trampus

However, readers will also see reasons why, despite the fascinating material it contains, the *Commentary* may have had difficulty in attracting attention. The book's organization is loosely patterned after Filangieri's. *The Science of Legislation* consists of five long volumes of an unfinished seven-volume work, and the *Commentary* effectively consists of two short volumes (the two parts of 1822 and 1824). The resulting problems of organization were never really solved. As Constant says in the opening "Plan of the Commentary," his chief point of diversion from Filangieri is that he prefers to leave to free choice what Filangieri wishes to see regulated by the state. But if the plan states Constant's overall perspective, it never provides the reader with any scheme of organization for the discussion. Constant bases each chapter on a topic and passage taken from Filangieri, and he follows Filangieri's order of proceeding, without ever giving an overview of the topics Filangieri discussed, and indeed skipping most of them. The result is that Constant's work does not have a very clear order, although very roughly the first two parts concentrate on the proper sphere of government, part one mostly devoted to legislation in general, and part two mostly devoted to economic regulation in particular. Parts three and four center even more loosely on criminal law and religion. The lack of focus that often afflicted Constant's writing is evident in the *Commentary* as well.

Nevertheless, the *Commentary* is a work of great interest, partly for what it says in itself, and partly for what it says about Constant, who since his period of relative obscurity in the late nineteenth and early twentieth centuries has come into his own as one of the leading figures in the creation of modern liberalism after the French Revolution. If Emile Faguet perhaps went too far in claiming that Constant "invented liberalism," he certainly played a seminal role. His well-known distinction between the freedom of the ancients and the freedom of the moderns—the former based on the primacy of the public sphere in antiquity, the latter based on the primacy of the private sphere in modern commercial societies—has become fundamental to much political thought.[5] That distinction was made in Constant's famous Royal Athenaeum speech of 1819 and in a less-famous passage in his *Principles of Politics* of 1810.

and Kurt Kloocke, "Reactions to Benjamin Contant's *Commentaire sur l'ouvrage de Filangieri,*" *Annales B. Constant*, 2012, no. 37, and 2013, no. 38.

5. See Emile Faguet, *Politiques et Moralistes du XIX*[e] *siècle* (Paris, 1885), art. "Benjamin Constant."

It is present in the *Commentary*. But Constant's work covered much more than that.

The *Commentary* is founded on the view that government should be limited to a strictly negative role in society: ". . . the functions of government are purely negative. It should repress disorder, eliminate obstacles, in a word prevent evil from arising. Thereafter one can leave it to individuals to find the good." "The functions of government are negative: it should repress evil, and let the good take care of itself." These two statements are found near the beginning and end of the *Commentary*, respectively. They act as bookends for all that comes between. This is Constant's political and economic credo, which finds expression in the *Commentary* in a variety of ways. Most of part one and much of the book as a whole is taken up with debunking Filangieri's and by extension much of the Enlightenment's and many of Constant's (and our) contemporaries' belief that legislation is all powerful, and that the legislator can single-handedly shape human societies in the desired way. The limits of legislation is a theme Constant repeatedly returns to, coupled with the corollary that in attempting to legislate for the good of humanity, despotism is often the unintended consequence. From legislation in general, Constant finds his way in part two to economic regulation in particular. The transition between politics (legislation) and economics passes through a relatively brief but ferocious denunciation of the evils of slavery and the slave trade in the French colonies. After this passionate plea in favor of government intervention (with the negative aim of preserving freedom), Constant proceeds to an extensive discussion of economic regulation. Here the first thing to be said is that Constant takes a resolutely liberal, *laissez-faire et laissez-passer* (a phrase he quotes, in whole or in part, on several occasions) view. The *Commentary* shows that in Constant's case there is no distinction to be made between economic liberalism and political liberalism. They both derive from his commitment to individual freedom.[6]

Constant's discussion of economic issues is broadly construed. Besides rejecting government intervention in the market, he discusses such related topics as Malthus's theory of population, the problem of poverty, and taxation. He proclaims himself a reluctant convert to Malthus's view of the inevitable growth of population up to and beyond the means of subsistence, but

6. See p. 3.

he rejects Malthus's remedies. Constant shows a great deal more sympathy for the poor than Malthus, and he refuses to legally discourage the poor man from marrying, despite the advice of both Malthus and Sismondi (Constant compliments Sismondi's *New Principles of Political Economy* on several occasions, but explicitly rejects it in this context). In the course of defending the poor person's right to marry and have children Constant draws a picture of poverty that shows that he was by no means insensitive to its hardships:

> It is not enough for you that the proletarian resign himself to have no part in any of the goods of which you possess a monopoly. It is not enough for you that he renounces fire, land, water, even air, for his condition obliges him to sometimes descend into the depths of the abyss, sometimes bury himself in workshops where he can barely breathe, and always to deprive himself of what he produces for you which he sees you enjoy at the price of his fatigue and sweat. One consolation remains to him, a consolation which Providence, touched by pity, has spread among all beings—you dispute his right to it. You want that that faculty given to all, of which the animals themselves are not deprived, be forbidden to your fellow because he is poor. I repeat, there is in this at least as much imprudence as iniquity.[7]

Constant's solution to the problem of poverty is freedom. He rejects the English Poor Laws' limitation on the freedom of the poor to move in search of work, as well as the restrictions on their right to enter a trade, requirements for expensive apprenticeships, etc.: "The poverty of the laboring class cannot be denied, and the laws of England are in this respect as absurd as they are atrocious. They weigh on indigence, they dispute its legitimate use of its faculties and its strength, they make its sufferings eternal, for they take from it every means of arriving at a more fortunate position." Given this situation, "the poor tax, a tax so regrettable in many respects, and which England will suddenly free itself from by a return to the principles of industrial freedom, is a kind of restitution consented to by the monopoly in favor of those whom it deprives of their rights." As a means of combating poverty in the long run, the *Commentary* goes on to champion parents' right to bequeath their property freely, rejecting both English entail and the Napoleonic Code's forced division of property among children: "When the disposition of property is free, it tends to division." Once all land has been made freely alienable by abolishing

7. p. 103.

entail, the actual cultivators of the land will be able to purchase it. This is important, because "when the poor man can acquire even one field, class no longer exists, every proletarian hopes by his labor to arrive at the same point, and wealth becomes in land as in industry a question of work and effort."[8]

Freedom—of movement, of industry, of trade, of bequeathing one's property—is always for Constant the best available remedy to any problem. A partisan of liberty, Constant is a partisan of a strictly limited government. But freedom can exist only with the aid of a government that is powerful in its proper sphere, which is negative yet crucial. Government naturally requires taxation, which for Constant is a necessary evil. He prefers taxes that "weigh equally on all, proportionally to their wealth." His suggestions favor an element of progressive taxation, and a combination of direct taxation and consumption taxes. But one form of tax he absolutely rejects—taxing capital, because this means destroying future economic growth.[9]

Constant's discussion of the justice system in part three raises many issues, some of them familiar to us, others less so. He devotes considerable effort to rejecting Filangieri's contention that only private individuals, rather than government officials, ought to be allowed to prosecute those they consider criminals. One of the consequences of modern liberty's preference for private life will mean that in this case too many crimes will go unprosecuted. He also defends the jury system. In an anticipation of William F. Buckley Jr.'s remark that he would rather be governed by the first four hundred names in the Cambridge phone book than by the faculty of Harvard, Constant says he would rather face a jury of twelve uneducated workers who owed nothing to the state and feared nothing from it, than one composed of twelve members of the Académie Française who all hoped for a government promotion. Curiously, his defense of the death penalty is based on consideration for jailors. Being a jailor, according to Constant, is inevitably morally corrupting. Being an executioner is worse, but we will need far fewer executioners than we otherwise would need jailors; therefore, better the death penalty than prison. Readers will be relieved to learn that Constant rejects the death penalty for crimes against property, and reserves it for crimes against persons.

The fourth part, shorter than the others, is divided between a discussion of

8. See p. 112.

9. See p. 160–61.

education (comments on which are scattered through the work) and religion. Constant champions freedom in the educational sphere as well. He fears both government political indoctrination and incompetence in a state-run system. The extent to which he wishes to banish government from education is not entirely clear, however. On the one hand he states that "Education belongs to parents, to whom the education of children is confided by nature. If these parents prefer domestic education, the law cannot oppose it without being a usurper."[10] On the other hand he also says that "One can look at [education] as a means of transmitting to the rising generation the knowledge of all kinds acquired by preceding generations. From this perspective, it is within the competence of government. The preservation and increase of all knowledge is a positive good. The government should guarantee us its enjoyment."[11] His conclusion is that "Public education is beneficial in free countries above all. Men brought together at whatever age, and above all in their youth, contract by a natural effect of their mutual relations a feeling of justice and the habits of equality, which prepare them to become courageous citizens and enemies of arbitrary power. Even under despotism, we have seen schools dependent on the government generate, despite it, the germs of freedom which it tried in vain to smother."[12]

Constant's final discussion of the origin of religion is full of references to his work *On Religion,* of which the first volume had already been published, and whose remaining three volumes were much on Constant's mind at the time. Constant mostly devotes himself here to disputing Filangieri's account of the origin of religion in general and of Greek and Roman religion in particular. His dislike for a priestly caste, evident throughout his writings on politics and religion, is prominent here too. It is in this section that he is most harsh toward Filangieri. The book concludes with a passionate defense of the freedom of thought, no matter how pernicious the ideas expressed may be. Constant was a thorough liberal, as can be seen from the *Commentary*'s final words: "Let us therefore cross out the words *repress*, *eradicate*, and even *direct* from the government's dictionary. For thought, for education, for industry, the motto of governments ought to be: *Laissez-faire et laissez-passer*."[13]

10. p. 28.
11. p. 219.
12. p. 223–24.
13. p. 261.

# Translator's Note

As the translator of Benjamin Constant's *Commentary on Filangieri's Work* I have, like Dennis O'Keeffe in his Liberty Fund translation of Constant's *Principles of Politics*, striven to "retain as much as possible of the general elegance and subtle rhetoric of Constant's writing while seeking to render it in accurate, graceful, and accessible English."[1] This has meant breaking up some of Constant's very long sentences, and lengthening some of his very brief paragraphs by annexing them to preceding or following ones where appropriate. As conventions change across times and languages, translations must change with them. The intention has always been to give the English reader of the twenty-first century the same ease and comfort that the French reader of the nineteenth century experienced when reading Constant. However, it must be admitted that in Constant's *Commentary on Filangieri's Work* the quality of the writing is very variable. Constant could write with elegance and subtlety when he wished, but he did not always take the trouble to do so. Nevertheless, for the most part even when Constant is not elegant, his meaning is clear, and the task of the translator is in this sense a straightforward one.

In certain respects, however, any translator of eighteenth- or nineteenth-century French social thought has to make choices that are less than straightforward. It is only proper to give the reader fair warning of how some of the most important of these choices have been made. For the word *liberté*, which presents the translator with the alternatives of "liberty" and "freedom," I have generally chosen *freedom*, on the grounds that *liberty* has an increasingly archaic or historical ring to readers today. The French terms *lumières, pouvoir,*

1. Dennis O'Keeffe, "Translator's Note," in Benjamin Constant, *Principles of Politics Applicable to All Governments* (Indianapolis: Liberty Fund, 2003), p. xi.

and *autorité* have been translated into the appropriate English words—words plural, rather than singular, because the meanings Constant wished to convey by those terms varies and depends on context. Thus while Constant most often used *pouvoir* and *autorité* as synonyms for "government," he sometimes used them in a more abstract sense. In those cases they have been translated accordingly, as "power" or "authority." *Lumières* has been translated as "education," "knowledge," and more rarely "enlightenment," depending on context. To those who argue that a word has only one meaning for a given author, I can only reply that this sort of consistency, if it is ever to be found in any writer, is not present in Constant's writings.

Whether the result of these choices has succeeded in producing an English-language text that is faithful to Constant as well as to both the French and English languages is a decision that must be made by the reader. In making my choices I have been greatly aided by my editor at Liberty Fund, Christine Henderson, and by the reader for the project, Jeremy Jennings. To both of them go my thanks for their help. All remaining inaccuracies and needless infelicities of style are the responsibility of the translator alone.

# COMMENTARY ON FILANGIERI'S WORK

# *Part One*

# CHAPTER ONE ❧ Plan of This Commentary

When I decided to add a commentary to the work of Filangieri, I was moved by two considerations. First, I took pleasure in rendering homage to the memory of a writer who deserved well of his country and his century. Second, his work's flaws gave me the opportunity to correct his ideas when they were wrong, to develop them when they were lacking in clarity and breadth, and finally to combat them when they were not fully in accord with the principles of political and, above all, of individual freedom, which I consider the sole purpose of human association, and which we are destined to establish either through progressive improvement or by terrible but inevitable convulsions. Filangieri never intended to contradict these principles, but the time when his book was published, and his personal character, noble and completely disinterested though he was, sometimes prevented him from marching with a sufficiently firm step along the direct path to truth.

One cannot say of Filangieri, as one can of Montesquieu—that ingenious and profound observer of what exists—that he was often the subtle apologist for what he observed. The immortal author of the *Spirit of the Laws* was frequently a zealous supporter of inequalities and privileges. He looked at these things, which had been consecrated by time immemorial, as constituent parts of the social order. A historian more than a reformer of institutions, Montesquieu asked no more than to preserve those institutions while describing them. However, his genius, and the bitterness inherent to genius, sometimes dictated language to Montesquieu that thundered against the very abuses for which his habits and social position inspired him with partiality and indulgence. Filangieri, on the other hand, was more distant from aristocratic prejudice than Montesquieu, and he did not disdain to declare himself a reformer.

He did not conclude that because something existed it ought to be respected, and if his will alone had been enough to destroy them, all abuses would have disappeared. But Filangieri did not have Montesquieu's genius. A sort of gentleness or reserve in his character led him to make concessions contrary to his principles, whereas the vehemence inseparable from a powerful mind forced Montesquieu, despite his moderation, to pronounce decrees which were incompatible with his concessions in favor of established systems. The result is that Filangieri, after having taken up the pen with a more hostile intent than Montesquieu, in reality fought abuses much more feebly. His attacks became compromises. He tried to mitigate evil rather than eliminate it. In his work there is a humble and painful resignation which often bows before the power it does not hope to disarm. Before the formidable revolution which shook and still threatens the world, perhaps this resignation was not imprudent. If men had been able to obtain redress for their grievances by reason mixed with prayers, rather than conquering it with blows which harmed the victors as well as the vanquished, perhaps things would have been much better. But today the price has been paid, the sacrifices consummated on both sides, and the language of free peoples, addressing themselves to their proxy-holders, cannot be that of subjects having recourse to their masters' pity.

One will thus find me frequently opposed to Filangieri, not as to the end, but as to the means. To make my idea clearer, I will give an example: Filangieri shows on every page that he is convinced that hereditary privileges are oppressive and harmful. However, he proposes the sacrifice of their prerogatives to the nobles themselves. By enlightening them with arguments, touching them with pleas, and putting before their eyes a picture of the evil they cause and which rebounds on them, he hopes to move their souls. He bases the success he flatters himself with on their generosity. Like Filangieri, I am persuaded that aristocratic inequality is a curse, but it is not from those who profit from it that I expect deliverance. I expect it from the progress of reason, not among a caste, but among the masses in whom strength resides, and from whose midst, through their representatives, reforms and the institutions to preserve those reforms will come.

This difference between Filangieri's doctrine and mine applies to everything which concerns government in general. The Neapolitan philosopher seems to always want to give government the job of limiting itself. In my opinion, this burden belongs to the nation's representatives. The time is past when it was said that everything should be done for the people, not by the people. Representative government is nothing but introducing the people to participation in public affairs. It is therefore by the people that everything is now done for the people. The functions of government are known and defined. It is not from the government that improvements must come, it is from opinion. Transmitted to the masses by the freedom which its expression should have, opinion returns from that mass to those whom it chooses as its organs, and thus rises to the representative assemblies which pronounce, and the councils of ministers which execute.

I think I have indicated sufficiently how the commentary diverges from the text. What Filangieri wanted to obtain from government in defense of freedom, I want a constitution to impose on the government. In my opinion, the advantages for industry that he begs from the government ought to be conquered solely by industry's independence. It is the same with morals and the same with education. Where Filangieri sees a gift, I perceive a right. Everywhere he calls for protection, I demand freedom.

As for the other flaws with which one can reproach Filangieri, in this respect indulgence is justice.

It is true that in this author one finds many maxims which appear trivial today. But in 1780 they had if not the merit of being new, at least that of being very good to repeat, for governments which already disdained them as commonplaces still treated them as paradoxes.

Filangieri often indulges in overemphasis and declamation, but he was writing in the presence of abuses, and one should pardon a little verbosity to conscientious indignation. He was also much more a well-intentioned citizen than a man of vast intellect. Revolted by the sufferings of the human species, and struck by the absurdity of some of the institutions which caused these sufferings, he seems to have taken up the pen much more as a philanthropist than as a writer led by his talent. He has neither the profundity of Montesquieu, nor the perspicacity of Smith, nor the originality of Bentham. He discovers nothing by himself. He consults his predecessors, gathers their thoughts, chooses those most favorable to the well-being of the greatest number, whose rights he establishes only in very diluted form, and arranges the materials gathered from the sorting process into the order which seems to him most convenient. This order itself is not always the most natural or the best. Filangieri wastes time proving what no one doubts, and he devotes entire pages to arousing feelings of enthusiasm or indignation in the reader's soul which the author of the *Spirit of the Laws* produces in two lines. But even in the Neapolitan author's wanderings we find a consciousness and love of the good. Since, when his book was published, opinion tended to favor improvements and recognized the necessity of limiting despotism, it is always in favor of improvements and in honor of freedom that Filangieri digresses or declaims.

From this characteristic of Filangieri (and I borrow this observation from his translator's preface), it follows that his opinion does not rise much above public opinion as it was forty years ago, and certainly the public opinion of that time was very much below the public opinion which thirty years of struggles, revolutions, and experience has educated. But this mediocrity of reason, if I may be permitted the expression, is in my view the chief advantage of Filangieri's work for us. We find in Filangieri's work the means of assuring ourselves of the progress of the human species in legislation and politics over the past half-century, and of comparing the principles formerly accepted by very enlightened men in these matters with those which are now the object of our examination and our daily debates. If this comparison leads us on the one hand to reject those exaggerations as the fruit of inexperience, which makes the best theories inapplicable; and if on the other hand it prevents us from falling back, by a retrograde impulse, under the yoke of the prejudices from which our predecessors freed themselves; the work for which Filangieri has served as the spur rather than the guide will not, I think, be without all utility.

According to the account I have just given of this commentary's plan, it is clear I had the choice either of following the thread of my own ideas, while recalling Filangieri's, or of subordinating my work to his and adopting the order of contents found in his work. The latter choice seemed preferable to me, even though it often made me separate what I would have liked to combine. But the reader will find it easier to juxtapose the commentary and the text, and when there is disagreement between Filangieri and his commentator, to decide between them.

## CHAPTER TWO ❧ From an Epigram by Filangieri against Improvement in the Art of War

> The sole purpose of all the calculations which have so long disturbed rulers' councils has been the solution of this problem: How can one kill the greatest number of men in the shortest possible time?
>
> INTRODUCTION, P. 1.

If one reads Filangieri with some attention, one notes several flaws of which there are examples in our eighteenth-century writers. One of the most striking is the need to make an impression, which led these writers to look for unexpected turns of phrase in order to give themselves an air of boldness and novelty. The definition of the problem which the sovereigns of Europe sought to solve by perfecting the art of war is strongly tainted with this vice. Certainly, there are many things to be said about rulers' mania for war, and about the guarantees to oppose to this mania. But an epigram which tends to error is certainly the worst beginning one could imagine. By creating the presumption that it is only going to be discussed with exaggerations, commonplaces, and jokes, it discredits in advance the examination of an important question.

Here, it seems to me, are the series of ideas which the Italian author ought to have followed in this respect. There are periods of society when war is part of human nature, and necessary to peoples. Then everything which can render war terrible, and thus shorter, is good and useful. Consequently, when the government concerns itself in such times with discovering "How can one kill the greatest number of men in the shortest possible time," the government is engaged in useful research, given the circumstances. For as soon as it is necessary to kill enemies, it is better to kill them immediately rather than more slowly, so as not to have to go back and do it again, and it would be desirable to find a sure means of killing today all those whom tomorrow one would be forced to kill all the same.

But there are also periods of society when, civilization having created new relationships between man and his fellows, and through them a new nature, war is no longer a necessity. Then one should apply oneself not to making war less deadly, but to putting obstacles in the path of all useless wars. Now the question is to know which of these periods we are in. It is obvious that we find ourselves in the second.[1]

Why were the peoples of antiquity warriors? Because, divided into small tribes, they fought, arms in hand, over a narrow territory. Because they were thrust against one another by necessity, they constantly fought or threatened one another. Even those who did not wish to be conquerors could not lay down the sword, under pain of being conquered. All bought their security, their independence, their entire existence at the price of war.

The world of today is in precisely the opposite situation from the ancient world. While each people formerly constituted an isolated family, the born enemy of other families, now a mass of men exists, under different names and various forms of social organization, but homogeneous by nature. This mass is strong enough to have nothing to fear from still barbarous hordes. It is civilized enough for war to be expensive. Its uniform tendency is toward peace.

We have arrived at the period of commerce, a period which must necessarily replace that of war, just as war necessarily had to precede it. This is not the right moment to discuss all the consequences of this change which, as I have just said, gave man a new nature. I will come back to these consequences later. It is enough to have stated the principle.

The period of war being over for modern peoples, clearly it is the duty of governments to abstain from it.

Yet so that governments do not deviate from this duty, it is not in government that we should put our trust. For governments, war will always be a means of increasing their authority. For despots, it will be a distraction they throw to their slaves, so that they feel their slavery less. For the despot's favorites, it will be a diversion they use to keep their master from understanding the details of their maladministration. For demagogues, it will be a way of

1. I have developed these ideas in my work on *The Spirit of Conquest*; I am only repeating them here.

inflaming the multitude's passions, and of leading it to extremes which favor their violent counsels and their partisan views. Thus, if one leaves governments—and under the name of governments I include all those who take power, demagogues as well as ministers—if, I say, one leaves governments free to start or prolong wars, the benefit peoples ought to receive from the progress of civilization will be lost, and wars will continue long after the time when they are no longer necessary.

It is therefore by taking the question of war away from rulers' arbitrary choice that we will succeed in preserving the governed from it. But how can we remove this question from rulers' arbitrary choice? By a representative constitution, according to which the nation's delegates have the right to deny the government the means of undertaking or continuing useless wars, and which subjects the holder of power who engages in such enterprises to a grave and inevitable responsibility.

This prejudges nothing about the question of the right of making peace and war proper, such as it has been discussed in our assemblies and such as our present Charte[2] decides. That in emergencies the constitutional monarch should have the prerogative of declaring war at the right time is a pure formality, provided that the funds necessary to sustain it can be denied to his ministers, and that these ministers are responsible for the declaration which they have suggested to the king.

We already see in this question (and it will be the same for many others) that the solution to the difficulty depends on the establishment of constitutional guaranties. Filangieri only obscures the question by a misplaced epigram. If war is necessary, the government is right to "want to kill the greatest number of men in the shortest possible time." As soon as war is unnecessary, it is criminal to undertake it. The number of dead and the instruments of destruction are irrelevant.

2. French constitution of 1814.—Trans.

# CHAPTER THREE ❧ On Encouragements for Agriculture

> We have not thought about rewarding the intelligent farmer.
>
> INTRODUCTION, P. 1.

Here already we perceive a symptom of Filangieri's mistaken system with regard to the influence of government protection. As he constantly comes back to it in his work, I am going to take the first opportunity to refute him here. But I must go back to the origin of his mistake, which was that of many enlightened men of the eighteenth century.

When the philosophers of that period began to concern themselves with the chief questions of social organization, they were struck by the evils produced by government's harmful interference and inept measures. But being novices in this science, they thought that a different use of that same authority would do as much good as its misuse had done harm. They did not recognize that the vice was in government intervention itself, and that rather than asking the government to act differently, one ought to have begged the government not to act at all. Thus you see them call the government to the aid of all the reforms they propose: agriculture, industry, commerce, education, religion, education, morality. They subject them all to the government, on condition that it act according to their views.

The last century counts very few writers who did not succumb to this mistake. Turgot, Mirabeau, and Condorcet in France, Dohm and Mauvillon in Germany, Thomas Paine and Bentham in England, Franklin in America—this is just about the list of those who recognized that, for all kinds of progress as for all kinds of needs, for the prosperity of all classes as for the success of all speculations, for the quantity of production as for its balance, one needs to trust to freedom and individual interest. One needs to trust the energy which inspires man to exercise his own faculties, and to the absence of all hindrances to it. The others preferred protection to independence, encouragements to guaranties, advantages to neutrality.

For the most part, the economists themselves made this error.[1] However, this was all the more inexcusable since their fundamental principle seems as if it ought to have preserved them from it. *Laisser-faire et laisser-passer* was their motto, but they applied it to hardly anything except prohibitions. Encouragements seduced them. They did not see that prohibitions and encouragements are but two branches of the same system, and that as long as you accept one, you are threatened by the other.

Of all the professions, agriculture was the one the economists most wanted to raise up from the degraded state into which it had fallen. Their favorite axiom, that land is the sole source of wealth, made them attach extreme importance to the work which made it productive. They became justly and legitimately indignant when they saw the oppression of the class which, in their eyes, was the most indispensable and hardest working. Thus arose their chimerical projects to raise up this class, to give it prestige and even fame.

The idea of giving rewards to the "intelligent farmer who, by his work or by new methods, had found means of increasing the public wealth" is therefore not Filangieri's at all. He could borrow it from the economists, for example from the marquis de Mirabeau,[2] author of *L'Ami des hommes,* but he seems to have been particularly attached to this idea. He comes back to it, more insistently and in more detail, in another part of his work (bk. 2, chap. 15). Trumping his original proposition, independent of monetary rewards, he wants to create a medal which would be worn by the sovereign himself, and with which the best farmers would be decorated.

If one considers the period when Filangieri proposed these childish and bizarre expedients, one will understand their absurdity. It was a time when the agricultural class was subject to laws and paid taxes which no representative they had chosen discussed or consented to. A time when, without a voice with which to make requests, or means to defend themselves, they submitted

1. By *economist* Constant is here referring to the writers often known as *physiocrats* in English.—Trans.

2. Mirabeau the elder.—Trans.

in silence to these biased laws and unequal taxes. A time when servitudes of all kinds weighed on them, interrupted their work, troubled their rest. A time when, finally, placed on the lower rungs of the social hierarchy, they bore all social burdens without appeal, for all the other classes pushed the burden lower down in order to exempt themselves.

To these misfortunes which were, so to speak, legal, let us add the occasional oppressions which resulted from this agricultural class's isolation, poverty, and defenseless position. These oppressions derived from the immense distance which separated the agricultural class from the supreme power, and which condemned its groans to vanish in the air; from the insolence of the intermediary powers which cut off its complaints; from the ease of oppressing, with or without the law, men equally ignorant of the laws' threats or their protections; from the rapacity of the treasury which spared the rich, and which had to compensate itself at the expense of the poor. This arbitrariness was all the more unchecked because it was exercised individually on obscure victims, and spread among a crowd of lesser agents, viziers of the village, pursuing their evil in the shadows. It was in such a situation, and as a remedy for such a situation, that Filangieri proposed encouragements for agriculture and honors for farmers. But agriculture had been struck at the root. The means of reproduction had been taken from it. Farmers were little islets, stripped of all their rights, burdened with all the work, condemned to all manner of privation. Even with good intentions, the government could not heal this incurable wound. Nature is stronger than the government, and nature wills that every cause have its effect, that every tree produce its fruit. All philanthropical projects are chimeras when they are not founded on constitutional freedom. They can serve as a text for the oratorical flights of well-intentioned rhetoricians; they can offer clever ministers the means of occupying their master's leisure in a new and amusing manner; they can, by fooling that master, assuage his guilt, should the spectacle of public misery create some remorse in him. But neither the agricultural class nor agriculture will profit at all from any of these impotent palliatives.

The situation of the agricultural class will be deplorable everywhere that class does not have, through agents of its own choice, certainty of legal and public redress. The situation of the agricultural class in France was deplorable before the Revolution. I call to witness the *taille*, the *corvée*, the militia, the *vingtièmes*, the head-taxes, the *aides*, the tithe, the perpetual mortgages, the transfer taxes, the alcohol taxes, and all those innumerable burdens, both monetary and personal, whose many and bizarre names would uselessly fill entire pages.[3] I attest to the not less numerous exemptions, so scandalously demanded and so easily obtained by the upper classes, as if their duties toward society were in inverse proportion to the advantages which society guarantied them. I attest to the impoverished and badly cultivated lands, bordered by sumptuous parks, and the huts, covered in thatch, which surrounded superb chateaus—silent protests, but which ended up acting only too energetically against such a social order.

Filangieri and the writers who followed him should have immersed themselves in these truths. Instead of dreaming about special encouragements, of vain distinctions tossed from the height of the throne—inevitably at random—and distributed according to the caprices of untrustworthy agents, they should have demanded the guaranties that every country owes the citizen who inhabits it, the guaranties without which all governments are illegitimate.

With these guarantees, agriculture, as well as every other sort of industry, can easily do without the authorities' protection. It is entirely useless for the government to involve itself in encouraging what is necessary. It is enough if it does not hinder it. Necessity will be obeyed. When there is no vicious action by government, production is always in perfect proportion to demand. I except unforeseen cases, sudden calamities, which in any case are pretty rare when one leaves nature free, but which governments by their erroneous measures create more often than one thinks. I will speak about them more in another part of this *Commentary*. In the usual order of things it is not encouragement but security that agriculture needs. However, security is only to be found in good constitutional institutions. When the farmer himself can be taken away because his neighbor is an informer, or because his enemy is some powerful man's valet; when the fruit of his work can be greatly diminished by excessive taxes because some landowner, a rich man or a noble, has had himself exempted; when his children, the useful associates of his daily operations, are taken from him to die in far-off wars, do you think that, worried about the present and frightened about the future, he will continue devoting himself to efforts whose profit may be taken from him? It is you

3. Eighteenth-century French taxes.—Trans.

who put despair and discouragement into his soul, and then you claim to encourage him. You torment, you oppress, you bankrupt the entire class, and you imagine that a little charity, or what is even more ridiculous, that a medal you invent and disdainfully confer on some individual your agents protect, will revive this impoverished and despoiled class. Your ineptitude or your despotism has made the soil barren, and you believe that your favors, like the presence of the sun, will return it to its original fertility. You show yourself, you smile, you distribute I don't know what vain and illusory honors, and this action, to listen to you, is going to be admired for centuries! What strange arrogance! Gross charlatanism, by which in the past some honest dreamers were taken in, but which, thank heaven, is more discredited every day. The emperor of China also deigns to guide a plow with his imperial hand, and to trace a furrow on a holiday. This does not prevent China from being the constant prey of famine, and parents from exposing on the riverbank the children they are incapable of feeding. This is because China is a despotic state, and when farmers are subject to the whip all year long, the honor one thinks one is doing them once a year neither compensates nor consoles them.

I will be forced to return more than once to the system of encouragements when Filangieri discusses industry. Consequently, I postpone further discussion which proves that even from a moral perspective this system is harmful.

# CHAPTER FOUR ❧ On the Conversion of Rulers to Peace

> The cry of reason has finally reached the throne. Rulers have begun to feel . . . that the real source of greatness does not lie in force and arms.
>
> INTRODUCTION, P. 2.

Is it really true that because reason has reached the throne, rulers have finally recognized that they owe more respect to human life and that true greatness is not in force and arms? I would be only too pleased to adopt this flattering conviction, but I cannot prevent myself from having certain doubts. I imagine myself in the time when Filangieri wrote these lines, and cast my eyes forward over the next forty years. I see the Seven Years' War end, but the War of the American Revolution soon begins. Joseph II threatens Prussia and attacks the Turks. Sweden launches itself rather foolishly against Russia. Poland is partitioned, and if this does not result in war, it is because the co-partitioners divide three against one. Finally, the kings of Europe form a coalition against France, which wants to give itself a free government. After ten years of ferocious combat, they are defeated, but then the French government gives up moderation and justice, and for another ten years the space from Lisbon to Moscow, and Hamburg to Naples, is again flooded with blood. Are these very satisfactory proofs of the empire of reason?

Nevertheless, there is an element of truth in Filangieri's assertion, which he disfigures by his well-meaning but little-deserved compliments to power. As I have previously observed (chap. 2), the warlike system is in contradiction with the current state of the human race. The age of commerce has arrived, and the more the commercial tendency dominates, the more the warlike tendency must weaken.

War and commerce are but two different means of arriving at the same end: possessing what one desires. Commerce is nothing but homage rendered to the strength of the possessor by the one who aspires to possession. It is an attempt to obtain by mutual agreement what one no longer hopes to conquer by violence. A man who was always the strongest would never entertain the idea of commerce. It is experience which shows him that war, that is to say the use of his strength against someone else's, is exposed to various resistances and failures. This leads him to turn to commerce, a gentler and more certain means of engaging others' interest in consenting to what agrees with his interest.

War thus precedes commerce. One is the impulse of an inexperienced desire, the other the calculation of an enlightened desire. Commerce should therefore replace war, but in replacing war it discredits it, and makes war odious to the world. This is what we see today.

The sole goal of modern nations is rest; with rest, comfort, and as the source of comfort, industry. War daily becomes more inefficient at attaining this goal. Its risks no longer offer, either to individuals or peoples, profits equal to peaceful work and regular exchanges. Among the ancients a successful war increased public wealth in slaves, tribute, and partitioned lands, while among the moderns a successful war infallibly costs more than it brings in.

The situation of modern peoples therefore prevents them from being warlike out of interest, and particular reasons, also derived from the progress of the human species and thus from the difference between periods, add to the general causes that prevent the nations of our day from being warlike by inclination. The new way of fighting, the change in weapons, and artillery, have deprived military life of what was most attractive in it. There is no longer a struggle against danger; there is only fate. Courage must be imprinted with resignation or consist of insouciance. One no longer feels that pleasure of will, of action, of the development of physical and moral faculties which made the old heroes, the knights of the middle ages, love hand-to-hand combat. War has thus lost its charm as well as its utility.

This means that a government which tries to talk about military glory today, and consequently of war as a goal, misunderstands the spirit of nations and of the times. Philip's son[1] would no longer dare propose to his subjects

1. Alexander the Great.—Trans.

the invasion of the universe, and Pyrrhus's speech to Cineas would seem the height of insolence or folly.[2]

Governments recognize truths as slowly as they can. Despite all their efforts, however, they cannot preserve themselves from the truth forever, and they have noticed the change that has taken place in the peoples' temperament. They pay homage to it in their public acts and their speeches. They avoid openly confessing the love of conquest, and they take up arms only with a heavy heart. In this respect, as Filangieri observes, reason today has made its way to the thrones. But in forcing governments to change their language, has it, as it pleases the Italian philosopher to hope, enlightened the minds or converted the hearts of those whom chance has invested with authority?

I regret that I do not believe so, for I do not see in their conduct more love of peace. I see only more hypocrisy. When Frederick attacked Austria to take Silesia, he said he only wanted to uphold ancient rights to give his realm an appropriate size. When England exhausted its men and its wealth to subjugate America, it only aspired to return lost children to the protective laws of the metropolis. When it brought devastation to India, it only intended to oversee its interests and assure the prosperity of its commerce. When a coalition of three powers broke up Poland, their only purpose was to return to the troubled Poles the tranquility disturbed by their internal struggles. When those same powers invaded a France which had become free, it was the tottering thrones they proposed to prop up. When today they crush Italy and threaten Spain, it is the social order which demands their intervention. In all this, the word *conquest* is never pronounced. But is the people's blood less likely to flow? What does it matter to them under what pretext it is shed! The pretext itself is at bottom nothing more than another insult.

Therefore, contrary to the over-confident Filangieri's suggestion, we must not trust ourselves to reason's influence on thrones, and to rulers' wisdom to preserve the world from the plague of unjust or useless wars. The wisdom of the nation must take part. I said in chapter 2 how it should participate.

2. See *The Spirit of Conquest*, chapter 1.

# CHAPTER FIVE ❧ On the Salutary Revolution Which Filangieri Foresaw

> A salutary fermentation is going to give birth to public happiness.
>
> INTRODUCTION, P. 11.

If one judged only by appearances, one could not help but feel sadness and pity for the human species when comparing the future Filangieri promises it here with the situation in which almost all the peoples of Europe find themselves today. What has become of that desire for improvement and reform which inspired societies' upper classes? Where is that freedom of the press which honored both the rulers who did not fear it and the writers who used it? The superstition whose defeat the Neapolitan writer celebrates—is it not the object of regret for all the holders of power? Incapable of reproducing it as it used to be—blind and cruel but sincere—they make efforts to replace it by command performances and calculated intolerance, no less harmful and much less excusable. Do we not see hypocrisy attempting to rebuild everywhere what the Enlightenment overthrew? Are not the foundations of fanaticism being laid in every country?

What does it matter that spiritual claims have bowed to political authority, if that authority makes religion into a tool and thus acts against freedom with double force? What use is it to us to have deprived aristocratic oppression of its ancient name of feudalism if it reappears under a new name, just as demanding and more astute? If the domination the old feudal lords lost should go to the large landowners, who are for the most part the feudal lords of times past? If large landholdings, made inalienable by entailments and always increasing because they are inalienable, recreate oligarchy? Finally, just as feudalism seeks to reappear under a less frightening name, has not despotism, which mores had made gentler, forsworn its philanthropic gestures? Has it not already replaced the outdated axiom of divine right with a terminology whose only advantage is that it is more abstract? Does it not use that terminology just as much to forbid to peoples all examination of the laws, and all resistance to arbitrary power?

This painful comparison of what has happened with what we had the right to hope for should not discourage us, however. Momentary disappointment was in the nature of things; ultimate success is as well.

When the principles of justice and freedom are proclaimed by philosophers, it often happens that the classes called superior rally to them, because these principles' consequences, still relegated to an obscure future, do not offend. It would be wrong to conclude from this that these classes will continue to want the system that they seem to—I will go farther—that they certainly believe they have adopted. In man's heart there is a need for approval which even power will be led by, when it flatters itself that it will not cost it any real sacrifice to satisfy. It follows that when public opinion is strongly aroused against despotism, aristocratic pride, or religious intolerance, the kings, nobles, and priests try to please opinion, and the privileged of various kinds ostensibly make common cause with the mass of the nations against their own prerogatives. Sometimes they are even sincere in the abnegation they manifest. While they win applause by repeating principles that do not seem likely to be applied any time soon, the intoxication of their words creates disinterested emotions in them, and they imagine that if it should happen (always convinced that it will not), they would be ready to do everything that they say.

But when the moment of truth arrives, interest demands the bill from vanity for the promises it has made. Vanity made them comfortable with the theory, interest makes them furious with the practice. They praised reforms on condition that they did not happen, like people who would celebrate the sun, provided the night would never end. In fact, dawn has come, and almost all those who had invoked it have declared themselves its opponents, and all the signs of improvement that Filangieri pompously lists for us have fled like vain glimmers of light.

As we see, this backward movement was inevitable, and it shows us a very important truth: reforms which come from above are always deceptive. If interest is not the motivation of all individuals, because some individuals' nobler nature rises above the narrow ideas of egoism, interest is the motivation of all classes. One can never expect anything effective or complete from a class which seems to act against its own interest. It may well abjure its interest momentarily, but it will always come back to it, and as soon as the moment comes to permanently consummate the sacrifice, it will retreat, voicing reservations and qualifications which it did not suspect itself amid its protestations of sacrifice and devotion. This is what we are witnessing today. The absolute monarchy, the clergy, the nobility, all want to take back the prerogatives they surrendered, accusing the people of theft for having taken what was offered, crying out against injustice and trickery with a precious naiveté, solely because they were taken at their word.

But should we infer from these recent efforts that our hopes are forever disappointed and that humanity's cause is lost beyond appeal? Certainly not. We should be grateful for the passing enthusiasm and vain imprudence of the various privileged classes. They popularized the principles they now condemn. In order to begin a war against the institutions which oppress them, nations often need leaders from the classes which profit from these institutions. Too much humiliation robs people of courage, and those who profit from abuses are sometimes the only ones capable of attacking them. These leaders call up the popular army, discipline it, and train it. It is lucky when they remain faithful to it! But if they desert, the army is [still] nevertheless in being. It easily replaces the apostates who abandoned it with men taken from its midst, and more identified with its cause. Thus, while victory may perhaps be delayed, it becomes more certain and more complete because there are no longer foreign interests among the victors who slow down the march or distort the goal.

Therefore fear nothing from momentary coalitions and declarations of circumstance, the forces ostentatiously deployed to frighten us. One does not abandon the philosophical flag without cost. Despotism, aristocratic pride, clerical power, all wanted to have the honor of it: they must also bear the costs. These costs can be decreased by a rational resignation. They can be cruelly increased by resistance. But the fate of the human species is decided. The reign of privilege is over.

Tyranny is only formidable, says an English author, when it smothers reason in its childhood. Then it can stop its progress and keep men in a long imbecility. But there is only a moment when all-powerful reason can be successfully proscribed. Once the moment has passed, all efforts are vain, the struggle has begun, the truth appears to all minds. Opinion separates itself from the government, and the government, rejected by opinion, resembles those bodies struck by lightning which contact with the air reduces to dust.

# CHAPTER SIX ❧ On the Union of Politics and Legislation

> It is really astonishing that among the many writers who have devoted themselves to studying law . . . each has only considered a portion of this immense edifice.
>
> INTRODUCTION, P. 12.

Filangieri's phrase contains the germ of a great truth, but he seems to have neither sufficiently understood it nor sufficiently developed it. He criticizes writers who have treated legislation separately from politics mostly from a literary angle, because they have not understood how to consider their subject as a whole, rather than from the much more serious perspective of the dangerous mistake they propagate. This mistake is all the more essential to combat because governments also propagate it with all their might. Governments would like to persuade peoples that good laws, ones appropriate for maintaining order among individuals, are all that is needed for security and general prosperity, without any need for recourse to constitutional institutions to protect these laws. This is to claim that a building's foundations are not necessary for its stability. Legislation separated from politics offers the governed no shelter, and presents no obstacle to the governors. Outside political guaranties there are no means of preventing those who hold power from violating the laws they have established. Also, the despots who are the most jealous of their absolute domination have not failed to give their slaves marvelous law codes, sure that these codes would have only the value that the master's will allowed. Two pages of a book, two words from a podium are better safeguards than the best-written law codes, those most perfect in appearance. They are better not only for freedom but also for justice, for that justice which each individual needs every day. For a law code is a dead and inert thing until the moment when men put it into practice. But if despots have to conform to it only when they feel like it, if no one can protest when they depart from it, all the merit of a law code vanishes.

This is the case with the distinction between legislation and politics, and equally with that which so many people want to establish between civil and constitutional freedom. The best legislation is worthless if a good political organization does not guarantee it, just as there is no civil liberty if constitutional liberty does not take it under its wing. Doubtless, even in countries ruled by arbitrary governments, all the civil liberties of all the inhabitants are not infringed upon, just as in all the countries ruled by the Turkish sultan, not all heads are cut off. But it is enough that such an infringement is possible, without any means of stopping it, for security to be nonexistent.

Today let us therefore challenge more than ever all efforts to distract our attention from politics and fix it on legislation. I say today more than ever, because today more than ever this trick is used as a last resort to fool us and give us the slip. When governments offer legislative improvements to peoples, peoples ought to respond by asking for constitutional institutions. Without a constitution, peoples cannot have any certainty that the laws will be obeyed. It is in constitutions, in the punishments they pronounce against unfaithful holders of authority, in the rights they assure citizens, in the universal publicity they ought to hold sacred, that the coercive force resides which is necessary to force the government to respect the laws. When there is no constitution, not only does the government make the laws it wishes, but it observes them as it wishes; that is, it observes them when convenient and violates them when advantageous. Then the best laws, like the worst, are only a weapon in the rulers' hands. They become the scourge of the governed, whom they strangle without protecting, and whom they deprive of the right of resistance without giving the benefit of protection.

# CHAPTER SEVEN ❧ On the Influence Which Filangieri Attributes to Legislation

Annotated plan of the work, p. 15.

Since the annotated plan Filangieri puts at the beginning of his book is nothing but an abridged analysis of the whole book, and therefore all the ideas contained in this analysis are found in the book itself, I thought I should abstain from any detailed observations here. But there is one observation which regards the writer's general system, which, even though indicated in the earlier chapters, needs to be restated and developed.

As I have said elsewhere, Filangieri fell into an error common to many well-intentioned philosophers. From the fact that government can do much evil, he concluded that it could equally do much good. In a certain country, he saw laws lending strength to superstition and limiting the growth of individuals' faculties. In another country he saw laws encouraging bad and absurd forms of education; in yet another country giving commerce, industry, and individual speculation the wrong direction. He thought that governments which took the opposite course would be as good for the happiness and progress of the human race as the others were harmful. Consequently, Filangieri's work constantly considers the legislator as a separate being, above the rest of humanity, necessarily better and more enlightened than they. Becoming enthusiastic about this figment of his imagination, Filangieri gave the legislator an authority over the beings subject to his orders which he only occasionally thought of containing or limiting. Thus he speaks to us "of the different tone which legislation should take among different peoples in different times" (p. 5); "of the manner in which, in destroying harmful errors, it should support with one hand what it destroys with the other" (p. 6); "of the laws which must be adapted to nations' childhood, follow the changes of their adolescence, wait for their maturity and guard their old age" (ibid.); "of the care the legislator must take to keep wealth in the state and distribute it equitably" (p. 11); "of the protection which must be given agriculture without neglecting the arts" (p. 12); "of the means of legally preventing excessive opulence which leads to excessive poverty" (p. 15); "of the official distribution of honor and shame, in order to powerfully influence opinion" (p. 18); "of the obstacles it is desirable to oppose to domestic education, independent of the laws, which should not be allowed except for a small number of citizens" (p. 21); "of the direction to give talents, the use which the legislator can make of passions, and the productive strength of virtues" (ibid.).

Thus, in this part of his system Filangieri confers on the legislator almost limitless sway over human existence, while elsewhere he objects very forcefully to "government encroachments." He holds this contradiction in common with a great many writers whom freedom nevertheless counts among her most zealous defenders. To explain this inconsistency, some discussion is necessary, and I need to ask my readers for a little attention.

Without realizing it, all those who have written about governments have simultaneously looked at them from two perspectives and have judged them, often in the same sentence, sometimes as they are, and sometimes as they would like them to be. In judging governments as they are, these writers have treated them very severely. They have exposed to public hatred and indignation the vices, mistakes, false calculations, bad intentions, obstinate ignorance, and envious passions of men clothed in power. But when they judged governments as they wanted them to be, they expressed themselves completely differently. Their imagination presented rulers as abstractions, and made them into beings of a different species than the governed, enjoying an incontestable superiority in virtue, wisdom, and education. Once noticed, this double perspective is easily explained. Since everyone wants to see his own opinion triumph, no one completely gives up on attracting the government's support, and the man who is thwarted by that authority does not want to see it destroyed, but only displaced.

Pick at random one of our most famous philosophers—Mably, for example. He devotes six volumes to retracing, history of France in hand, the misfortunes of peoples and the crimes of power. The facts he gathers and comments on certainly do not show the rulers to be better than the ruled. Every fair mind would be led to conclude from these facts that government should be limited as much as possible, and that the whole portion of human existence which does not absolutely have to be subjected to it should be exempt from its harmful action.

But now follow Mably in his theories. The authority that he found so harmful and dangerous in practice he suddenly depicts as beneficial, equitable, enlightened. He surrenders man entirely to it as to a protector, a guardian, and a guide. The law, he says (and he ignores that the law is not made by itself and that it is the work of governments), should seize hold of us from the first moments of our lives, surround us with examples, precepts, rewards, and punishments. It should direct, improve, and enlighten that numerous and ignorant class which, not having the time for examination, is condemned to accept truth itself by faith and like prejudices. All the time the law abandons us is time that it leaves the passions to tempt us, seduce us, and subjugate us. The law should excite a love of work, engrave respect for morals in the souls of the young, strike the imagination by well-coordinated institutions, reach to the bottom of our hearts to tear out guilty thoughts. Instead of limiting itself to repressing harmful actions, the law should prevent crimes rather than punish them. The law should regulate our least movements, preside over the spread of knowledge, over the development of industry, and over the perfection of the arts; it should lead as if by the hand the blind crowd that must be instructed and the corrupt mass that must be corrected.[1]

Reading about all that the law should do, who would not believe that it descended from heaven, pure and infallible, without need of intermediaries whose errors falsify it, whose personal calculations disfigure it, whose vices sully and pervert it? But this is not the case if the law is the work of men. If it is stamped with men's imperfections, weakness, and perversity, who does not realize that the work does not merit more confidence than its authors, and that they themselves have no right to inspire us more in one capacity than another? We fear them as rulers because they are despots; we fear them

1. I should warn the reader that having intended some time ago to publish, in a series of periodical articles, an essay on the limits the law should not cross, I began by establishing several of the ideas I develop here. It would have been impossible for me to skip ideas which were the basis of my whole doctrine, and I have thought it all the better to reproduce them, as I very early gave up on the mode of publication that I had adopted before starting this *Commentary*, so that very few copies of the articles were printed, and the writing has been considerably changed.

as peoples because they are blind and ignorant. A change of name does not change their nature at all. It seems to me that here are strong enough reasons to mistrust men, even when they find it convenient to call themselves legislators.

Long ago I said,[2] and I repeat: abstract and obscure language has created illusions for writers. One could say that they had been duped by the impersonal verbs they used. They thought they were saying something when they said: men's opinions must be directed; men should not be left to the wanderings of their minds; thought must be influenced; there are opinions which can be usefully used to trick men. But these words—"one must," "one should," "one should not"—are they not used about people? One would think that they were about a different species. However, all these phrases imposed on us amount to saying that men should direct the opinions of men; men should not leave men to their own devices; there are opinions which men can use to trick men. The impersonal verbs seem to have persuaded our philosophers that there were some beings other than men who governed.

It is assuredly far from my mind to want to weaken respect for the law when it is applied to objects within its competence. I will describe them soon. But extending the law's competence to everything, as Mably, Filangieri, and so many others do, is to organize tyranny and to return, after so many long declamations, to the state of slavery from which we were hoping to free ourselves. It is once again to subject men to unlimited force, which is equally dangerous whether we call it by its true name, despotism, or by a gentler name, legislation.

I therefore reject all this part of Filangieri's system, from which, furthermore, he himself departs as soon as he goes into detail. Legislation, like government, has only two purposes: first, to prevent internal disorder, and second, to repulse foreign invasion. Everything beyond this limit is usurpation. Legislation therefore ought not to "take a different tone among different peoples or among the same peoples in different times." In all times, real violations—that is, acts which harm another—ought to be repressed, and those which do not harm anyone ought not to be. Legislation ought not to be "concerned with destroying errors," nor, when it destroys errors, "with supporting with one hand what it destroys with another." Errors should be destroyed only

2. *On Constitutions and Guaranties,* 1814.

by themselves, and they are destroyed only by experience and examination; legislation has nothing to do with it. There should be no question of laws "which are adapted to the childhood of nations, to their adolescence, to their maturity, their old age," because once again, in the childhood as in the adolescence, maturity, or old age of peoples, attempts against life, property, and security are crimes and should be punished. All the rest should remain free. Furthermore, when a nation is in its infancy, its legislators are in infancy. The title of legislator does not confer any intellectual privilege.[3]

Legislation should not try to "fix wealth" in the state and to "distribute it equitably." Wealth is fixed in a state when there is freedom and security, and in order for there to be these two things, it is enough to repress crime. Wealth is distributed and divided by itself in perfect equilibrium, when the division of property is not limited and the exercise of industry does not encounter any hindrances. But the best thing that could happen to either is the neutrality, the silence of the law. Legislation (as I already said in chap. 3) is not needed to "protect agriculture." Agriculture is effectively protected when all classes have guaranties and are sheltered from persecution. The law has no need "to prevent excessive opulence," because excess is only introduced among a people when the law solicits it and in a certain sense calls for it. It is usually with the help of laws, institutions, and hereditary privileges that colossal fortunes are formed and maintained. Afterwards one makes laws to oppose their immod-

3. I beg the reader to notice that I am not attacking Filangieri's basic idea, that there should be a relationship between a people's laws and the state of opinion, education, and civilization of that people. This relationship is certainly indispensable, but in one of his metaphors Filangieri always seems to give the legislator the gift of judging and determining this relationship. It is here that the error resides. It is against the hypothesis of a class miraculously gifted with supernatural sagacity, out of proportion with contemporary nations, that I object to with all my strength. This hypothesis serves as an apology for all oppression. Sometimes it justifies the refusal of the most opportune improvements, and sometimes it justifies prematurely attempted improvements, or innovations which are nothing but scourges. Today it is under this pretext that nations' leaders oppose the restitution of the rights nations demand and the destruction of abuses which arouse indignation. Peter I tormented the Russians in the opposite sense a hundred years ago; fifty years ago the marquis de Pombal bent the Portuguese under an iron yoke; forty years ago Joseph II made Bohemia, Belgium, Austria, and Hungary unhappy under the same pretext.

No one doubts that there ought to be a relationship between laws and popular ideas, but to establish this relationship one must have recourse to freedom, and most of the time one should not make laws, but get rid of them.

erate growth, and that is another evil. Get rid of laws which favor them, and you will not need laws to repress them. This will be a double advantage. For the first torment and debase the poor man, while the second torment and corrupt the rich. The first arm the various classes of citizens against each other. The second arm the class of citizens who serve as an example to the rest against the institutions. The distribution of "honor and shame" is exclusively the province of opinion. When the law wants to intervene, opinion balks and annuls legislative decrees. "Education" belongs to parents, to whom children are confided by nature. If these parents prefer domestic education, the law cannot oppose it without being a usurper. Finally, "talents" do not need the law to give them "direction." "Passions" should be repressed when they lead to actions contrary to public order but the law should not meddle with them, either to create them or use them, "and the productive force of virtues" is not the law, but freedom.

In the outline of his book and in several parts of the book itself all of Filangieri's expressions are essentially vague and incorrect: this is the work's great flaw. One can see clearly that the author's ideas were not sufficiently developed. He had realized that almost all the obstacles to men's happiness and the development of their faculties come from the very measures that governments take under the pretext of aiding their development and assuring their happiness. However, he was not sufficiently convinced that the obstacles were not to be overcome by different governmental measures, but through the absence of all positive measures. In correctly exposing the problem with what existed, he constantly used expressions which implied direct action. This flaw in the writing keeps the work from having a clear impact and the reader from reaching the conclusion confirmed by all the facts, which is that the functions of government are purely negative. It should repress disorder, eliminate obstacles, in a word, prevent evil from arising. Thereafter one can leave it to individuals to find the good.

I will come back to each of these goals, briefly indicated here, when Filangieri's chapters successively lead me to them. Here I have only sought to announce the fundamental truth. The examination of each particular question will only bolster this truth with more evidence.

# CHAPTER EIGHT ❧ On the State of Nature, the Formation of Society, and the True Goal of Human Associations

> I take care not to suppose a state of nature previous to society. . . . Society is born with man: but this primitive society was very different from civil society. . . . It was necessary to create a public strength superior to each of them out of all individual strengths . . . which had the power to forever place the instrument of their preservation and tranquility in men's hands.
>
> BOOK I, CHAPTER 1, P. 43.

We ought to be grateful to Filangieri for having put aside questions relative to man's primitive state. The writers of the eighteenth century made these questions very fashionable, but they are both insoluble and futile. In the history of all origins there are primordial facts whose cause one should not look for behind their existence. Existence is a fact that must be accepted without trying to explain it. All attempts at explanation send us back to that trivial and comic problem which nevertheless defies reason: which came first, the chicken or the egg? The only philosopher who expressed himself sensibly on this question was the one who said: We follow those who precede us and we precede those who follow us. It is with the mode of existence of each species as with existence itself. This mode is also a primordial fact, a law of nature. Religious people can attribute it to the creator's will, unbelievers to necessity, but this fact is not explicable, as other phenomena are, by the succession of causes and effects.

Man is not social because he is weak, for there are weaker animals which are not at all sociable. He does not live in society because he has calculated the advantages society gives him, for in order to calculate those advantages, he would have had to have already known society. In all this there is a vicious circle and a *petitio principii*.[1] Man is sociable because he is a man, as the wolf is unsociable because he is a wolf. It makes as much sense to ask why one walks on two legs and the other on four. Filangieri was therefore right to take society's existence as a base, and to start from this first fact in order to examine how society should be constituted, what its purpose is, and what are the means of attaining this purpose.

His definition of the goal of society is fairly precise: it is preservation and tranquility. But here the author stops and does not draw the conclusions which ought to follow from this principle. If the purpose of society is the preservation and tranquility of its members, everything which is necessary so that this preservation is guaranteed and this tranquility untroubled is within the sphere of legislation, for legislation is nothing but society's effort to fulfill the conditions of its existence. But everything which is not necessary for the preservation and maintenance of tranquility is beyond the social and legislative sphere.

Now two things are indispensible for the preservation and tranquility of societies: one, that the association be sheltered from internal disorders; the other, that it be safe from foreign invasions. It is therefore within the sphere of society's responsibility to repress these disorders and repulse these invasions. Thus legislation should punish crimes, organize an armed force against external enemies, and impose on individuals the sacrifice of a portion of their personal property to pay for the expenses of these two purposes. Punishing crimes and resisting aggression—this is the sphere of legislation within the limits of the necessary.

It is even necessary to distinguish two kinds of crimes: actions harmful in themselves and actions which are harmful only as violations of contracted obligations. The jurisdiction of legislation over the former is absolute. It is only relative with regard to the latter. It depends on both the nature of the engagement and the demand of the individual who has been harmed. Even when the victim of a murder attempt or a robbery would like to pardon the guilty party, the law should punish him, because the action committed is harmful in and of itself. But when the breaking of an engagement is agreed to by all the contracting or interested parties, the law has no right to keep it

1. Logical fallacy—"begging the question."—Trans.

in force, just as it does not have the right to dissolve it at the demand of only one of the parties.

It is clear that legislative jurisdiction must extend to these boundaries, and that it can stop there. One cannot imagine a people among whom individual crimes remained unpunished, and which would not have any means prepared for resisting attacks on it by foreign nations. But one can easily imagine a nation whose government had no other mission but to watch over these two objects. The existence of individuals and that of society would be perfectly assured. The necessary would be done.

Filangieri seems to have instinctively grasped this truth in several parts of his book, but he does not establish it clearly enough anywhere. He allows a vagueness to linger in all his expressions which has always been and is, in effect, the source of many abuses. To convince ourselves of this, let us reread the whole paragraph devoted to explaining, as the author says, "the origin and purpose of civil society, and the origin and purpose of laws, and consequently the sole and universal object of legislation."

> It was necessary to create a public strength from all individual strengths, superior to each of them individually. It was necessary to create a moral entity whose will represented all wills, whose strength was the assembly of all strengths, which, directed by public reason, interpreted natural law by developing its principles, fixing rights, regulating duties, and prescribing the obligations of each individual towards society and towards the members who compose it. This moral entity would establish a standard among citizens which would be the rule for their actions and the basis of their security. For the maintenance of order it would create and preserve balance between needs and the means of fulfilling them. Finally, it would have the power of permanently putting into men's hands the instrument of their preservation and tranquility, the only purposes for which they had sacrificed their primitive independence.

When interpreting each of Filangieri's expressions, it is undoubtedly possible to show that he restricts the competence of legislation within its just bounds. But by a different interpretation one could also extend that competence to everything. If legislation is a moral entity whose will always represents all wills, then all the wills thus represented no longer have any individual existence which belongs to them. If it is legislation which interprets natural law, it is only through that legislation, which is however something conventional and artificial, that man can know nature. An eternal silence is imposed on the internal feelings that nature has given man as a guide. If it is legislation which fixes each individual's rights, individuals have only the rights which legislation agrees to leave them.

Understood in this way, Filangieri's system does not differ at all from that of Rousseau, which I have opposed in another work, and whose terrible consequences and incalculable dangers I believe I have shown.[2] Legislation would be an unlimited and despotic power, according to Filangieri, just like society according to Rousseau, for whose benefit the entire individual would be surrendered. One cannot object too strongly and too persistently to this doctrine. I will not repeat here the series of arguments which I used in the work just mentioned. I will limit myself to repeating the conclusions.

There is a part of human existence which necessarily remains individual and independent, and which by right is beyond all social or legislative competence. Society's authority, and thus that of legislation, exists only to a relative and limited extent. At the point where the independence of individual existence begins, the authority of legislation stops. If legislation crosses this line, it usurps.

Individual rights are a part of human existence which should remain independent of legislation. They are rights which legislation should never touch, rights over which society has no jurisdiction, rights which it cannot invade without making itself as guilty of tyranny as the despot who has no other title to authority than a deadly sword. The government's legitimacy depends on its purpose as much as on its source. When this authority is extended over purposes which are outside its sphere, it becomes illegitimate. When legislation brings an interfering hand to bear on that part of human existence which is not within its sphere of responsibility, does it matter from what source it comes, does it matter whether it be the work of a single man or of a nation? If it came from the entire nation, except the citizen it torments, its acts would not be any more legal. There are actions which nothing can clothe with legality.

> Law has been defined (I borrow this just and profound remark from a writer whose name I have forgotten) as the expression of the general will. This definition is very false. The law is the declaration of men's relations with each other.

2. *Lessons in Constitutional Politics,* vol. 1, pt. 1, pp. 173–76.

> From the moment society exists, certain relationships among men are established. These relations are in conformity with human nature, for if they were not in conformity with human nature they would not be established. Laws are nothing but these relations experienced and observed. They are not the cause of these relations which on the contrary are prior to them. They declare that these relations exist. They are the declaration of a fact. They do not create, determine, or institute anything, except forms to guarantee what existed before their institution. It follows that no man, no portion of society, or even society as a whole can, properly speaking and in an absolute sense, attribute to itself the right to make laws. Laws are nothing but the expression of the relations which exist between men. These relations preceding the law, a new law is nothing other than a declaration which had not yet been made of what previously existed.
>
> The law is therefore not at the legislator's disposition. It is not a spontaneous creation. The legislator is to the moral universe what the physician is to the material universe. Newton himself could only observe the universe and tell us the laws he recognized or thought he recognized. He certainly did not imagine he was the creator of those laws.

As I have observed above, Filangieri frequently approaches these principles in the course of his book, but he never explicitly states them. In more than one chapter we will even see him accord legislation a broad competence to which he does not seemingly assign any limit. I will prove in my later discussion that the doctrine I establish is not dangerous to good order, and that government, restricted within its legitimate limits, is no less strong and attains its purpose even more surely. By allowing government to transgress these limits, one weakens and compromises it. Individual rights, in all their latitude and their inviolability, are never opposed to the just rights of associations over their members. The repose and happiness of all is better guaranteed by the independence of each, in everything which is not harmful to others, than by any of the attempts, open or disguised, violent or equivocal, which are constantly repeated by authority and unfortunately blessed by some short-sighted philosophers, to endow society, that abstract and fictive being, at the expense of individuals, the sole real and sensible beings.

## CHAPTER NINE ❧ On Errors in Legislation

> Nothing is easier than to commit an error in legislation: but there is nothing more deadly to peoples, nothing more dangerous from which to cure them. The loss of a province and all the ill-successes of a war are short-lived misfortunes. A moment of good fortune, a single battle, sometimes repairs the losses of several years, but a political or legislative error is the inextinguishable source of a century of hardships, and its destructive influence extends for centuries to come.
>
> BOOK I, CHAPTER 3, P. 53.

From the fact that it is easy to commit errors in legislation, and that errors of this kind are a thousand times more harmful than all other calamities, it seems to me that one should decrease the chance of these errors as much as possible. If to decrease this chance men are reduced to sacrificing a portion of the advantages which they hope to obtain from legislative action, they must resign themselves to the sacrifice, provided that it does not entail the destruction of the social state. One should consent to laws doing perhaps a little less good, in order to be assured that they will cause much less evil. In restricting their intervention within the fairly narrow limits of public security, this goal is attained. The fewer occasions the legislator has to act, the less he will be exposed to error.

In the first chapter of *L'Ami des hommes*, the marquis de Mirabeau established a very just distinction between positive and speculative laws. He said that positive laws limit themselves to maintaining; speculative laws extend to directing. He did not draw any broad conclusions from this distinction. His purpose was not to set the limits of legislation, and although in the rest of his book he was constantly led by the force of circumstances to restrict the speculative functions of legislators, he nevertheless accepted their rights. He only tried to indicate how these functions could be usefully and advantageously exercised. My purpose is different. But I will adopt the same distinction in order to follow its incontestable results to the end.

When the government or legislation punishes a harmful action, or when they repress the violation of a contractual agreement, they fulfill a positive function. When they rigorously punish an action which is not harmful under the pretext that it could indirectly lead to an action which would be harmful; when they impose on individuals certain obligations or rules of conduct which are not a necessary part of the agreements contracted by these individuals; when they hinder the disposition of property or the exercise of industry; when they try to take over education, or dominate opinion, whether by punishments or rewards, they arrogate to themselves a speculative function.

In his positive functions the legislator does not act spontaneously. He reacts to facts and previous actions which have taken place independently of his will. But in his speculative functions he does not react to facts or actions already committed; rather, he foresees future actions. He therefore acts spontaneously, and his action is the product of his will. The positive functions of the legislator are of an infinitely simple nature, and in their exercise the action of power is neither equivocal nor complicated. His speculative functions are of a different nature. They have no fixed basis or clear limit. They are not exercised on facts, but are based on hopes or fears, on probabilities, on hypotheses—in a word, on speculation. For that reason alone they can be infinitely varied, extended, and complicated.

The positive functions often permit the government to remain motionless. The speculative functions never permit it rest. Its hand, which sometimes limits, sometimes directs, sometimes creates, and sometimes restores, can sometimes be invisible, but it can never remain still. One after another, you see the legislator put up barriers of his choice this side of crime in order to establish punishments for crossing these barriers later, or else prohibit actions neutral in themselves, but whose indirect consequences seem dangerous. Or he makes coercive laws to force men to do what seems most useful to him. At other times he extends his authority over opinion, or modifies or limits the enjoyment of property. He arbitrarily regulates its forms and determines, orders, or prohibits its transmission. He subjects the exercise of industry to numerous hindrances, alternatively encouraging or limiting it. Thus actions, speeches, writings, errors, truths, religious ideas, philosophical systems, moral affections, intimate feelings, customs, habits, mores, institutions—what is most vague in man's imagination, most independent in his nature—all become the legislator's domain. His authority spreads over our entire existence, confirms or combats our most uncertain conjectures, and changes or directs our most fleeting impressions.

There is therefore this difference between the speculative and positive functions: the latter have fixed limits, whereas as soon as they are accepted, the former have none. The law sending citizens to the frontier in order to defend the border when attacked would be a positive law, for its purpose would be to repel aggression and prevent the territory from being invaded. The law authorizing the government to make war on all peoples suspected of contemplating an attack is a speculative law, for there would be no previous fact, no action committed. There would be a presumed action, speculation, conjecture. Note also how in the first case the function of the legislator and of the executor of the laws would be limited. The one would not pronounce except against a fact, the other could not act if the fact did not exist. But in the second hypothesis, authority would be limitless, for conjecture would always be at the discretion of the holder of authority.

From this difference between positive and speculative laws, it obviously follows that when the legislator limits himself to the former, he cannot go wrong. Conversely, by venturing into the second he exposes himself to all sorts of mistakes. A law against murder and theft, punishing well-defined actions, can be more or less well made; it can be either too indulgent or too severe, but it cannot go in a direction opposite to its purpose. A law to prevent the decline of trade or remedy the stagnation of industry runs the risk of mistaking for means of encouragement things which are the opposite. By trying to encourage commerce, it can destroy commerce; by trying to favor industry, it can obstruct it.

If therefore the grave, varied, and prolonged harm done by mistaken legislation ought to lead us to reduce the possibility of these errors as much as possible, it is clear that everything which relates to the speculative functions should be excluded from the legislative domain. By this route, as by all others, we thus arrive at this sole, unchanging result, the only reasonable and salutary one: repression and defense are the legitimate, that is to say necessary, purposes of the law. The rest is luxury, and harmful luxury.

In restricting the law's action to this narrow circle, we doubtless give up the realization of many brilliant dreams and put an end to a thousand gigantic hopes. The imagination can conceive of an extremely useful employment of legislation, in its indefinite extent, by supposing that it will always be exercised in favor of reason, the common interest, and justice; that it will always choose means of a noble nature and certain success that it will succeed in subjecting human faculties without degrading them; that it will act, in a word, like Providence as the devout conceive it, by combining the force which commands and the conviction which penetrates the bottom of hearts. But to adopt this seductive supposition, one must accept a principle that the facts are far from proving, which is that those who make the laws are necessarily more enlightened than those who obey them.

It may be thus among the savage hordes that colonists bring under orderly government, but it is not the same with civilized peoples. When a small group of people, which as yet possess only the basic ideas necessary to physical existence, receive by conquest or in any other way laws which teach them the basic elements and subject them to the basic rules of the social state, the authors of these laws are certainly more enlightened than those whom they instruct. Thus one may believe that Cecrops, if he existed, had more knowledge than the Athenians, Numa than the Romans, Mohammed than the Arabs.

In my view, to apply this reasoning to an association which is already ordered is a great mistake. It is true that in such an association a substantial number educates itself only with great difficulty, devoted as they are by the nature of circumstances to mechanical occupations. The men charged with making laws are incontestably superior to that portion. But there is also an educated class to which these legislators belong and of which they make up only a small part. It is not between them and the ignorant class, it is between them and the instructed class that the comparison should be made. Reduced to these terms, the question cannot turn to the advantage of the legislator. "If you suppose," says Condorcet, that "the public authorities are more enlightened than the mass of the people, you must suppose them less enlightened than many individuals."[1]

If this is the case, if the legislator does not have the privilege of distinguishing better than the individuals subject to his power what is advantageous and what is harmful, what will we gain for happiness, order, or morals by

1. *First Mémoire on Education.*

extending his attributes? We create a blind force whose use is abandoned to chance. We draw lots between good and evil, between error and truth, and chance decides who will be invested with power.[2]

This is not to say that laws are not altogether respectable when they limit themselves to their sphere. The possibility of legislative error is not a winning argument against the possible or rather the certain dissolution of all society, a dissolution which would result from the complete absence of laws. Furthermore, limited to what is strictly necessary, the laws' intervention is simultaneously more necessary and less dangerous. When the laws limit themselves to the maintenance of external and internal security, they require only ordinary intelligence and education in order to be well made. This is really a very great advantage. In destining the multitude for mediocrity, nature wanted mediocrity to be in a position to understand the rules proper to preserving peace and good order in society. Just as in legal verdicts men find it sufficiently good to be judged by their peers, in matters of legislation they will find it sufficiently good that their peers have made the laws. But just as the questions submitted to juries should be simple and precise, so it is necessary for the laws' object to be precise and simple.

I foresee that the opinion I give here is of a nature to excite many loud objections. One of power's tricks consists in always describing legislation, government, and the management of affairs as a very difficult task. The crowd believes this, because it believes docilely whatever is repeated to it. The holders of authority gain by making themselves into profound geniuses solely due to the fact that they are burdened with such arduous functions. But there is something remarkable in their charlatanism in this respect: at the same time that they pose the principle, they fight its most necessary consequence with all their strength. If power requires so much capacity in order to be exercised, is it not clear that it ought to be confided to the most capable?[3] The masters of

2. *Ideas on Sovereignty, Social Authority and Individual Rights,* chap. 2 and 3.

3. "How many false ideas do we see raised about the mode of election," says a writer who is very opposed to popular government and greatly desires to restrict all eligibility to the aristocratic classes. "The capacity to elect is no more a right than the capacity which makes one able to hold positions. It is a commission conferred by law for the benefit of all. To make good laws, one needs good legislators, and the qualities of a legislator being rare, they must be found where they are." Does this reasoning not apply equally well to the monarchy, and does it not tend to prove that it should be elective?

the world are far from consenting to this. When it pleases them to be admired they speak of the obstacles they have to overcome, the pitfalls they avoid, the perspicacity, wisdom, superior understanding with which they must be endowed. But when one is led to conclude that one should look and see if in fact they possess these high qualities, this perspicacity, this wisdom, they immediately put themselves on another footing. They affirm that whatever the limits of their faculties, government belongs to them and that it is their property, their right, their privilege. It follows from their system both that the art of ruling men requires superhuman intelligence, and that one can trust in the most blind of all chances, birth, to confide the exercise of this art to the first comer.

I think I am being more favorable to the rulers' real interests than the rulers themselves by demonstrating that government restricted to its legitimate limits is not such a difficult thing. I think I am rendering an eminent service to hereditary constitutional monarchy by this demonstration. I do it freely, because at the present period of our species in Europe, hereditary constitutional monarchy can be the freest and most peaceful of governments.

But to extend government's jurisdiction to objects which are outside of its sphere is to distort the question. It is to entrust innumerable and unlimited functions to a small number of men, in no respect better than the rest. These functions are less necessary than the positive functions, since society would exist all the same if they were not performed. Yet they are almost impossible to perform well, since superior understanding is required, and more dangerous to perform badly, since they touch on the most delicate parts of our existence and can dry up the sources of prosperity. Therefore everything confirms my principle. Have positive laws, giving that expression the meaning given it by the marquis de Mirabeau, for you cannot exist without those laws. Do not have any speculative laws, for you can do without them.

Above all, be extremely careful to reject the usual pretext for all laws of the latter kind, the argument of utility. Once this argument is accepted, you will be forced despite yourself toward all the problems inseparable from the blind and colossal force created under the name of legislation.

Utilitarian reasons can always be found for all commands and prohibitions. To forbid citizens from leaving their homes would be useful, for this would prevent all kinds of crimes which are committed on the road. It would be useful to require everyone to present himself every morning before a magistrate, because then one would more easily discover vagabonds and thieves who hide and wait for a chance to commit a crime. Twenty years ago this logic transformed France into a vast prison.

Utility is not susceptible to exact proof. It is an object of individual opinion and thus of debate and of unlimited contestation. Nothing in nature is neutral. Everything has a cause, everything has an effect, everything has real or possible results, everything can be useful, everything can be dangerous. Once authorized to judge these possibilities, legislation has no limits and can have none. "You have never," says a very intelligent Italian,[4] "you have never in your life tied up anything at all with string or thread without giving it an extra turn or making an extra knot. It is our instinct, in small things as in great, to go beyond the natural measure." Led by this tendency inherent in man, the legislator acts in every direction and commits those innumerable errors that Filangieri describes. As I have shown, he must commit them, for he is no more infallible than individuals. I say that he is not more infallible, and if I wanted I could prove that he is less.

There is something in power which distorts judgment. Strength's chances of error are much greater than those of weakness. Strength finds resources in itself, whereas weakness needs reason. Imagine two equally enlightened men, one vested with any kind of power, the other a simple citizen. Do you not feel that if the first were put in a prominent position, pressed into making decisions he must adopt at a given moment, and committed to these decisions that become public, he would have less time for reflection, more interest in persistence, and thus more chance of error than the second? The second man examines at leisure, makes no public commitment, has no motive for defending a false idea, has not compromised either his authority or his vanity, and finally, if he becomes impassioned for this false idea, has no means to make it triumph.[5]

And do not expect to find a remedy in this or that form of government. Because in a representative government the people choose those who impose laws on them, you think that they cannot make a mistake. You are making a mistake yourself. Supposing a perfect system and the best-guaranteed freedom of election, it will follow that the opinion of the elected will be in

4. Galiani, *The Grain Trade,* p. 250.

5. *Ideas on Sovereignty, Social Authority and Individual Rights.*

conformity with that of the voters. They will therefore be at the level of the nation. They will be no more infallible than it is.

I will add that the qualities the people choose often do not include superior education. To conquer and above all to retain the multitude's confidence, it is necessary to have tenacity in ideas, partiality in judgment, deference to prejudices still in favor, more strength than finesse, and more promptness to grasp the whole than delicacy in discerning the details. These qualities are sufficient for what is fixed, determined, and precise in legislation. But transported into the domain of intelligence and opinion, they are somewhat raw, unfinished, and inflexible, which thus works against the intended purpose of improvement or perfection.[6]

A very witty Englishman said to me one day: In the House of Commons, the Opposition is more intelligent than the Ministry. Outside the House of Commons, the educated portion of the English people is more intelligent than the Opposition. In tolerating speculative laws—that is, taking legislation beyond the sphere of necessity—you thus subject the human race to the inevitable mistakes of men vulnerable to error, not only through the weakness inherent to everyone, but through the additional effect of their special position.

What reflections I could add if I wanted to speak here of the flaws inseparable from all collective decisions, for they are nothing but forced compromises between prejudices and truth, interests and principles! Or if I wanted to examine the means legislation must use in order to be obeyed, to describe the influence of coercive or prohibitory laws on citizens' morals, and the corruption which the multiplicity of laws introduces among the government's agents! But I have already touched on this subject in another work,[7] and furthermore I will be brought back to it in the course of this commentary.

To sum up: errors of legislation have multiple disadvantages. Independently of the direct harm they cause by forcing men to adapt to them and conform their habits and calculations to them, they are, as Filangieri observes, as dangerous to eliminate as to respect. Individuals can doubtless make mistakes, but if they stray, the laws are there to repress them. On the contrary, errors of legislation fortify themselves with the force of law itself. These errors are

6. Ibid.

7. *Course on Constitutional Politics.*

general and condemn man to obedience. The mistakes of private interest are individual: one person's mistake has no influence on another's conduct. Since all error harms the person who commits it, error is soon recognized and given up when the law remains neutral. Nature has given man two guides: interest and experience. He learns from his own losses. What motive for persistence would he have? Everything he does is private. Without anyone noticing, he can retreat, advance, change course—in sum, he can freely correct himself. The situation of the legislator is the reverse in everything. Further removed from the consequences of his measures and not feeling their effects so immediately, he discovers his mistakes later, and when he discovers them, he finds himself in the presence of hostile observers. He has reason to fear losing prestige if he corrects himself. Between the moment legislation deviates from the correct path and the moment when the legislator perceives it, much time passes; but between the latter moment and when the legislator decides to retrace his steps, even more time passes, and the very act of retracing his steps is not without danger for both the legislator and society.

Thus whenever there is no absolute necessity, whenever legislation does not have to intervene so that society will not be overthrown, whenever finally it is only a question of a hypothetical good, the law must abstain, allow things to happen,[8] and be silent.

8. *Laisser-faire.*—Trans.

# CHAPTER TEN ❧ Some Remarks by Filangieri on the Decline of Spain

> Spain owes not only to the expulsion of the Moors . . . but to false principles of administration . . . the deplorable state of agriculture, industry, population and commerce.
>
> BOOK 1, CHAPTER 3, P. 54.

Doubtless Filangieri is correct to include the expulsion of the Moors and the absurdity of several of the commercial laws which rule that kingdom among the causes of Spain's decline. We will have more than one occasion to return to the disastrous influence of these prohibitive laws, of which all European governments formerly made such ample use. The lessons of experience and the efforts of all sensible men still cannot get rid of these laws, which are recommended by all governments' flatterers, all the promoters, all the ignorant speculators, all the greedy businessmen. They frequently seduced Montesquieu himself. So hateful to governments is belief in freedom's good effects! As for the expulsion of the Moors, today happily it is put alongside the St. Bartholomew's Eve massacre and the revocation of the Edict of Nantes. Despite the shamelessness of writers in government pay, the progress of the century has gained this: were such measures repeated, they would perhaps find accomplices, but they would not meet with approval from afar.

Nevertheless, these causes, to which Filangieri assigns the destruction of an empire always favored by its climate and position, and for several centuries aided by a unique combination of circumstances, are only secondary and accidental. Or rather they are themselves the effect of a general and permanent cause, the gradual establishment of despotism and the abolition of all constitutional institutions.

Spain did not suddenly fall into the state of weakness and degradation in which that monarchy was mired when Bonaparte's invasion awoke a generous people from its stupor. Its decline dates from the destruction of its political freedom and the suppression of the Cortes. Formerly inhabited by thirty million people, it has seen its population gradually fall to nine million. Sovereign of the seas and mistress of innumerable colonies, it has seen its navy decline to the point where it was inferior to those of England, Holland, and France. Arbiter of Europe under Charles V, terror of Europe under Phillip II, it has seen itself crossed off the list of powers which have determined the world's destiny during the last three centuries. All this did not happen in a day. It was done by the stubborn work and silent pressure of a government which limited human intelligence, and which, in order not to fear its subjects, paralyzed their faculties and kept them in a condition of apathy.

The proof of this is that if we look at England, we see commercial laws no less absurd, no less harmful, no less unjust among the English. In the massacres of Catholics, above all in Ireland, and in the execrable regulations which reduced all that portion of the Irish people to the condition of helots, we see the counterpart of the persecution and to a certain extent the banishment of the Moors, yet England has remained in the first rank of nations. It is the political institutions, the parliamentary discussions, and the freedom of the press which England has enjoyed without interruption for 126 years which have counterbalanced the vices of its laws and its government. Its inhabitants' energy of character has been maintained because they were not disinherited from their participation in the administration of public affairs. This participation, even if it was almost imaginary, gave citizens a feeling of their own importance which kept up their activity. An England ruled almost without exception by Machiavellian ministers, from Sir Robert Walpole down to our own day, and represented by a corrupt parliament, has nevertheless preserved the language, the habits, and several of the advantages of freedom.

If one objects that the Spanish constitution was already nonexistent under Philip II, I would respond that despotism's effect is not immediate. A nation which has been free, and which has owed the development of its moral and industrial faculties to its freedom, lives for some time after the loss of its rights on its old capital—on its acquired wealth, so to speak. But once the reproductive principle is dried up, the active, enlightened, industrious generation gradually disappears, and the generation which replaces it falls into inertia and bastardization.

If one raises as an objection the example of other European states, who are no less strangers to constitutional institutions than Spain but who have not been subject to the same decline, I will explain this difference easily, by proving that these states retained a kind of freedom that was uncertain and without guaranties but real in its results, even though precarious in its duration. This gives me an opportunity to suggest some ideas about the political effects of the discovery of printing that I believe are important and that I think I was the first to develop.[1]

Formerly, in all European countries there were institutions associated with many abuses but which, by giving certain classes privileges to defend and rights to exercise, kept up activity among these classes and thus preserved them from discouragement and apathy. To this cause must be attributed the energy of character existing up to the sixteenth century, an energy of which we no longer find any trace by the time of the revolution which shook thrones and reforged souls. These institutions had been everywhere destroyed, or changed so much that they had lost almost all their influence. But around the time they collapsed, the discovery of printing gave men a new means of interesting themselves in their country. It allowed a new spring of intellectual movement to well forth.

In countries where the people do not participate actively in government, that is, everywhere where there is no freely elected national representation with very considerable prerogatives, freedom of the press to some extent replaces political rights. The educated part of the nation interests itself in the administration of affairs when it can express an opinion, if not directly, at least on the general principles of government. But when there is neither freedom of the press nor political rights in a country, people detach themselves entirely from public affairs. All communication between the rulers and the ruled is cut off. For a while, the government and the government's supporters may regard this as an advantage. The government does not encounter any obstacles, nothing thwarts it, but it alone is alive; the nation is dead. Public opinion is the life of states. When public opinion is wounded in its principle, states perish and fall into dissolution. Consequently, and note this well, since the discovery of printing, certain governments have favored the expression of opinion by means of the press. Others have tolerated this expression, and others have smothered it. The nations among which this intellectual occu-

1. *On the Spirit of Conquest*, 1814.

pation has been encouraged or permitted are the only ones which have retained strength and life. Those whose governments have imposed silence on all opinion have gradually lost all character and vigor.

Such was the fate of Spain, subject as it was more than any other country in Europe to political and religious despotism. The moment constitutional freedom was taken from the Spanish, since no new path was open to their intellectual activity, they became resigned and fell asleep. The state suffered in consequence. Its death sentence was pronounced.

We must not believe that the gains of trade, the profits of industry, or even the necessity of agriculture are sufficient motivation for human activity. The influence of personal interest is often exaggerated. Interest is limited in its needs and crude in its pleasures. It works for the present without looking farther into the future. The man whose opinion languishes and is smothered is not excited for long even by his interest. A sort of stupor overtakes him, and just as paralysis spreads from one portion of the body to another, it also extends to one after another of our faculties.

Those who hold power would like their subjects to be passive in servitude and active in work, insensitive to slavery and ardent in all enterprises that have nothing to do with politics, resigned serfs and able tools. This combination of opposite qualities cannot last. It is not given to power to awaken or put to sleep peoples according to its convenience or its passing fancies. Life is not something that one alternately takes away and gives back. Human faculties come together: enlightenment applies to everything. It makes industry, the arts, the sciences progress, and then, analyzing this progress, it extends its own horizon. But its basis is thought. If you discourage thought in itself, it will be exercised apathetically for any purpose whatsoever. One might say that, indignant at being expelled from its proper sphere, thought wanted to avenge itself for the humiliation inflicted on it by a noble suicide. Human existence attacked at its core soon feels the poison reach even its furthest parts. You think you have limited only some superfluous freedom or taken away some useless pomp, but your poisoned weapon has wounded it to the heart. Human intelligence cannot remain stationary. If you do not stop it, it advances; if you stop it, it retreats; it cannot remain at the same point. Thus, although governments want to kill opinion and think they are encouraging interest, they discover that their clumsy double operations kill them both, to their great regret, and intellectual activity soon slows within the government itself. Where there is no public opinion a nation's lethargy communicates itself to its government. Unable to keep the nation awake, the government ends up going to sleep along with it. Thus everything is silenced, everything weakens, everything degenerates and dies.

Such, I repeat, was the fate of Spain, and neither the beauty of the climate, nor the fertility of the soil, nor the domination of the two seas, nor the riches of the New World, nor, what was even more, the eminent faculties of that now admirable nation could save it from this fate. So true was it that it was the government which burdened this people's lot, that as soon as a foreign invasion suspended this government's action, the nation's energy fully reappeared. What the coalition of Europe's governments had been unable to do, what the bureaucratic ability of Austria and the belligerent ardor of Prussia had vainly attempted, the Spanish did. They did it without kings, without generals, without money, without armies, abandoned, disavowed by all the sovereigns. They had to repulse not only Bonaparte and French valor, but also the docile and zealous collaboration of the rulers whom he had forced or accepted into the ranks of his vassals.

Some partisan writers have attributed much heroism to religion, to ancient mores, to doctrines scrupulously transmitted from one century to another, and above all to the absence of what they call revolutionary ideas; but religion, ancient mores, and hereditary doctrines had been unable to prevent Spanish power from decaying, its industry from languishing, and its glory from being eclipsed. Bent beneath the yoke, each Spaniard was detached from his own destiny, which his will could not influence. Put back in possession of his natural portion of influence by an unexpected revolution and invested with the right to defend his country and himself, every Spaniard felt his strength reborn and his enthusiasm set alight. The absence of government returning the full use of their faculties to all, the full extent of these faculties was immediately rediscovered. No virtue, no talent was absent from the roll-call: so much is the most unequal struggle preferable to servitude!

Do you require additional proof of this important truth? By a deplorable fate, an oppressive government followed this inspired struggle, these patriotic victories. Informers and courtesans, a race hostile to kings and peoples alike, fooled a monarch who was led astray by inexperience and the prejudices of the day. Suddenly apathy, collapse, disgust for work, stagnation of industry, interruption of trade, fall of credit—all the symptoms of decadence and ruin which had signaled the decline of old Spain—reappeared in a Spain delivered from the foreigner. However, the causes to which its triumphs had allegedly been linked had lost none of their intensity. Spain possessed both its excessive worship and its attachment to its ancestors' mores. But freedom had departed: it has now returned and already it is reopening all the springs of prosperity.

While I was writing this about Spain, a thought came to me; why should I silence it?

At the moment when a magnanimous nation which had just broken its fetters associated its deliverance with the king who governed it, at the moment when that king himself consecrated the new social pact by sacred oaths, how did it come about that in other parts of Europe some men seemed to have made it their task to smother the seeds of good, eternalize hatred, and resuscitate suspicion? How did it happen that in France, tools of I don't know what faction, ambassadors created by themselves, or missionaries of I don't know what secret power, dared offer criminal help to the ruler they compromised, and pursued a constitutional monarch with insolent and hypocritical pity? Do they not know that it was thus that foreigners caused the fall of the unfortunate Louis XVI? Have they forgotten that their crazy threats, their alleged information, their incendiary pamphlets helped royalty's more direct but not more dangerous enemies?[2] Safely seated far from the theater of agitation and danger, it matters little to them what pits they dig beneath the feet of nations and around thrones.

Enlightened and generous Spaniards, these men have already caused you many hardships. Since 1814 they have perpetually preached to your rulers both the legitimacy of absolute power and the justice of the frightful means necessary to preserve it. Their opinion seemed disinterested. Who can determine the authority it ought to have? Their voice came from afar: one would have thought it impartial, like that of an equitable posterity. Who can know to what degree it has influenced your misfortunes?

Of all your enemies, these men are the most inexcusable, perhaps the only inexcusable ones. Without passion and without immediate interest, they coldly applauded the persecutions, the sufferings, the tortures inflicted by your defenders. Let the victims' blood fall on them!

2. I developed this idea a few months ago in an article in *La Minerve* titled, "On the plots of French counter-revolutionaries against the life and safety of the King of Spain."

Despite these contemptible and perfidious adversaries, you will peacefully follow your noble path. You know that justice is the basis of freedom, that in order to found a constitutional monarchy one must respect its first principle, the inviolability of the monarch, and that the will of the majority is only legitimate when it does not wound any of the minority's rights. You also know, by immortal and glorious experience, that your will alone is enough against Europe united. You resisted Bonaparte: heaven will not create a second Bonaparte. Napoleon was not able to defeat Spain, and the generals he defeated will be no more fortunate against Spain than was he before whom they succumbed. If there was one who had success accompanying his flag, it was because he defended a holy cause. Abjuring this cause, he will lose his strength, and Salamanca and Ciudad Rodrigo will in future be only the witnesses of his shame and his defeats.[3]

3. Constant is referring to the Duke of Wellington.—Trans.

# CHAPTER ELEVEN ❧ On Filangieri's Observations about France

> If we pass from Spain to France, we will again see a nation which, after having dominated Europe . . . found . . . in the ignorance of its legislators the principle of its decline.
>
> BOOK I, CHAPTER 3, P. 56.

With regard to France, Filangieri commits a mistake analogous to that which I have brought to light with respect to his reflections on Spain. Just as he attributed the decline of the latter kingdom to the expulsion of the Moors and to bad commercial laws, so he assigns the cause of the decline of the former to the revocation of the Edict of Nantes and the encouragements Colbert gave exclusively to industry, without regard for and without concessions to agriculture.

Unquestionably Colbert fell into many errors, and according to my principles concerning the neutrality governments ought to observe in everything which regards industry, commerce, and individual speculation, it would be very surprising if I were to make myself the apologist of this minister formerly so much praised. The revocation of the Edict of Nantes was also a great crime and an act of delirium. But Colbert would not have been able to give in wholly to his erroneous theories about the necessity of giving manufacturing a forced and artificial activity, nor would Louis XIV have been able to banish the Protestants from a country they enriched, if France had been safeguarded by a free constitution against the despotism of kings and the fanciful ideas of ministers. Nevertheless, several differences between France and Spain deserve to be noted.

Intellectual oppression has never weighed on us to the same extent as on our neighbors over the Pyrenees. The French were not completely deprived of all political rights until Richelieu. I already said in the previous chapter that defective institutions which nevertheless invest some powerful classes with certain privileges they are permanently interested in defending possess many disadvantages, yet they also possess the advantage of not letting the whole nation be degraded and bastardized. The beginning of Louis XIV's reign was disturbed by the Fronde,[1] in truth a childish war, but one which was the remnant of a spirit of resistance accustomed to action, and still acting almost without purpose. Despotism greatly increased around the end of that reign. Opposition still continued, however, taking refuge in religious quarrels, sometimes the Calvinists against the Catholics, sometimes the Catholics among themselves. The death of Louis XIV was the beginning of the relaxation of authority. Freedom of opinion gained ground daily.

I do not mean to say that that freedom was used in the most decent and most useful way. I mean to say only that it was exercised, and that as a result one cannot list the French of any period, down to the revolution of 1789, among the peoples condemned to complete subjection and moral lethargy. However, it is certain that when Filangieri wrote, France had fallen from its rank and forfeited its power, and that its national character had changed. But where did this decline, this change, this decadence come from?

It is easy and convenient to attribute general effects to partial causes. Freedom's enemies amuse themselves greatly with this way of resolving problems because every time we go back to principles, the necessity of freedom suddenly appears, while if we take a given detail, a given individual, a given accident for the solution of the problem, freedom is not significant. Some will tell you that France's weakness in the last century was because of the unsuccessful wars in which Louis XIV engaged around the end of the preceding century. Others will blame this weakness on the corruption the Regency introduced to all classes, and the weak resistance to the progress of this corruption by Louis XIV's successors, who were voluptuous, lazy, or weak and showed themselves incapable of fully exercising royal authority.

As for the corruption for which Louis XIV's successors are accused of

1. Period of civil and political unrest in Paris, 1648–53.—Trans.

providing the example and favoring and tolerating the progress, it was the necessary consequence of the moral oppression which Louis XIV in his senility exercised over a nation already too enlightened to bear it: the reaction was proportionate to the action. This reaction was beginning even before Louis XIV's death. Memoirs of the time tell us of intercepted letters, "equally offensive to God and the King."[2] These letters were written by courtiers who lived under his strict authority. But the old ruler weighed on his old court, which itself imposed fraud and dissimulation on the rising generation. With the death of the king, the torrent to which his despotism had opposed dikes breached them all. By breadth and boldness, reason compensated itself for the constraints to which it had impatiently submitted. One can affirm, and this ought to be an instructive lesson for those who govern, that every time lies have ruled, the truth has avenged itself with interest. Hardly had Louis XIV disappeared than the Regency appeared. Mme de Prie replaced Mme de Maintenon, and depravity sat down on hypocrisy's tomb.

Conversely, give France a free constitution. A monarch's superstition will be without influence on a people with the right not to ape its master's opinion. There will be no reaction toward license, because there will not have been pressure for false zeal and bigotry.

One can say as much of the weakness of the rulers who followed Louis XIV. The lax mores of Louis XV and Louis XVI's indecision would have been matters of very little importance in England, because the king's personal character means nothing in a constitutional government. I will go further. It is fortunate that Louis XIV's successors had lax morals and were weak, for this caused the difference I have noted between France and Spain, which is all to the advantage of the former. If Louis XIV had, like Charles V, been succeeded by a severe, easily offended ruler, competent enough to oppress the nation without causing an uprising, it is probable that France would have fallen into stupor and apathy. In this respect perhaps we ought to congratulate ourselves on the orgies of the Regency and the immorality of Louis XV's court. The license of the great came to the rescue and benefitted the people's freedom.

Under a government that was serious, oppressive, and supported by an implacable Inquisition, Spain lost all activity and interest in public affairs. France had an arbitrary government, but one which was illogical and frivo-

2. Letters of Mme de Maintenon.

lous and opposed by an opinion which found a thousand exits through which to escape, and so France retained interest in public affairs. France preserved, if not the right, at least the ability to concern itself with them, and if the two monarchies perished, it was in a different way, each in conformity with the cause of its decline. Paralyzed Spain was never of any use during the two centuries of its lethargy, neither to itself nor to Europe, despite the sublime qualities which were seemingly buried in the character of its inhabitants. France, in its most profound abasement, spread enlightenment around it, preserved intellectual life in literature, and finally gave the noble signal for freedom.

# CHAPTER TWELVE ☙ On the Decline Filangieri Predicted for England

> England is today on the edge of ruin, and its sudden decline has its source in its laws' errors.
>
> BOOK I, CHAPTER 3, P. 57.

All Filangieri's observations on the vices of English laws, on the absurdity and cruelty of the commercial prohibitions in force in Adam Smith's homeland, on the inequality and injustice of the relations England established and wanted to perpetuate between itself and its colonies, are obviously true. The legislation of that famous island in everything which relates to industry, to manufactures, to fixing the price of daily wages—in a word, to the existence of the man reduced to living from his labor—resembles a permanent conspiracy by the class of the powerful against the poor and laboring class. Innumerable proofs would be easy to assemble. Even leaving barbarous times aside and only consulting laws from the reign of Elizabeth to the present, one cannot open the English statute book without seeing harsh punishments, tortures, and death given for actions which it is impossible to consider crimes. The export of a ram or a lamb brings confiscation of property or loss of the left hand, and a second offense brings death. Whoever approaches the coast with raw wool is struck with a no less severe penalty, suspected of having wanted to export unprocessed raw material. If some workers, dying of poverty with their families, unite to obtain salaries proportional to the price of food, they are punished as rebels. In this country in which every inhabitant boasts of being able to wander in freedom, the indigent man needs the consent of the parish where he intends to live in order to move from one parish to another, for fear that deprived of the means of subsistence he may become a burden on his new fellow citizens. In their own country the pregnant woman, the old man, and the orphan thus meet at every step artificial barriers which transform their country into an inhospitable land where poverty is proscribed, because property has retained the original ferocity of usurpation.

In his indignation at this sight, it is not astonishing that Filangieri thought he saw the causes of ruin where he saw so many iniquities displayed. Nevertheless, more than forty years have passed since he predicted a near and inevitable decline for England. His predictions have been repeated annually by writers of diverse opinions, some in good faith, others attacking what is bad in England in order to discredit what is good in it. These gloomy prophecies not having been realized, today I think we go to the other extreme and imagine that because England has long been threatened without being harmed, it is permanently immune from the consequences of its vicious institutions.

This subject is extremely important, not only from a doctrinal point of view, but with regard to the future destinies of the European republic. Two powers dispute over Europe as over their prey. These two powers are England and Russia. I do not have to concern myself here with what would become of Europe under Russian influence. To depend on Russia is to depend on an individual. Everything which rests on a single head is fleeting. Governed by absolute rulers, Russia cannot keep an identical system for two imperial generations. What an absolute ruler has begun, his successor abandons; what the first threatened, the second spares or protects. The facts prove this truth to us. Toward the end of the Seven Years' War, the death of an empress saved Prussia, and at the beginning of this century, the fickleness of an emperor would have saved France, if an immoderate ambition had not provoked Russia in the midst of its snows. Thus Russian influence would present Europe with the particular problem that kings, the vassals of this barely civilized giant, would be the playthings of incalculable caprices. If by their submission they bought its assistance against their peoples they would soon see themselves the victims and dupes of this shameful bargain. But once again, this question is foreign to what concerns me. I must now discuss English influence.

England is in a completely different position from Russia. Its constitutional institutions give it all the advantages of aristocratic government. The king in the British constitution is what the supreme power ought to be, a moderator raised above the sphere of agitation, appeasing, disarming, or dividing the other powers. The real daily action is in the ministry, a group of men always more or less distinguished by talent or experience. As a collective body they are sheltered from the vicissitudes of heredity, which successively brings to office childhood and old age, weakness and violence, cowardice and presumption. In short, they form a kind of senate, constant in its views, uniform in its step, and preserved by its composition from the fickleness and caprices inseparable from a succession of individuals who replace one another by right of birth.

Whatever party divisions there have always been, the English government, in passing from the hands of one of these parties to another, has in reality never deviated from its aristocratic principle. Chatham's Whig ministry fifty years ago was no more cosmopolitan or less jealous of the prosperity and rights of the continent than the Tory ministry of Lord Castlereagh today. In the former there was certainly something noble, broad-minded, and generous that is not to be seen in the latter. The doctrines of freedom, even limited to domestic affairs, always give this appearance to those who profess them. But when, returning to the ranks of the opposition, Mr. Pitt's father made demands on behalf of oppressed America, he still cried, "Peace with America and war with Europe!"

For Englishmen of all opinions, the European continent is not a combination of allied countries peopled with beings of the same nature, but a continual object of more or less Machiavellian speculation, and if they do not treat it as they do India, it is because we are Indians too able and too tough for them.

The question of how to know whether England's decline is nothing but a momentary chimera, or if the moment is approaching when that decline will happen is therefore, I repeat, extremely important. It is the question of the industrial, commercial, and even political independence of Europe. But I should note that by decline I do not mean only a momentary weakening, against which the constitutional institutions of England would always react. I mean the destruction of these institutions and the social order based on them, and through this a mortal blow given to England's internal prosperity and external influence.

The two causes that writers who predict England's fall usually allege as producing this result are (1) the poverty of the laboring class and (2) the enormity of the public debt.

The poverty of the laboring class cannot be denied, and the laws of England are in this respect as absurd as they are atrocious. They weigh on its poor, they dispute their legitimate use of their faculties and strength, and they make their sufferings eternal, for they take away from them every means of arriving at a more fortunate position. As a result, when other causes bring about a great crisis, the effect of these disastrous laws would unquestionably be to add to the disorders and calamities of that crisis. But the vices of these laws, however great they are, will not alone produce the convulsion that they would aggravate if it came from outside.

The class of the poor is always divided. Pursued by needs which are hourly reborn, it surrenders to the first hope it is given of satisfying even half its pressing needs. Hunger, the motive of its uprisings, at the same time forces it to give in to every temptation presented to it. Left to itself, this unfortunate class, against which all the other classes conspire, can rattle its chains but not break them. It remains in chains after having struck its masters with them, and is formidable only when the higher ranks furnish it with leaders.

But in England these higher ranks are all leagued against this unhappy class. In a country where political freedom exists and where persons and properties have nothing to fear from arbitrary power, all those who possess something form a coalition in favor of the established order as soon as anarchy presents itself. Thus English constitutional institutions preserve them from the consequences of their industrial and commercial mistakes, which makes all the more strange the folly of those writers who simultaneously propose to us to borrow that people's prohibitive laws while inviting us to preserve ourselves from its constitutional system.

Furthermore, among the measures and precautions taken to contain the lower class, if several are hostile and rigorous, there are also some which consist in sweeteners and palliatives of at least limited efficacy. Thus the poor tax, a tax so regrettable in many respects and from which England would instantly free itself by a return to the principles of industrial freedom, is a kind of restitution consented to by the monopolists in favor of those whom they deprive of their rights. It is a fine, the price with which prohibitions purchase continued existence. Although insufficient, this tax keeps up the poor man's hopes, and thus calms his irritation.

I will add that, despite its attachment to its harmful regulations, England has over the past century relaxed its old limits on industry a little. Its most barbaric laws are rarely executed, and the courts receive with favor subtle distinctions tending to free as many professions as possible from prohibitive statutes. For example, the apprenticeships established by Elizabeth have been limited to professions which existed under her reign.[1] Thus in this respect freedom gains ground, and the industrial laws, which are moderated or evaded, should not be regarded as a direct and immediate cause of revolution.

It is the same with the enormity of the public debt, which Filangieri and all the writers who afterwards worked the quarry of political economy have seen as a source of upheaval. This debt is doubtless a great curse. In the end its progressive growth must make it unbearable. But up to now, the English public debt, which in some respects ties private fortunes to those of the state, makes supporters for the existing order rather than enemies. It will remain thus as long as the English government has the good sense to see that when a debt is considerable, one should be much more concerned about paying the interest than reducing the principal, and that the greatest reduction is never so profitable as to be worth the least obstruction given to credit by the means employed to reduce it. With this principle, a country can long defy all calculations and brave all human probabilities. A less indebted England would perhaps attract many fewer or much less zealous defenders of the government responsible for and guaranteeing its debt. But in the minds of the state's creditors, the fear of losing capital struggles against the desire to get back their rights, and the reform invoked in theory is rejected in practice, because a real and complete reform would perhaps have bankruptcy as a preliminary or a consequence.

England's danger thus resides neither in the poverty of the laboring class nor in the enormity of the debt. It is in the annihilation, which I believe henceforth inevitable, of its aristocratic principle. This needs further discussion.

As I have said, England is fundamentally nothing but a vast, opulent, and vigorous aristocracy: immense lands combined in the same hands, colossal wealth accumulated likewise, a numerous and faithful clientele grouped around each great landowner, the clients putting at the proprietor's disposition the political rights they seem to have received constitutionally only

1. "One has to have been an apprentice in order to make wagons, but not carriages." Blackstone.

in order to surrender them. In the end, a national representation composed partly of government employees and partly of the aristocracy's choices is the result of this combination. Such has been the organization of England down to this day.

This organization, which in theory seems very imperfect and even very oppressive, was mitigated in practice. This was partly by the good effects of the freedom conquered in 1688, as well as by several circumstances particular to England, circumstances that I think have not been sufficiently noticed when people have wanted to transport elsewhere certain institutions having to do with privileges, and have borrowed from the British constitution with modifications. For the sake of honesty I will even agree that I have not always sufficiently preserved myself from this mistake.[2]

Unlike that of several other countries, the English aristocracy has never been the enemy of the people. Called upon in the most distant centuries to demand what it called its rights against the crown, it had not been able to make good its claims without establishing certain principles useful to the mass of citizens. The Magna Carta, even though written in the middle of feudalism and imprinted with many vestiges of the feudal system, consecrated individual freedom and trial by jury without distinction of rank or persons. In 1688, a large part of the English peerage concurred in the revolution which founded constitutional government in England. Afterwards, instead of devoting itself to domesticity and waiting rooms, this part of the nobility remained at the head of an opposition party, which it served with both its prestige and its wealth, while at the same time being strengthened by it.

Thus by collectively making itself one of the pillars of freedom, the aristocracy gained the dependent class's affection in every way, and did so by patronage which time made almost hereditary as well as by the fidelity with which it fulfilled its duties. The great landholdings of the English lords were in part leased by wealthy farmers who cultivated them from father to son on terms that remained the same for a very long time. Their houses were filled with numerous domestics whom the master paid well, and who seemed to him to be a burden inseparable from his rank. Each of the great lords was to some extent the leader of a small people whose fortune depended on him, and

2. This applies above all to what I said of the peerage in my work on constitutions and guaranties.

who served him with zeal and with the various means which each individual of this people possessed.[3]

Because of this the English aristocracy was in no way hateful to the mass of the nation. Even the laws which emanated from the popular party in the periods when it held power were never directed against the nobility. One must not object against my argument the abolition of the House of Lords during the civil wars. This revolutionary measure was not at all in harmony with the true national feeling. The nobility's privileges, modified by custom more than by law, were preserved in Great Britain without exciting the irritation which they caused elsewhere.

The war of the French Revolution suddenly upset this combination of freedom and aristocracy, of clientism and patronage. By adding greatly to the tax burden, this war created a disproportion between the wealth of the great and the needs of the population which depended on them, and this destroyed all balance. Impatient at a torment they were not used to, the great and the wealthy wanted to free themselves from it. Landowners raised their rents or changed their farmers. Masters sent away their many domestic servants. In these actions they saw only a means of saving money, but it has been the seed of a change in the foundation of the social order. The symptoms of this change are already visible, even though its cause is unknown.

Everywhere the masses of the nation are not repressed by an overwhelming force, they do not consent that there should be classes that dominate them, unless they believe they see in the supremacy of these classes utility for themselves. Habit, prejudice, a kind of superstition, and men's tendency to consider that whatever exists should exist, prolong the ascendancy of these classes even after their utility has ceased. But then their existence is precari-

3. The accuracy of this picture of England around the end of the last century has been contested by several English writers, who have reproached me for having attributed to present times customs and feudal institutions which have not existed since Henry VII. Certainly I am not unaware of the distance which separates constitutional England from the England subject to feudalism. But when institutions are gradually destroyed, relationships and customs survive. The farmers of the great English landowners were certainly not attached to the soil thirty years ago, but the leases and the families which enjoyed them remained the same, and this stability created a link of clientism and patronage between these families and the landowners. As soon as the landowners saw raising rents as a speculation, this link was broken. There were no longer any patrons and clients, but men acting equally according to their interest, and deprived of affection as well as exempt from duties toward one another.

ous, and the survival of their prerogatives becomes uncertain. Thus the clergy saw its power diminish as soon as it was no longer the sole depositary of the knowledge necessary to social life. Peoples no longer wanted to implicitly obey a class they could do without. The authority of the lords began to decline when they no longer offered their vassals sufficient protection to compensate them for their submission to privileges which they had agreed to respect. The great English lords possessed neither a monopoly of the sciences, like the clergy, nor of protection, like the medieval barons, but they had that of patronage, and they rendered this monopoly tolerable for the lower classes by attaching to themselves and winning over a vast clientele. They let them go. They thought—and this is a mistake which the aristocracy always makes—that they could free themselves from the burdens and keep the profit. But the clients, rejected by their patrons, by that very fact felt themselves returned to a footing of equality. They understood this silently and instinctively, and the entire moral disposition of England was changed. The old farmers who paid more, or the new farmers who replaced the old, were no longer the landowners' dependents. They were men who, having dealt with the landowners according to the law, recognized only those laws in whose name more onerous conditions had been imposed on them as intermediaries. The dismissed servants reinforced the class which had nothing to lose, a class already very numerous in England because of its detestable prohibitive laws and its "parish laws," so horrible toward the poor. This caused a large portion of the people who formerly supported the aristocracy to become its adversary.

This first result, getting rid of the dependent class, produced a second, and these two effects have mutually reinforced each other. Up to the present, part of the aristocracy openly defended freedom. Feeling sheltered from popular storms, it was agreeable to it to limit the power of the throne for its benefit. The nobles of the opposition were flattered to flaunt themselves as the tribunes of a people they directed. Today this very portion of the British aristocracy sees that it is no longer at the helm, and it is frightened of the democratic principles which are making progress. Consequently its path is uncertain. It no longer asks for all that it used to ask for, and it does not want all that it asks for. For example, of all the old Whigs who began by demanding parliamentary reform, there are very few who still speak of it, and there is not one, I dare say, who would do it, if it could be done by an act of his will. Also the opposition, properly speaking, has lost the confidence of the mass. This is a problem. Those who want to lead the people beyond bounds profit from the fact that the people have only them for leaders. In order to understand the full extent and importance of such a change, one observation will suffice.

The moment of England's greatest distress was that of the end of the war brought about by the peace of 1814. The war caused this distress, but peace was the signal for its outbreak. During the war English activity was directed toward those kinds of industry and financial speculations driven by a gigantic struggle against Bonaparte and his vassal kings. A population of entrepreneurs, manufacturers, shipbuilders, contraband smugglers—a sort of military population—was brought into existence. It replaced the manufacturing and industrial population of peaceful times, and came to the rescue of that part of the population which remained without direct employment by indirectly associating it in its enterprises and profits. This population's prodigious activity, necessitated and favored by circumstances, created not only an illusion, but also a reality which daily made up for the inconveniences of such a position. From this came the sort of miracle by which the more enemies England had, the more she seemed to grow in strength and power.

Peace came. For a moment activity had to stop, along with the war that had created it and which alone had fed it. It had to stop before it was replaced by other forms of financial speculation and industry, because long-neglected channels could not immediately reopen and the direction of capital could not be changed as quickly as a treaty had been signed. Because of this, taxes became intolerable. What had helped make them bearable was the rapid circulation of capital employed in military enterprises, and the no less rapid profit made on that capital. With these springs no longer acting, not only were the taxes going to crush the taxpayers, but as the latter no longer had anything with which to employ the laboring class, extreme poverty had to result for that class too. This indeed is what happened.

At this time, mobs reduced to the most desperate extremes formed in various provinces and even in the vicinity of London. These mobs, given the strength which long-established freedom always gives a constitution, did not put the state in danger, but in any other country they would have created fears of total anarchy. Peasants entered the capital in bands to ask for bread. Coal merchants, hitching themselves to their wagons, came from various counties to seek help from the prince-regent. However, in such a crisis, when the workers were without work, the manufacturers without consumers, the landowners without income, and the poor without food; and when crowds, driven by hunger to badly organized and random pillage, braved punishments equal to those they would have brought on themselves by political crimes, not a single word of rebellion was pronounced, and no sign of sedition displayed. The people, in despair and led by misery to many illegal acts, nevertheless appeared completely untouched by any intention of rising up against the government and attacking the state's constitution in the slightest.

By contrast, the following year, even though distress had diminished and the people had found some means to live and the poor had found work, conspiracies were hatched, dangerous associations were reported, and it was found that a fairly large number of the lower class nourished desires and projects of uprisings. They were willing to run the risks of a revolution without direction, without a fixed goal, and without an end. I agree that the gravity of these symptoms has been exaggerated. The frightful expedient of sending spies to excite ignorant minds and incite revolt in order to denounce it contributed to these uncoordinated movements. A few wretches seduced those who had the misfortune of hearing them, and they probably also accused those they were unable to seduce. Since extraordinary measures had been taken, it was necessary to give the utmost verisimilitude to alarming hypotheses. However, there was a real basis for these hypotheses.

The basis was that the moral state of England had changed. The dismissal of the aristocracy's clientele and their abdication of patronage (for to no longer wish to fulfill their obligations was to abdicate patronage) brought about a change in the social order. The English aristocracy did to itself what royal power did to the aristocracy in other countries.

Here is the cause of a possible and perhaps approaching revolution. This cause did not exist when Filangieri wrote. Despite the vices of its prohibitive system, despite the enormity of its debt, England was still unshakeable in its institutions, because its institutions were in accord with interests and opinions which were still in accord with the interests of the mass. Today these institutions are in direct opposition with those interests, and it is difficult for them to resist.

What still saves the institutions is that the opposition has retained the right to manifest itself in all its violence, despite sometimes oppressive laws. The opposition is dissipated by this manifestation. Repressed, it would produce a terrible explosion, and the government, which complains that it does not have sufficient repressive means at its disposal against the opposition, owes its salvation to the very impotence it deplores.

Comparing these observations to those of Filangieri, I think one will find that the latter, already inaccurate and superficial when the Italian author wrote them, are completely inapplicable to the present state of things. The danger which threatens England does not chiefly derive from either the poverty of a large part of the population or the growth of England's debt. The danger comes from the fact that as the aristocracy is the foundation of England's institutions, the moment that foundation is shaken, the institutions must totter. Should one conclude from this that the aristocracy must be strengthened? The attempt would be vain. One does not paddle upstream, one does not go against the current but with it, and the boat should be navigated so as not to be shattered on the shoals. England must preserve what is good in its present organization: a national representation, freedom of discussion and of the press, judicial guaranties. It must renounce its concentrated landownership, which creates millions of proletarians, and its aristocracy, which no longer has a clientele nor, as a result, any utility.

P.S. During the printing of this work, several facts have combined to corroborate my assertions.

Some agricultural associations, composed of wealthy landowners in various parts of the kingdom, have taken resolutions which all, in different forms and more or less directly, end by proposing bankruptcy. Among these resolutions, those of the agricultural association of the county of Worcester, presided over by Sir Thomas Winnington, merit serious attention:

> It has been unanimously resolved in this assembly:
>
> 1. That the distress of agriculture and other sufferings of the agricultural interests have been fully demonstrated.
>
> 2. That the committee of the House of Commons has opposed all effective remedy, by stating in principle that the cause of this distress has been the increase in prices caused by the forced circulation of paper money, and in supposing that today these prices will naturally go back down to the level which had been disturbed by the circulation of paper money.
>
> 3. That the association's opinion is that the prices of all objects, production, work and rents have doubled since the existence of paper money, that the increase in taxes is based on these doubled prices, and that the bulk of the national debt and the debt of individual obligations was contracted after these prices doubled.

> 4. That the association cannot comprehend how it would be compatible with good faith that the price of production and labor, that is the income of the landowner and farmer, be reduced to the level previous to the forced introduction of paper money, while the interest on the debt and the salary of place-holders and sinecures, that is the income of the state's creditors and that of government employees, be exempt from this reduction.

If one translated these resolutions into an ordinary style, one would find that they mean that since the reestablishment of payment in specie decreases the cost of foodstuffs and consequently the income of those who produce and sell them, one must, in justice, decrease in equal proportion the interest on the public debt and the salaries of government employees.

As for reducing salaries, this measure is obviously just. As no one is forced to accept salaried jobs, no one has the right to complain about their low pay, since everyone is free to refuse them.

But reducing the debt or the interest on that debt is a completely different kind of question. I will not stop to demonstrate the iniquity of such a violation of sworn faith. I will not even insist on what would be impolitic about it. Every person who is not a stranger to the first notions of public credit knows that there are blows from which it cannot recover, or at least that it does not recover from except when a complete upheaval destroys the government guilty of these blows, and a new government presents itself and seems to offer more guaranties. Thus after the fall of the Directory, which had declared bankruptcy in 1797, France's credit could be reborn under Bonaparte, who had overthrown the Directory. Because he was not responsible for the Directory's infidelities, one could attribute to him the intention of repairing the faults of a government of which he was simultaneously the heir and the conqueror. But if the English government failed to meet its obligations, it would never regain confidence. It would require other men, other things, other institutions, other forms; in a word, a revolution. If that revolution did not happen, what would the English government be in Europe without credit? Its population does not allow it to intervene in continental quarrels by itself. England is important only through its allies. But England has no allies except those it bribes, and it bribes them only through loans. If the source of these loans dries up, what becomes of England? England would then occupy a place in European politics no more important than Sardinia.

I say nothing of the internal upheaval which reducing the debt would entail. A phrase that escaped the authors of the resolutions I have just transcribed is enough to show this. They say that the debts and obligations of individuals were contracted after the doubling of the price of foodstuffs and labor, just as much as the national debt. They do not add, it is true, that individual debts ought to be reduced like the public debt, but this conclusion follows from their principles. Injustice has its logic, as preemptory as the logic of fairness. Those who wish to despoil the state's creditors today, in order to decrease the taxes which pay them, will all the more voluntarily apply the rule they invoke to their own creditors because they will be justified in applying the principle.

There is certainly a considerable distance between the resolutions of a few provincial associations and the determinations of parliament dominated by ministers who know their position pretty well. However, note the progress of ideas over four years. In 1817, a petition based on the doctrine now adopted by the Worcester agricultural association was signed by four thousand individuals of much lower class in the open air; no one paid it the least attention. In 1818, another petition in the same sense was addressed to the House of Commons. It was not read, on the grounds that it was much too long. In 1819, a minister treated all requests for reducing the debt as projects guilty of the crime of high treason. In 1820, some reformers were prosecuted for having said that state creditors were "rapacious creatures." So much for the resistance. Now the progress: In the last session Mr. Littleton, a large landowner, said that these same state creditors were "monsters of consumption," and for this expression, stronger than "rapacious creatures," he was not even called to order. Finally, in 1821, we see that the same language is used not by some reformers or by an isolated man imbued with their doctrines, but by the owners of vast landed properties, by men who are in large number and belong to the highest classes.

And if I am now asked what is to be done in order not to founder on the rock toward which an almost irresistible force is pushing England, I will respond that I see the causes, I perceive the effects, but that when the remedies are of a nature to harm all active interests and encounter obstacles in all organized forces, there would be inexcusable presumption in pointing them out. I will say, however, that for England, shaken to the core, to change its foundation by violent and sudden innovations would be dangerous. Let it use the remnants of its artificial resources, while they still exist, to gain time, and during this time let it create fewer artificial resources for itself. Let it help the poor by abolishing its prohibitive laws. Free industry will be worth more than taxes which perpetuate the poor's misery while helping them go on from day to day. Let it permit ease to be born of itself; by no longer forbidding the division of landholdings, let it renounce its aristocratic concentration of wealth as of power. Perhaps in this way, before the inevitable end of its artificial life, England will succeed in procuring the seeds of a political life more in harmony with the imperious and invincible tendency of European societies. I say perhaps, for I do not know if it is too late.

# *Part Two*

# CHAPTER ONE ❧ Object of This Second Part

It is with a mixture of satisfaction and regret that I leave the field of politics.

On the one hand, it is possible that by prescribing complete silence for myself regarding the highest questions of social organization, I surrender the discussion of some useful idea which at some point would have been applied. The triumph of useful ideas is always just a matter of time, but delay is sometimes harmful to individuals and even to contemporary generations.

On the other hand, since European statesmen have adopted as their maxim that all improvement should come from the government alone, be granted exclusively by it, and be granted only when the peoples have not made any attempt to impose conditions or trace limits on authority, it seems to me that no one ought to intervene about what has to do with government. No one can do so without risking useless dangers and, what is worse, without calling down on his head a moral responsibility which seems to me too great a burden.

In fact, is it not undeniable that by demonstrating the existence of an abuse or the necessity of a reform, one is liable to create the desire for reform in the minds of a multitude who suffer from that abuse or who would gain from that reform? And who can foresee the results of a desire born from conviction and made more ardent by the obstacles themselves? But if this desire leads nations to demands which are too bold, or to illegal actions, it will follow that they will be deprived for a much longer time of the good they demand. I do not wish to contribute to this sad result in any way.

I do not exaggerate the influence that writers exercise. I do not think it is as extensive as governments suppose. However, this influence exists. It is to it that we owe the abolition of religious severity, the elimination of hindrances on commerce, the prohibition of the black slave trade, and many improvements of various kinds.

In any other time this conviction would have added courage; now it halts the conscience. It is established that light ought to come only from above. If light came from below, it would suggest wishes to peoples, which would be a reason for the fulfillment of those wishes to be indefinitely postponed for fear that their realization would be imprudent. I will therefore be silent about politics. The authorities have claimed for themselves alone the totality of our destinies.

It is true that if these considerations were taken very strictly, they would possibly apply to the subjects which will occupy me in this second part as much as to those I thought I should forbid myself. It will be difficult for me to mention even a financial or commercial mistake without seeming to give advice or indicate a solution. However, these subjects are further from those which give offense, and I hope to be able, with the necessary precautions, to speak freely about population, commerce, and taxes.

# CHAPTER TWO ❧ On the Black Slave Trade[1]

> The frightful coasts of Senegal would not have become markets where Europeans go to trade in humanity's inviolable rights at bargain prices. . . . Only Pennsylvania no longer has slaves. The progress of enlightenment makes us hope that this example will soon be followed by the rest of the nations.
>
> BOOK I, CHAPTER 4, PP. 70–71.

When we consider the measures taken by the various governments of Europe against the abominable traffic that Filangieri pointed out for public indignation forty years ago, when we read the ministers' speeches in every assembly and the royal ordinances in all countries, we are tempted to believe that the wishes of the Italian writer have been at least partly fulfilled. But in comparing facts with theories, what happens with what is promised, we see that the result of the laws obtained and promulgated has been to make worse the fate of the unfortunate race we wanted to protect.

A sad and natural consequence of badly executed prohibitions is that the precautions necessary to evade them introduce concealment and haste into the actions which greed inspires despite the laws. This makes them doubly irregular, and when they bear on feeling beings, doubly cruel. The black slave trade has become much more horrible since it was hindered by ineffective prohibitions. When it was permitted, the government which tolerated it ex-

1. The black slave trade having long been considered from a commercial as well as a political perspective (to the shame of the human species), I thought I could, despite the limits I have imposed on myself in this *Commentary*, discuss a subject about which everyone is in at least verbal agreement, and which is of such essential interest to humanity.

ercised at least some supervision over the slave boats, the number of blacks penned into these deadly dwellings, the healthiness of the food intended to prolong their sad existence, and the punishments inflicted on them by their torturers. Since the trade has been forbidden, the ships which serve it are constructed to more easily escape pursuit and to compress into a narrower space captives who are nevertheless in greater number. Fear of unexpected inspection leads their captains to lock up their prey in closed containers where the agents' eyes cannot detect them, and when discovery is inevitable, these containers and the victims they hide from sight are thrown into the sea.

These horrors are confirmed by authentic documents. One can consult the debates of the British parliament, the discussions of the French chambers, and the Reports of the African Society of London. I pass over the details here. They would be out of place in this work.

As a result the abolition of the slave trade, as it has been executed up to the present, has done more evil than good. The greed of the traders who speculate in human blood is no less, and their barbarity is increased by the obstacles they encounter.

This persistence in the most horrible crime that has ever been committed, I will not say by civilized peoples but by the most ferocious hordes, comes from two causes which are related to one other. The first cause is the immensity of the profits combined with the indulgence of the laws. The second is the state of opinion in several European countries on this question.

Of all forms of smuggling, the black slave trade is certainly the most lucrative. It returns five to thirteen times the capital employed.[2] The only means of counterbalancing the lure offered to greed by such enormous profits would be rigorous legislation. But the punishments pronounced against the trade are almost everywhere much more gentle than those directed against crimes infinitely less odious. While death is distributed by our law codes for crimes caused by poverty, despair, and passion, the slave trade, which is a combination of kidnapping, arson, theft, and murder, and which is accompanied by the coldest and most considered premeditation, is only punished in France, for example, by confiscation, from which the guilty shelter themselves

2. See the Reports of the African Society, the account by the Duc de Broglie to the Chamber of Peers in the session of 28 March 1822, and above all a prospectus for a ship intended for this trade, a prospectus published by some businessmen from a port town with incredible shamelessness.

through insurance, and by loss of profession, which is eluded by ostensibly sailing under someone else's orders.

People object that more severe punishments would be reluctantly applied by the courts, and that their indulgence would leave unpunished the accused, whom they would not want to surrender to harsh treatment which they found excessive. The same men, who do not fear that lack of punishment would result from judges' compassion toward political crimes, declare that it is impossible to obtain the same obedience, and the same execution of the law, from these judges when it comes to the most revolting crime against all the principles which preserve justice and the dignity of the human species.

I will soon say what truth there may be in this observation, but I do not think it is sufficient to excuse the mildness of the present laws. There are, I dare hope, many men among those who would be jurors to whom a moment's reflection would make clear the abuse and the crime of such indulgence.

As for me, I declare that it can sometimes be necessary to pronounce a death sentence against the citizen who, misled by his opinions or even by his ambition, has conspired against freedom or troubled his country's peace; but I will always deplore this necessity, because political crimes do not imply perverse intentions or the corruption of the heart. Whereas if I was a juror, and the laws offered me a way to deliver society from the tiger who had carried off or bought his fellows; packed them into a filthy hole in the bottom of a boat; let some perish in the torments of disease, hunger, thirst, or slow agony; and perhaps thrown into the sea the sick and infirm, seeing in them nothing but damaged merchandise, I would certainly not hesitate a second to let the sword of justice fall upon him. I don't think that the least feeling of pity would rise in my soul against the verdict I would pronounce.

At the bottom of the sophism I have just described, however, there is an element of truth which gives weight to what is false in it, and this brings me to the second cause which perpetuates the black slave trade among us. One cannot deny that in several European states, particularly in France, the abolition of the slave trade preceded the time when enlightened opinion was unanimous on this subject. This abolition was presented on the continent in the form of a decree imported from England; consequently, people have always sought its motivation in politics and interest more than in justice. It thus preceded the moral conviction which makes reforms effective. It was imposed by authority, and public opinion supports legal measures less strongly when these measures take initiatives which opinion thinks belong to it. The traders whose greed was limited by the laws were not generally condemned. They were considered victims of a trade prohibited because of the jealousy of a rival people, rather than as guilty individuals punished for an odious and infamous crime.

Concerning the black slave trade there thus occurs what occurs in all human affairs. Reforms which precede opinion, however evident their justice, are never either effective or complete in their effects. The enemies of these reforms find support in habits and prejudices that are not yet destroyed. It is only when enlightenment is sufficiently widespread that the goal can be attained and the laws executed.

This is so true that the two countries where this abominable commerce is most highly condemned and most actively and in good faith repressed are America and England. As for America, its government's intentions do not seem suspect to me. It is placed in such fortunate circumstances that the vices of the old European politics cannot be introduced there. An immense territory, a population that can spread out at will, and complete security with regard to any invasion preserve America from most of the difficulties which hinder and corrupt our governments. But this is not the case with the English government or ministry. The prohibition of the slave trade is in its interest, we are told, in the interest of its commerce, and this apparent humanity toward the blacks is nothing but a clever conspiracy against the prosperity of other peoples.

To refute this objection, which a natural national mistrust disposes us to think is very strong, I will borrow the words of a man who has carried out long and thorough research on the facts relative to the abolition of the slave trade, and who as a peer of France cannot be suspected of leaning toward England's commercial interests.

> English commerce [he says] has never asked for the abolition of the slave trade; it has never shown itself to be its originator or its supporter. On the contrary, it has pronounced against it. For twenty years it waged the fiercest fight to maintain it. It did not let itself be deprived of the trade except after having fought tirelessly, and after having exhausted itself in efforts and imprecations. Even today, if some English traders dared raise their voices, perhaps they would ask that the slave trade might be made possible under a foreign flag, perhaps they would regret

> that the last disguise and the final refuge had been taken from their detestable speculations. . . . The present English ministers have not seen the abolition of the slave trade as an advantage. For more than twenty years they were numbered among the adversaries of this holy cause. They voted to the last in the final minorities, persisting in their opposition until the end. They predicted, as this measure's inevitable consequence, both the ruin of the colonies and universal bankruptcy. . . . It is not their policy which has triumphed, it is not their work whose success is assured. In working for the definitive destruction of the black slave trade, they are making, so to speak, honorable amends for their past errors. They have been defeated by the ascendancy of public opinion, by the strength of reason and truth. Today it is the force of reason and truth which drives and dominates them.[3]

The strength of this reasoning seems evident to me. If today the English government is in good faith in creating obstacles to the slave trade, it is because opinion in this regard has been prepared in England by long discussion and by the indefatigable perseverance of the most respected men.

In general people do not sufficiently recognize the power of demonstrated truths. Whatever unfavorable judgment the human species may merit, there is a degree of evidence which interests do not resist. The ancients, much less advanced than we with respect to enlightenment, possessed all the natural ideas which serve as the basis of morality. However, they tolerated slavery in its most odious excesses. Having been reconciled by practice to a thing execrable in itself, their conscience was not aroused by the word *slave*. In the Europe of our day, the idea of commanding a man's work without paying for it, or of passing judgment without trial over the life of an innocent man, would revolt the least enlightened and least scrupulous among us.

But we have yet to arrive at this point when it is a question of blacks. Unfortunately, part of the European public still does not consider them as belonging to the human race. This part of the public, which would blush at the thought of perpetrating murder or stealing on the highway, participates without scruple in a trade which has seduced it by its profits, and which drugs itself with sophisms so as to hide the fact that there is an equivalence between it and the murderer or arsonist. When this truth is well recognized; when

3. Discussion by the Duc de Broglie.

the laws make no distinction between crimes that are in fact at least equal; when, independently of the laws, an indignant public opinion pursues the businessman who has participated in the slave trade in the streets and the public square, almost the entire commercial population will refuse to touch it. Only a few wretches will be left, equally without means as without shame, who for a dubious profit will join the ranks of pirates and bandits outside the society which will punish them.

Therefore we must work tirelessly to produce this moral conviction. We must not, like Filangieri, limit ourselves to stating principles, proving that in theory the slave trade is a violation of all rights; we must demonstrate by facts that in practice it is a combination of every crime. We must describe every aspect of the cruelty with which today it still soils the maritime annals of all nations. Everywhere we must put on record, and constantly repeat, how thirty-nine blacks, having become blind because they were packed into the bottom of the hold, were thrown into the sea;[4] and how twelve slaves, shut into containers in order to hide them from the searches of an English ship,

4. This fact is all the more remarkable because it is known only through a scientific work whose author was so far from intending to arouse minds against the slave trade that he very much regretted having inserted this horrible detail into his account, and made haste to eliminate it from an edition expressly created to replace the first. This is one more reason to give it all the publicity possible and to denounce it to all those who retain some feeling of humanity.

> The ship . . . of two hundred tons burden, left . . . 24 January 1819, for the African coast, and arrived at its destination the following 14 March. The ship cast anchor before Bouny, on the Malabar river, in order to engage in the black slave trade there. . . . The blacks, who numbered 160, packed in the hold and the steerage, contracted a considerable redness in their eyes, which spread from one to another with amazing rapidity. . . . The blacks, who had previously remained in the hold, were made to come on deck one after another, in order to give them better air to breathe: but it became necessary to give this measure up, salutary as it was, because many of these blacks, affected by nostalgia (the desire to see their native country again), threw themselves into the sea while embracing one another. The illness spread among the Africans in a rapid and frightening manner, and soon became dangerous to all, and created fears among the crew. . . . The suffering increased daily, as well as the number of the blind, so that the crew, already afraid of a revolt among the blacks, was terrified at the thought of being unable to sail the ship to the Antilles if the last sailor, who alone was untouched by the infection, became unable to see like the others. Such an event had occurred aboard the *Léon*, a Spanish ship which sailed before the ———, and of which the entire crew, blinded, had been forced to give up directing the vessel, and recommended themselves to the charity of ———, almost as unfortunate as they. . . . Arrived at Guadeloupe 21 June, 1819, the crew was in a pitiable state. . . . Among the blacks 39 had become blind and were thrown into the sea. *Bibliothèque opthalmologique of Dr. Guillié.*

were likewise probably thrown into the waves when the captain of the slaver no longer hoped to escape from the English.[5]

We must add that the slave trade's crimes are not limited to these unbelievable atrocities. To the number of these crimes, and among the acts for which the slave merchants are responsible, we must add the state into which they thrust the small nations whom they seduce with their foul suggestions and bargains. They inflame all the vices and passions of these barbarous nations, pervert their rude institutions, and poison their domestic relations. The petty tyrants of these countries condemn entire families pell-mell for minor or imaginary crimes, post their soldiers in ambush in order to assault unarmed travelers, fall on sleeping villages at night, drag into slavery the men, women, and young people old enough to serve, and massacre the aged and the infants. Famine, devastation, and wars undertaken to obtain prisoners are the immediate effect of the presence of Europeans who, as speculators, or rather as accomplices in this spectacle of desolation, furnish weapons, feed hatred, and maintain divisions.

And if, as is always done, one tries to weaken the impression these horrors must produce by reminding us of the barbarities committed by the blacks who rebelled on Saint-Domingo,[6] one must reply: yes, the blacks who broke their chains were ferocious, they punished horrible cruelties with horrible

5. On 4 March 1820, the boats of the English vessel *Tartar* stopped the *Jeune Estelle*. . . . The alarm and agitation that were observed in the faces of all the people on the ship aroused suspicion, and the ship was inspected as a result. During this examination, one of the men of the *Tartar*'s crew, having knocked on a very carefully sealed barrel, heard a voice like the moans of a dying person come out of it, and two young black girls of twelve or fourteen years of age were found shut up in it, in the last stage of suffocation, and who, thanks to this lucky chance, were saved from the most frightful death. . . . It must be recognized that the captain had embarked fourteen slaves on board the *Jeune Estelle*. . . . Another visit resulted in saving from death a black who, however, was not one of the twelve who were being sought. A kind of platform had been built on top of the barrels which contained the ship's water, composed of detached planks, shaped like a steerage, around 23 inches tall. . . . Under this platform, the body covered with one of these planks, pressed between two barrels, was found the unfortunate black just referred to. It was a matter of great astonishment for all the witnesses of this frightful spectacle to find him still alive in such a situation. . . . However we asked ourselves what had become of the other twelve slaves. . . . The officers of the *Tartar* remembered with a feeling of horror that when they had begun to give chase to the *Jeune Estelle*, they had seen several barrels floating behind them, and they suspected that each of these barrels contained one or more of these unfortunates. *Official evidence deposed before the committee of the House of Commons.*

6. Haiti.—Trans.

cruelties. But whose fault was it? Did they come to coasts inhabited by Europeans to bring fire and massacre there? Who dragged them to these coasts? How were they transported? By what right are they kept? What were their duties toward foreigners guilty of kidnapping and murder against them? What treaty was there between these two races of men, if not on one side the treaty of chains and the whip, and on the other that of the torch?

To judge the question justly, here is how it must be posed. On the Barbary coasts there are also pirate peoples who carry off the Europeans they can catch. If one of these Europeans, imprisoned in the bagnio of Tunis or Algiers and covered in chains, bound with ropes, nourished on stinking food, exhausted with work, covered with blows, was freed from this frightful yoke and found his way back to his family and his country, and if in telling you about his rescue he said to you: I set fire to the prison where I was held, I killed the thief who had carried me off, I killed him and his family—would you condemn that European? If he was your friend, your son, or your brother, would you reject him as a criminal?

The governments which consider publicity about the crimes to which the slave trade gives birth an evil, and which from national pride want to spare the shame of them from their subjects who engage in it, and from those of their agents who tolerate it, are making a bad calculation of their own real interest. The slave trade need not be the most atrocious of crimes, but by the very fact that it is prohibited, it is in governments' interest that the prohibition be carried out. It is always in the interest of governments that laws be obeyed. Disobedience is contagious, and the sight of an existing law that is despised is corrupting for peoples and dangerous for authority.

The slave trade is contrary to governments' interests in that those who engage in this frightful commerce find themselves in a state of hostility to and a struggle against society because of the prohibition which they defy and the pursuit which threatens them. Rebels to the law, criminals to nature, armed smugglers trafficking in human flesh and blood, they are thrown onto a path where they can only become daily more determined and ferocious public enemies.

By a benevolent dispensation of Providence,

> [said Mr. Wilberforce in the English Parliament, twenty-five years ago] normally, in the moral as in the physical realm, something good is created along with

> evil. Hurricanes purify the air; persecution encourages enthusiasm for the truth; pride, vanity, profusion often contribute indirectly to the happiness of the human species. Nothing is so horrible that it has no palliative. The savage is hospitable, the thief is bold, violence is in general exempt from perfidy, arrogance from baseness. But here there is nothing of the kind. It is the privilege of this detestable trade to deprave equally the good and the evil, and to dirty even crime. It is a state of war which courage does not ennoble, a state of peace which does not preserve one from either devastation or massacre. These are the vices of polite societies without the delicacy of mores which temper them, it is the primitive barbarism of man deprived of all innocence, it is a pure and complete perversity, completely detached from any honorable sentiment, and from all advantage that one can contemplate without indignation or confess without opprobrium.

Finally, the slave trade is contrary to governments' interests in that it corrupts not only those who engage in it, but also those who profit from it. The hope of replacing the miserable slaves whose lives have been shortened by excessive work and atrocious treatment through the slave trade prevents the colonist from even taking care of that unfortunate race. This hope accustoms the colonists to watching with indifference as these beings, subject to their yoke, expire of misery or suffering, or under horrible tortures. And such is the deplorable effect of habit that more than one colonist who, in his social relations with his equals is an honest, upright, and estimable man, has, perhaps without thinking about it, ordered or tolerated more crimes on his property than the guilty man whom the laws punish with death on the scaffold.

This latter reflection, in truth, is not only applicable to the slave trade; it scourges with almost equal force slavery itself. Slavery corrupts the master as much as the slave, and the executioner as much as the victim. However, the friends of humanity resign themselves to the continuation of slavery, provided that the slave trade be effectively prohibited. But let us at least create a barrier which will be effective and powerful for the future. And by a happy consequence of a first act of justice (for good leads to good as evil leads to evil), the abolition of the slave trade will make the slavery that we do not dare abolish gentler. The colonists will be forced by their interest to treat their slaves better, to give them healthier food and shelter, to preserve them from debauchery, to encourage marriages among them, to care for and treat well their pregnant women, and to help them educate their children. They will thus help prepare, by an imperceptible and voluntary process, the new relations which must exist one day, in the colonies as elsewhere, between the class which limits itself to consuming and that which is fated to produce.

For the rest, however imperfect and however distressing the present state of things may be, let us not despair of an inevitable improvement. Filangieri's prediction will come to pass—the abolition of the slave trade, even if so far it only exists in theory, is a shining proof of truth's omnipotence. "Less than forty years have passed," says the duc de Broglie, "since a young clergyman,[7] unknown, without friends, without fortune, first denounced the black slave trade in a Latin dissertation addressed to the University of Cambridge. Seven years later, all the men of genius of Europe joined together in support of that cause; fifteen years have already passed since it triumphed in the two worlds."[8]

7. The reference is to Samuel Wilberforce.—Trans.

8. Since this chapter was written, we have been able to observe with pleasure several verdicts pronounced against slave ships, and many circumstances combine to strengthen the hopes M. de Broglie expressed.

# CHAPTER THREE ❧ On Population

> I am going to rapidly summarize all the means the ancient legislators, and above all those of the Greeks and Romans, imagined for the multiplication of the human species.
>
> BOOK II, CHAPTER 1, P. 203.

Filangieri's ideas on population must appear extremely commonplace today; they were so in his time. The marquis de Mirabeau, taking the same side of the question as the Neapolitan author, rises far above him by his elegant expressions and the finesse of his wit, and M. de Montesquieu, even though on this matter he was mistaken as on many others, nevertheless says more of substance about them in one of his sentences than Filangieri in his eight chapters.

But it is not just because they are old and trivial that we can criticize the ideas Filangieri presents; it is still more because some are false and the others very problematic.

They reduce themselves in point of fact to two. Filangieri thinks (1) that the example of the ancients in their laws on population can be useful to modern nations, and (2) that population growth is always a good thing. The first of these ideas is extremely dangerous in administration, as in politics, in religion, and in all things. In my "Essay on the Spirit of Conquest" I tried to prove that the state of the human species in antiquity was so different from what it is in our day that nothing applicable to one of those times is acceptable in the other.

In order not to get away from my subject, I will rapidly review Filangieri's citations. I will set aside the Hebrews, a nation apart, whose numbers are an article of faith rather than a statistical fact. As for the Persians, we know nothing for certain about the population of that vast empire. It is probable that the Greek historians, so as to enhance their fellow citizens' victories, exaggerated the number of soldiers that Xerxes and Darius brought along with them, but even if we give those historians' accounts more than reasonable trust, it would still be very hazardous to draw conclusions about the number of inhabitants of Persia from the number of those warriors.

The invasion of Greece was not the effect of an overabundant population, like that of the Roman Empire by the peoples of the North. It was the work of an angry despot who poured his slaves and nomads over the little country that he wished to devastate, without any sense of proportion and without rhyme or reason. What proves that the cause of this invasion was neither need nor a natural tendency is that two victories in fairly close succession put an end to that enterprise, so that later nothing like it was attempted again. The defeated kings of Persia waited until Alexander came and attacked and destroyed them.

If we reflect that the Persian Empire was composed in large part of pasturelands where wandering tribes lived with their flocks, we will recognize that that empire must have been much less peopled than would have been the case if its inhabitants had been solely devoted to industry and agriculture. To cite as an example in a chapter on population a people half of whom devoted themselves to pastoral life or to pillage is a bad idea.

Religious precepts do not change the nature of things in any way, and the dogmas of Saddur that Filangieri praises cannot mean that hordes of shepherds and thieves found sufficient means of subsistence to encourage the growth of population, or that the population grew beyond the means of subsistence. But we see that the Italian writer was impressed by a single idea. In extracts from the Zendavesta he found exhortations for the multiplication of the species, and without examining their real effect, he admired the means in itself.

This was a great mistake. Supposing that in Bactria, where the Zendavesta was probably compiled, religious exhortations produced the result the legislator intended, trying to transport this means of action to our modern, industrious, and enlightened time would be chimerical. I am far from thinking that the progress of enlightenment removes all kinds of influence from religion, but the influence of religion is now no longer a direct influence which can be called legislative. It softens mores, it elevates the soul, it gives the whole of human life a purer and more moral tendency, but it cannot fight the power of interest or the evidence of calculation. The Gospels could well recommend marriage with as much and more insistence as the Zendavesta, but there would not be a single marriage more among a people who had reached the refined state we have. The reason for this is simple. This refined state makes marriage the greatest of scourges for one who contracts it without having assured the means of subsistence for the children he is liable to have. Since the rules which protect property would condemn the family created by this imprudent individual to permanent poverty, religious precepts in contradiction with this state of things would certainly be violated or evaded.

If the poor person braves this danger and procreates limitlessly, it is because he is blinded and led on by an irresistible and imperious urge which wants satisfaction at any price. A religious precept which would transform a pleasure into a duty and almost a penance would have rather the opposite effect, since given society as it is, this precept could be translated into other words as follows: Bring into the world the greatest number of children you can, so that the hunger which you cannot satisfy and the illnesses you cannot care for will take the majority of them from you at a young age, and so that the others, struggling against privation and destitution, and finally giving in to the temptation of crime, will fill the prisons and die on the scaffold.

When Filangieri moves from Persia to the republics of Greece and Rome he walks on more solid ground. He finds fixed institutions, written laws, and established punishments and rewards. He lists them with pleasure and praises them with heartfelt effusion. But these lists and elegies end with a pretty striking conclusion: Every time circumstances, governments' vices, the corruption of private mores, or any obstacles whatsoever were opposed to population, the institutions, the laws, the hope of reward, and the fear of punishment were all useless. Should he not also have concluded from this that when such obstacles do not exist, the laws' intervention becomes superfluous? Leave people alone, at least in what depends on a natural urge which is difficult to restrain, and which would be impossible for you to direct. The real encouragements to population growth are the absence of hindrances, the more equal division of property, and, by the same process, the increase of the means of subsistence, not the speeches of an old tyrant like Augustus, wanting to repopulate the empire he had devastated for his convenience, protesting in official harangues against corruption—his regime's foundation, without which it could neither have been established nor preserved.

I say all this in accord with the common hypothesis that the highest level of population is always desirable. I will examine this question shortly. Meanwhile I thought I ought to refute this foolish admiration for laws which were ineffective even in their own time, and which would be much more intolerable today. Moreover, Filangieri is not the only one guilty of such admiration, since the most distinguished writers of the eighteenth century gave him all the examples he could want.

# CHAPTER FOUR ❧ Continuation of the Same Subject

> Fortunate century, fortunate republic, where paternity is the citizen's first duty!
>
> BOOK II, CHAPTER 1, P. 309.

This philanthropic exclamation by Filangieri leads us to examine the real question in this matter, a question about which our economists of the last century did not have the least idea. Is it favorable to happiness, to the physical and moral perfection of the human species, that population should increase indefinitely?

In order to resolve this question, one must start with several facts that have become incontestable. It is certain that population tends to increase. Its increase can be slowed down or encouraged by circumstances, but when extraordinary calamities or a completely insane government do not depopulate a country, the doubling of the population always takes place over a given period of time. This time is fairly short. In America, where men are not crowded against one another by the narrow limits of the land they inhabit but can still freely spread out over immense uninhabited lands, this period is from ten to fifteen years. Elsewhere it is twenty, while in France twenty-five, and if we take this latter rate for the general rule, we will be assured of not establishing too restricted a term.

Now is it possible to hope that the means of subsistence will always increase as a consequence of this increase of population? Here we have to set aside a response which seems plausible, but which however is purely specious, because it only defers the real difficulty. There are many uncultivated lands on our planet; the most cultivated countries are not farmed to the extent they could be. Population can therefore increase without any difficulty until the entire soil possessed by the human species and all that it can still occupy is rendered fertile.

But, in the first place, man clears the land less rapidly than he multiplies. It is not near uncultivated lands that the greatest multiplication of the species takes place. It is impossible to overcome the obstacles and cross the distances required in a way that maintains an exact balance between the growth of population and the quantity of cultivated land. Further, the expedient of putting uncultivated lands into cultivation is only a temporary remedy. The time must come when the product of the soil which furnishes the subsistence of the human race will reach the highest level our imagination can conceive, and if the multiplication of our species takes place at an ever-accelerating rate, this time will come soon. With man continuing to multiply, this time—characterized by the peak of civilization and agriculture—will be immediately followed by an ever-increasing disproportion between population and the means of subsistence.

My readers will easily perceive that in this description of a very real and very serious problem unexpectedly thrown in the way of all the systems of population, in favor of which our philosophers have endlessly declaimed, I have done nothing but combine the basic ideas of a famous Englishman—ideas for which the evidence in his book is irresistible, because they are accompanied by all the developments and all the facts that the limits of this *Commentary* have forced me to leave out. In thus giving a very brief account of Mr. Malthus's observations and the conclusions he draws from them, I have not been moved by any feeling of partiality. Later we will see that while agreeing with him in principle, I have little confidence in the remedies he proposes. Of his remedies those which are gentle seem to me of little effectiveness, and those which promise more efficacy are difficult to execute and above all painful, and I do not like men to arrive at the good through the bad. This is a complicated operation with which Providence alone should be charged. But if it can be demonstrated that the infinite growth of population must bring an unfortunate disproportion between the means of subsistence and the population, what becomes of our philosophers' wishes and exhortations? What would happen if those wishes were fulfilled? Or if the human species showed itself susceptible to those exhortations? We would arrive a little sooner at the time when the equilibrium between needs and demands would only be reestablished through the slow agony and painful death of the superfluous among the needy; a time when all lands being cultivated and producing all they can produce, the excess population would appeal to their fertility in vain; a time when all countries being equally overburdened with population, emigration and colonization would be illusory palliatives. Finally, we would arrive at a period when, destitution and famine arming the now innumerable non-landowners against the tiny minority of landowners, the laws in favor of property would be struck impotent, and society would perish under the very weight of the ravenous population whose imprudent multiplication it had encouraged.

As a result of the habit people sixty years ago had of admiring the poorest countries and the most tyrannical governments, provided one was separated from them by time or distance, Filangieri praised the Chinese. Among the Chinese, the land was entirely used for subsistence: rice covered the whole surface of their empire, and the rivers bore people's floating houses so that the land their houses would have occupied could be devoted to agriculture. Filangieri did not reflect that in a state where the land was entirely used to provide for human subsistence, and where as a result one could not increase its production at all, one single birth beyond the number for which death left a vacancy would disturb society's entire economy. The child who would then be born would be condemned to die of hunger, and the bachelor, who in marrying would have fulfilled one of the citizen's first duties, would see his family die of poverty as the prize for accomplishing this duty. What a strange blindness of the systematic mind! What strange effects principles adopted on faith have! It is China that Filangieri cites to us as the model in regard to population, the China which, by the daily results of its overabundant population, would be much better suited to enlighten us as to the dangers of excessive population! It is there that terrible famines carry off thousands of unfortunates; it is there that the poor are reduced to throwing into rivers the children they can't feed. If they have built floating houses on these rivers, one might be inclined to say that it was so as to be closer to the abyss which must swallow up the miserable beings to whom they gave life only in order to immediately take it away.

But Filangieri wrote at a time when our philosophers, impelled by the need to criticize European institutions which I am certainly far from justifying, found it easier and safer to attack them through indirect comparisons. To make these comparisons more striking and more conclusive, they looked far away for subjects of praise. It mattered little to Filangieri that China, governed by the bamboo rod, offered the shameful spectacle of the human species' degradation more than any other country, just as it mattered little to Mably that Sparta was exactly the opposite of a free state as the moderns conceive it, and it mattered just as little to Voltaire that the Brahmins exercised a theocratic power over Hindustan which immobilized all human faculties. One praised China, the other Lacedaemon, the third India, in the same way that Tacitus, indignant against his own compatriots, wrote his fiction about the tribes of Germania.

Equity demands an exception in favor of Montesquieu. Genius will never bow for long or completely before the views and prejudices of a party, and in one of his concise and energetic sentences, the author of the *Spirit of the Laws* scourged China with just and severe reprobation.

I recognize, however, that the conclusion of Filangieri's chapter is more reasonable than its point of departure would allow one to hope. Take away the obstacles, he says, without bothering yourself with baits and encouragements. Let authority give nothing, but let it take nothing away; as Pliny said, let it not nourish, but let it not kill, and children will be born everywhere. It is in fact this truth which should serve as a rule to governments in everything concerning population. Population will soon reach the highest point it ought to reach, if governments are willing to respect the means nature has given man for providing for his family. With freedom of industry assured, it will be unnecessary to insult bachelors, and when each person is able to use his faculties to his greatest advantage without hindrance, marriage will no longer offer the man of the laboring class, along with the chance of seeing his burdens grow, the perspective of seeing his means diminish and his position become hopeless.

# CHAPTER FIVE ❧ On Malthus's System Relating to Population

> What obstacles halt population growth, and what means should be employed to get around or destroy them?
>
> BOOK II, CHAPTER 2, P. 224.

In the previous chapter I said that in describing M. Malthus's system on population I was not moved by any feeling of partiality. This system repels me more than it pleases me. When I decided to examine it carefully, in order to judge it from a position of knowledge, I approached it as an arduous task, the kind necessary when submitting to a painful operation or looking at something unpleasant for a long time. But one is not permitted to deny the evidence, and I remain convinced of the truth of the principle proclaimed by the English author. Subsistence follows population unevenly, and famine will arrive before subsistence if population growth is unchecked. Thus, submitting to a proven truth, I asked myself if I would adopt the conclusions M. Malthus draws from it.

I will begin by declaring that these conclusions are not the ones that have been presented to us in several works intended to combat this system. In most of the French refutations there is a mixture of bad faith and humor which serves only to falsify all questions by distorting the opinions which are attacked. The mania for being witty does not abandon our writers when treating the most serious subjects. They told themselves once and for all that ridicule is the most powerful weapon, and the clumsiest, just like the most adroit, want to use it. The result is that in France there is an exaggeration, an infidelity, a pretention to lightness and gaiety in almost all the criticisms of important discoveries or new ideas published, which creates obstacles to any candid and impartial investigation. From this derived the absurd judgments pronounced against Dr. Gall's profound and ingenious observations, against the literary theories of several German critics, against Mme. de Stael's system of perfectibility, and finally against the work in which M. Malthus was the first to deepen our understanding of the great question of the population of the human species.

This writer did not claim that it was necessary to employ coercive and barbaric regulations against the excessive increase of births. He did not defend infanticide, nor did he recommend vice and corruption as practical remedies against the multiplication of our race. But he thought that by indirect means one could impose one more hardship on the poor in addition to those to which they were condemned by their disinherited position, and which were already numerous enough. He attributed a more extensive influence to a principle he called moral constraint than this principle can have, in my view. He thought one could increase its effects by withdrawing public aid, and several of his ideas on these subjects seem to me to be lacking a reasonably incontestable practical possibility, if not the correct logic that a distinguished mind easily succeeds in establishing on paper. Above all, I admit with regret, they are deficient in feelings of sympathy and pity—an essential part of a virtue which however M. Malthus professes, I mean the virtue of humanity.

There is certainly something harsh and severe in the reasons M. Malthus piles up to prove that the poor have no right to society's aid. In general I am no more a supporter than he of public aid, which is typically badly administered and badly apportioned, and which takes from man, by luring him with false hopes, the salutary feeling which teaches him that each person should count only on their own hard work, and not expect his subsistence except from his own efforts. But to pronounce from the height of the evangelical pulpit that from now on parish assistance will be refused to children whose parents cannot feed them is too frank a declaration of a state of permanent hostility between those who have everything and those who have nothing. This may be true, but it seems to me neither good nor prudent to proclaim it, and when speaking of the unfortunate person who has given in to the most imperious desire, the most irresistible tendency, the English author cries out:

> Let us leave this guilty man to the punishment pronounced by nature. He has acted contrary to the reason which has been clearly shown him. He cannot

blame anyone, and he should take it on himself if the action he has committed has unfortunate results for him. Access to parish assistance should be closed to him, and if private charity offers him help, the interest of humanity imperiously requires that this help not be too abundant. He must know that the laws of nature, that is to say the laws of God, have condemned him to live painfully as punishment for violating them. He must know that he can exercise against society no kind of right to obtain the least portion of nourishment beyond what his work can purchase, and that if he and his family are sheltered from the torments of hunger, they owe it to the pity of a few charitable souls who deserve all his gratitude for it.[1] When, I say, one reads such sentences one is tempted to cry:

I give thanks to the Gods that I am not a Roman
So that I can still retain something of the human.[2]

And if we weigh all the expressions of this terrible anathema, we will perhaps find that several are dubious and presume assent to certain fundamental dogmas that the human heart refuses and the mind itself can dispute.

Is it really true that the laws of nature—that is to say, the laws of God—have attached such severe punishment to the imprudent multiplication, if you will, of our species? Is it really just to call to this society's aid the curse of God, when, on the contrary, religion shows him opening his arms to the poor

1. The quotation is a translation of Constant's French. Although Constant read English, his citations of Malthus, always in French, are borrowed from the translation by J. J. Paschaud published in Geneva in 1809, based on the fourth edition of the *Principle of Population*. Malthus's original language, in the fourth and later editions, is as follows:

> To the punishment therefore of nature he should be left, the punishment of want. He has erred in the face of a most clear and precise warning, and can have no just reason to complain of any person but himself when he feels the consequences of his error. All parish assistance should be denied him; and he should be left to the uncertain support of private charity. He should be taught to know, that the laws of nature, which are the laws of God, had doomed him and his family to suffer for disobeying their repeated admonitions; that he had no claim of *right* on society for the smallest portion of food, beyond that which his labour would fairly purchase; and that if he and his family were saved from feeling the natural consequences of his imprudence, he would owe it to the pity of some kind benefactor, to whom, therefore, he ought to be bound by the strongest ties of gratitude.

Malthus, *An Essay on the Principle of Population*, vol. 2, bk. 4, chap. 8. For convenience, I have used the sixth edition, Thomas Robert Malthus, *An Essay on the Principle of Population, or a View of its Past and Present Effects on Human Happiness; with an Inquiry into our Prospects respecting the Future Removal or Mitigation of the Evils which it Occasions,* 6th ed. (London: John Murray, 1826). Accessed from http://oll.libertyfund.org/title/1945.—Trans.

2. Corneille, "Horace," II, 3.—Trans.

and the weak and receiving them into his bosom? All to save society, society which has power and laws and weapons on its side, not from a direct attack which disturbs its order, but from an inconvenient burden on those who are the exclusive owners of something which, after all, could not be a monopoly? Our institutions exist, they must be defended, they must be obeyed; but as a consolation to the class disinherited by these institutions, let us at least leave them the hope of heaven and divine charity.

I do not know if I am mistaken, but every time an involuntary condemnation rises in every heart I think there is something defective and shocking in the principle which calls forth that condemnation. However, I have always noticed that when a mother who asked for charity for her hungry children was reproached for having so many of these unfortunate creatures, a feeling of indignation was visible among those who witnessed such a reproach.

Here I cannot forebear making an observation which, it seems to me, ought to lead to serious reflection. I do not know at what social state we have arrived, but when population is a danger because there is not sufficient subsistence, and at the same time the abundance of necessary goods is proclaimed as a curse, must there not be something wrong with this social state?

However, I repeat that it is rather in his expressions than in the acts he recommends that M. Malthus has let himself get carried away by his system. His occasional aberrations change nothing with regard to the truth of the principle on which this system is based. Yet enlightened as the author is, he has not recognized that in considering what he calls moral constraint as a remedy for the ills he points out, he has given in to an excess similar to that for which he reproaches Condorcet and Godwin.

To foresee a time when indefinite perfectibility will have made property disappear, made work useless, and endowed men with a limitless lifespan is doubtless chimerical. To hope that the human species, and among humanity the uneducated class, will succeed in overcoming the attraction of the sexes by considering the evils which follow from excessive population, and that this attraction between the sexes will be subjugated without shameful vices replacing it, is to give oneself up willingly to dreams and illusions. One can amuse oneself with the picture of a society where each member would try to attain happiness by perfectly fulfilling his duties. A society where every action aroused by the desire for immediate pleasure, but which subsequently would lead to greater pain, would be considered the violation of a moral law. A society where, whatever the suggestions of blind passion, a man who earned enough to nourish two children would never put himself in a position which would force him to feed four or five, where time passed in privation would be employed for savings, and where at the same time the period between puberty and marriage would be a perpetual exercise in continence and chastity.[3] But in all honesty, do you really think you can defeat nature in this way? The urge which gives the most timid courage and throws the laziest into a frenzy, the urge which was made the most irresistible because the survival of the species depended upon it, this urge which defies death, pain, all reflection, and all fears—will it surrender to some metaphysical reasoning, to calculations of distant probabilities which perhaps will not happen, and which will have still less force as no criminal law will support them with its authority?

And here the flaw of the arguments we refute appears fully. "The most irresistible and most universal of our needs," says M. Malthus, "is that of being fed and having clothes and a house. . . . There is no one who does not feel how the desire to satisfy such needs has advantages when it is well directed, but in the contrary case we also know that it becomes a source of evils. Society has been forced to punish directly, and severely, those who employ illegitimate means to fulfill this pressing desire."[4] The author concludes from this that since we have been able to prevent man from illegitimately providing for his subsistence, we can in the same way prevent him from multiplying imprudently.

But on M. Malthus's own admission, we have been able to attain the former goal only by criminal laws, and very severe ones at that. But to do him justice,

3. *On Population,* vol. 3, pp. 20–22.

4. Malthus's original:

> The most powerful and universal of all our desires is the desire of food, and of those things, such as clothing, houses, &c. which are immediately necessary to relieve us from the pains of hunger and cold. It is acknowledged by all, that these desires put in motion the greatest part of that activity, from which the multiplied improvements and advantages of civilized life are derived; and that the pursuit of these objects, and the gratification of these desires, form the principal happiness of the larger half of mankind, civilized or uncivilized, and are indispensably necessary to the more refined enjoyments of the other half. We are all conscious of the inestimable benefits that we derive from these desires, when directed in a certain manner; but we are equally conscious of the evils resulting from them, when not directed in this manner; so much so, that society has taken upon itself to punish most severely what it considers as an irregular gratification of them.

Malthus, *An Essay on the Principle of Population*, vol. 2, bk. 4, chap. 1. See note 30 for the source.—Trans.

he is far from proposing such measures. It follows that there is no equivalence between the two cases. Yet his system has the danger that it may lead writers less wise than he to invoke the law against the attraction of the sexes covered by the sanction of marriage, the same as if it were applied to combat hunger, and we will then fall into a succession of absurd and ever-increasing problems. We will come to the proof of this in a moment.

However, before providing this proof, let us consider the question further. Let us measure the hardship which we prescribe for beings morally and physically similar to us from the confines of our studies, well heated and well fed, with our wives, or sometimes women who are not our wives, nearby. We do not condemn the laboring and unfortunate portion of our species merely to unnatural continence, hardship, or even the illness that continence produces just as much as the contrary excess. Not only do we condemn them to these evils, we condemn them to a more lasting and bitter misfortune which awaits that cruelly treated class precisely at the end of its sad career.

For I accept all the assumptions necessary to make the English author's utopia possible. Workers in their youth will abstain from both marriage and from the illegitimate pleasures which console bachelors today. The majority of the human species will daily secure a victory over their senses that the most austere Christian saints regarded as the most difficult, a victory for which eternal salvation did not seem too high a recompense to the primitive Church. In the midst of temptation, the youth of today will display an impassivity which the hermits of the Thebaid barely attained through mortifications, fasts, and penances which make us shudder. The young farm laborer or artisan, reaching the age when the image of a woman makes the blood boil, will remain as calm in the presence of seduction as St. Simeon Stylites on top of his column. Still more, I accept that he will not throw himself into any other extravagant pleasure to compensate. He will live chastely, without drowning his sorrows in wine, without distracting himself with amusements, without allowing himself to use the smallest bit of his savings to procure himself a moment's relaxation. Is it really sure that his efforts will lead to the goal to which he aspires? One must agree that the thing is not certain. Despite his practical stoicism, the worker may reach old age without his savings ever being enough to allow him to marry. In what position will he be then? Isolated, without help, without family, without affections, without an arm to support him if he is ill or guide him if he is blind, he will have consumed his life in painful abstinence, only to find himself at the end of his days in a condition of deplorable abandonment. I like political economy well enough, and I applaud the calculations which teach us about the results and probabilities of our sad and doubtful fate, but I wish one would not forget that man is not solely a mathematical symbol, that there is blood in his veins and a need for attachment in his heart. Doubtless marriages by the poor have many material disadvantages, but is it nothing to open to these beings, deprived of everything, treasures of affection which for them replace the treasures of wealth which we are so afraid they will take from us? Marriage is desirable and indispensable for the poor man above all, despite all the disadvantages of the multiplication of children whose subsistence is uncertain. The rich man can do without it. He always has the wherewithal to make people imitate conjugal, brotherly, or filial affection for him. He is sure of being able to surround himself with the appearance of all the affections there might be, and such is the poverty of our nature that I will almost say that wealth gives the affections it commands a kind of reality. Around the great and wealthy there is an atmosphere of tenderness which is not always entirely false. But the poor man, where will he find this care, this aid, this sympathy? He will not be able to buy them like us, in order like us to give himself illusions later on about their source, their depth, and their extent. Marriage alone gives him a being who identifies herself with him, who bears with him the burdens that our social order pitilessly casts upon him, who works with him, suffers with him, and begs for his bread with him.

Everyone knows the response of the blind man who was criticized for feeding his dog: "And who else will love me?" he said. These few words seem to me an eloquent refutation of the cold and straitlaced system which, for the greater comfort of the wealthy classes, wants to deprive the poor classes not only of the strongest of physical pleasures, but of all the consolations which come from the conjugal bond and parenthood. One would almost say that today we have arrived at the point where the birth of a child who does not have his subsistence assured alarms us like the approach of a thief ready to take from us what we have. This is, I think, to take the privileges of property too far.

In saying all this, I do not reject the conclusions that have been drawn from a true principle. I accept everything that can be alleged against giving encouragement to population growth. These direct encouragements necessarily bring about, as M. Malthus says, an increase in mortality. Thus do not encourage marriage by artificial means: do not impose it as a duty, but do not prohibit it like a crime. Since, like me, you believe that Providence has made of this world a place of trials, let these trials be borne partly by the class favored by fate. Do not always choose the poor man when ordaining privations. If the poor class multiplies, let the rich class tighten its belt and put up with it. By your own admission, several centuries must pass before the population becomes such that, with the careful cultivation of our entire globe wherever possible, subsistence will become insufficient. We will deal with it then. Meanwhile, let us allow things to take their course. Nature, by its rigors, and personal interest, through its calculations, will limit population, and charity will help, especially if you do not make charity a crime.

# CHAPTER SIX ❧ Some Writers Who Have Exaggerated M. Malthus's System

> Everything which tends to make subsistence difficult tends to diminish the population.
>
> BOOK II, CHAPTER 2, P. 224.

I promised to show that M. Malthus's system, as presented by its author, contains the great danger that less-wise writers would use its authority to invoke the law against the marriage of the indigent classes, and thus to exercise the most painful and unjust of all punishments on them. It is with regret that I see among the supporters of such a prohibition, which in my opinion would be as oppressive as it would be immoral, one of our best economists, a man who in many respects possesses and merits the esteem of enlightened Europe; an historian distinguished by his erudition, tireless research, and new insights; a philosopher, finally, who defends with zeal and talent the cause of real freedom: M. Simonde de Sismondi, author of an excellent history of the Italian republics, who has undertaken a history of France, in what has been published so far much superior to all those which have preceded it. No less active in the field of political economy, in 1819 he published some new principles of that science, and it is in this work, otherwise full of just and ingenious ideas and philanthropic views, that he wrote the following sentence, which I cite exactly in order not to be accused of distorting what I refute.

> It is a duty not to marry when one cannot assure one's children the means to live; it is a duty not towards oneself, but towards others, towards these children who cannot defend themselves, who have no other protector. The magistrate is called to make all reciprocal duties respected: there is no abuse of authority when he forbids the marriage of those who are most likely to forget this duty. Marriage

> is a public act, a legal act. It has been justly taken under the laws' protection because it is also under their inspection. The marriage of beggars should never be permitted. It is an odious connivance of authority in the sacrifice they intend to make of their children. The marriage *of all those who do not have any property* should be subjected to severe inspection. One should have the right to ask for guarantees for the children to be born. One could require a guarantee from the employer, require a commitment to keep the man who is marrying on his payroll for a certain number of years; in the end to work out with the industry proper to each canton means of raising the father of a family a degree on the social scale, while never allowing marriage to those who remain on the lowest level.[1]

I will not go on about the immediate consequence of celibacy forcibly imposed on the whole class of the poor. The consequence would obviously be libertinage taken much farther than it is now. The author admits this problem, but since he considers it only from a partial and narrow perspective, he gives it little importance. However, there are other perspectives from which it would have been good to examine it, and a little thought would have shown that the problem would become very serious.

First of all, the disapproval, condemnation, and contempt attached to debauchery would cease as soon as debauchery, so to speak, would be prescribed for those denied marriage. You can make of numbers what you like, but men will remain men, and from twenty to forty years of age the need to reproduce will dominate them in a way that cannot be repressed. But there is an innate justice in all minds which does not attach any guilt to actions except when they are really criminal, and when it is not beyond human strength to abstain from them.

Among the upper classes, one has never been able to make the duel dishonorable, because at the bottom of his heart everyone feels that prejudice having combined the refusal to fight or take vengeance for an affront with

1. *New Principles of Political Economy*, vol. 2, p. 308. One rather odd thing is that M. de Sismondi furthermore seems to completely forget the principles which motivate his severity against the marriages of the poor, and which alone excuse that severity. He says, on p. 97 of his first volume, when speaking of a farmer who would double his harvest every year: "Who would consume this increase? We respond: his family, which will doubtless multiply; but the generations do not grow as fast as the food. If our farmer had the hands to repeat the supposed operation every year, his harvest of wheat would double annually, and his family could at most double every 25 years."

social shame, no one can be forced to bear this shame and submit to it. In the same way, everyone will feel that 25-year-old workers cannot live in chastity, and if, even today, we do not judge very severely those who stray from it, we would regard the illegitimate commerce of the sexes as a necessity created by the law and as perfectly innocent on the part of those who gave in to it.

If I wanted to go into all the repulsive and difficult details of this matter, I would recall that this necessity has been so well recognized in several countries[2] that the magistrates themselves thought they had to allow those detained in prison periodic pleasures in order not to encourage much more shameful vices. We are not so indulgent in France. Thus the mores of the prisons where we keep lower-class men are a subject of complaint and regret for all good citizens.

But once libertinage is no longer a subject of disapproval it will become a matter for repression, more so than today (for I imagine that one does not want to favor illegitimate births while forbidding marriage). The consequence would be that the struggle between law and nature, that struggle that is always fatal, would take place every moment of the night and day among the poor. But it is not good that a man should become accustomed to violating the laws. He passes rapidly from one violation to another. The great social secret is to give individuals the means of satisfying themselves legitimately. To put legal obstacles before something that one cannot prevent is to discredit legislation in the eyes of the people, and when discredited in those of its commandments which impose artificial duties, it is soon discredited in those which prescribe real duties.

But this is not all. Let us go on to the execution of the project. It will not take long to realize that the difficulty involved becomes much greater.

In effect, when we compare the need to reproduce with that of being fed or clothed, and when one seeks to conclude from the fact that fear of punishment prevents the famished or naked man from stealing food or clothing, that the same fear of punishment would forbid the action by which the species multiplies itself, one forgets several differences which make the two hypothetical cases very different. When an unfortunate steals a loaf of bread or takes a coat, he does an immediate, direct, and positive injury to the owner of the coat that he wears or the bread he devours. There is therefore someone who

2. In Holland, for example.

has an interest in complaining. Justice is immediately informed. It is spared the work of surveillance, which is half its work, and the most difficult half. But when it is a question of the union of the sexes, it is an entirely different matter: ordinarily the guilty party, rather than doing someone a positive harm which would lead them to denounce him, gives pleasure, which in the long run doubtless has unfortunate consequences but which certainly does not provoke an immediate accusation. In the case of theft, there is an injured party; in the case of the union of the sexes, there is only an accomplice. Thus the penal law which strikes the thief will not touch one who imprudently runs the risk of becoming a father. We punish rape, seduction, and adultery because there are plaintiffs in the person of the offended parents or spouse! But in the simple union of two individuals who broke the proposed law there would be no one with an interest in complaining. On the contrary, there would be two people interested in keeping silent and hiding.

Moreover, the intention is not to punish the haphazard and secret union of the sexes; rather, one wishes to refuse to sanction this union. Beggars should not be able to get married; workers must be authorized to do so by special license.

As for the beggars, I think it is rare that two persons, having no other occupation than begging, present themselves before a competent authority to contract a marriage. This appears to me all the more difficult because almost everywhere today begging is forbidden, and I do not see how the men whom one pursues in order to secure their arrest, and whom one seizes when they are found, will present themselves to the magistrates. They would be taken to the prison prepared for them before they could reach the altar.

It is therefore vulnerable men who are likely to become beggars—that is, workers who have no other capital than their hands—whom one wishes to confine to enforced celibacy. They will be asked for guarantees before their children are born; one will require a similar guarantee from their master who gives them work. Thus one will create a kind of serfdom; one will make of the workers a caste reduced to the most deplorable dependence; and, in the name of political economy, one will in actual fact reconstitute the most oppressive feudalism.

Who will be judge between the worker and the master if the latter refuses the requested authorization? Who does not see the door being opened to arbitrariness, caprice, personal hatreds? What master would want to commit himself, as the author proposes, to employ for a number of years a man who, by the very fact that he no longer fears being fired, will become either more negligent, or more lazy, or more insubordinate? And what will you do if, tired of working for a master who will think he has exaggerated rights and who might perhaps want to abuse those rights, the worker leaves the master to whom the law chained him, so to speak, as the price of his marriage? Do you want him to be pursued as a fugitive serf was pursued? This would be to turn the workers into a race of pariahs and would revive in Europe—this Europe, where industry has promised to establish the highest degree of individual freedom—the tyrannical and absurd institutions of India and Egypt.

One more word, and I will finish this refutation of an idea that does not withstand examination. If you attach to property the exclusive right of tasting the strongest and sweetest pleasure which nature has given us, do you not fear to increase beyond all limits and all prudence property's prerogatives? It is not enough for you that the proletarian should resign himself to having no part in any of the goods of which you possess a monopoly. It is not enough for you that he renounces fire, land, water, even air, for his condition obliges him sometimes to descend into the depths of the abyss, sometimes to bury himself in workshops where he can barely breathe, and always to deprive himself of what he produces for you and sees you enjoy at the price of his fatigue and sweat. One consolation remains to him: a consolation which Providence, touched by pity, has spread among all beings—yet you dispute his right to it. You want the faculty given to all, and of which the animals themselves are not deprived, to be forbidden to your fellow because he is poor. I repeat, there is in this at least as much imprudence as there is iniquity.

One should certainly not imagine that by expressing myself in this way, I am attacking the intentions of an author whom I respect, and to whom I am simultaneously attached by agreement in opinion on many points and by the memory of an old and lasting friendship. But I think that the enthusiasm with which he adopted M. Malthus's system, and the desire to make this system more practically applicable than the English author had, led him into some grave mistakes. He wanted to achieve by law what is impossible to do by law. And, as happens to the best minds too strongly taken by an idea, when he did not see any effectiveness in the means M. Malthus proposed, he thought to solve the problem by invoking the intervention people always resort to when everything else fails, and which when it leaves its proper sphere habitually does more evil than good. By this I mean the direct and threatening intervention of government.

# CHAPTER SEVEN ❧ On a Contradiction by Filangieri

> Instead of forcing its subjects to abandon their country, she (England) ought to hinder their frequent emigration by wise regulation.
>
> BOOK 1, CHAPTER 3, P. 57.

What we have just said about the advantages and disadvantages of population obliges us to go backwards to note a strange contradiction in our Italian author. According to the principle which he himself recognized, and which in fact is incontestably true, I mean the necessary and constant relationship which exists between population and the means of subsistence, it is clear that emigration is what most favors the multiplication of the human species. Wherever there is an empty space, a birth fills it. And yet the same writer who wants population to grow endlessly exhorts England, a few pages later, to forbid her subjects to emigrate. But men often forget one half of their opinions when they want to make the other half prevail. They take each of them in isolation as so many dogmas, and when they have put together everything they think they have to say about a subject, they think they have finished their task and begin the same work on a new subject without worrying too much about or noticing the contradictions into which they may fall. It is true that the readers' inattention often comes to the writers' aid, and that among the distractions which cross our path and the interests which carry us away, each idea serves as an amusement or a weapon without our feeling the need to make a whole out of them, satisfied as we are to have attained our goal or to have provided for the conversation of the moment.

One doesn't hinder emigration by regulations, and the advice that

Filangieri here addresses to the English government reveals again the mistake of a philosopher who considers man a passive agent in the hands of authority. In speaking of wise regulations, Filangieri doubtless thought of them as gentle and moderate, but by the very fact that these regulations would avoid too severe penalties they would be more easily infringed. Their violation would force the government to increase the rigor of punishments, so that whatever the caution with which the government had entered into this course, it would be led to the highest degree of violence and severity. The only regulations one should make in order to hinder emigration are free constitutions, just laws, and solid guarantees. Assure these goods to a people, and you can be certain that its citizens will not emigrate. Refuse these goods to a people, and all your regulations will not prevent it from leaving a country where its existence will be precarious, its rights threatened, and its industry hindered. I ask every man of good sense and good faith, by what measures will you keep on English soil those starving proletarians whom the laws do not allow to earn a living for themselves and their family? And if, by some impossibility, you managed to close all exits to them, what would be the result for prosperity or the public peace? Individually, robbery; collectively, sedition.

I consider the question here only from a political point of view. What would I have to say if I engaged in moral considerations?

Existing society has consecrated the right of property; that is, it has wished that the land should belong without dispute to one who has occupied it from time immemorial, or after a transaction whose forms it has prescribed. It has further wished that production, the fruit of labor, belong either to the producer or to those who by legal agreements furnish him with the materials and the means to produce.

Necessity excuses what society has done in this regard, but the condition is nevertheless harsh and severe. Three quarters of the human species are born disinherited. Land, common to all in the natural order, becomes the monopoly of a few in the social order. These, in order to conquer it, as has been forcefully said, have only to take the trouble to be born. This is the way things are. Two compensations remain and console the deprived class: one is work, the other emigration.

By the first, the poor man finds in his hands and his industry an equivalent for the property which idle owners are forced to give him part of, in order that he make the rest produce for their profit. By the second, if in one country his efforts are unavailing, he can look elsewhere for a sky more propitious and for circumstances more favorable.

Who would have believed it? The government has frequently contested these two expedients. Prohibitive laws have hindered the worker's industry in the country, and decrees against emigration have forbidden him to take his industry elsewhere. I declare that with such legislation there is no excess we should not expect and no disorder which can surprise us.

Will we be told that we demand of governments an indifference and apathy which harms their interests? That they could not resign themselves to seeing the country depopulate itself, their lands remain fallow, and their industry perish for lack of capital every time a so-called emigration mania took hold of the minds of an ignorant and credulous class, seduced by untrue writings and false promises? We will respond that the mania for emigration will not take hold of a people or a class if the government, by its persecutions, by the hindrances which it opposes to the development of human faculties, in a word, by what we could more justly call the regulatory and legislative mania, did not force that class or that people to emigrate.

And note this well: the tendency to emigration is not the result of any of the physical drawbacks which nature has divided among the various countries of the planet. The Lapp does not leave his frozen climate, and nations exposed to the heat of the sun bear the hot weather. Habit, family ties, and childhood memories all chain man to the place where he is born. Even when need chases him from it, or when adventurous youth leads him away, the spirit of return, to use an expression which the law has consecrated only because it found it at the bottom of our hearts, accompanies the traveler in his distant pilgrimages and sooner or later brings him back under his father's roof, which he would like to leave to his children. There is nothing more unbearable for a man than the harm he receives from his fellows. The rigors of nature are necessities; the rigors of government are injustices. We submit to the one; the other revolts us.

Thus, while we see peoples resign themselves to the extremes of the seasons, the harshness of a climate, and the sterility of the soil, and while mountain peoples bear on their back humus to fertilize the summit of the peaks, the gentlest sky and the most fertile plains cannot keep men who tremble beneath an oppressive government. Neither the fogs of the Hebrides nor the moors with which the slopes are covered make the Scottish peasant leave his native country; his fathers breathed the fog for centuries and profited from the dry heather. Today the lords' greed, a greed all the more intolerable in that the excess of civilization draws these lords to the towns, does not leave the class which depends on them the compensations which formerly resulted from the patriarchal life of the northern peasants on their lands.

We have spoken much of English national pride, and in fact this pride has long raised seemingly insurmountable barriers between England and all the continental nations. Now, despite this pride, France is flooded with Englishmen who have become landowners or manufacturers on foreign soil. Artisans and farmers bring us their experience and their precious discoveries, and Great Britain finds the most dangerous scourges of its industry in its own children. What has caused this change? It is because prohibitive laws for the poor man and enormous taxes for the rich have become scourges in England from which they wish to free themselves at all costs. Against the constant pressure of these scourges, neither national pride, nor patriotism, nor habits, nor childhood memory can prevail.

One must not exaggerate the influence of love of country in our modern times. I have already recognized the comparative weight of this feeling, and it can compensate up to a certain point for governments' ineptitude and injustice; governments, however, should rely on this moral force only with distrust and discretion. Among us love of country cannot exist the way it existed among the ancients. Commerce has brought nations together and has given them mores that are quite similar. Leaving one's country, which was a problem and almost a torture for the people of antiquity, has become easy and often agreeable for us. When Cicero said, "*Pro qua patria mori, et cui nos totos dedere et in qua nostra omnia ponere, et quasi consecrare, debemus,*"[1] his native land contained everything that was most dear to a man: to lose his country was to lose his children, his friends, all the objects of his affections; it was to face the ignorance and coarseness of unknown and semi-barbarous peoples; it was to renounce all intellectual communication, all social pleasure. Now, surrounded by well-ordered and hospitable nations, we bring with us what is dear to us, and we find, with slight variations, everything that we do not bring. What we love in a country is the ownership of our goods; the secu-

1. "The fatherland, for which we ought to be willing to die, to which we owe our whole selves, and in which we ought to invest everything and virtually consecrate it."—Trans.

rity of our persons and our family; the progress of our children; the development of our industry; the possibility, according to our individual situation, of work or leisure, of financial speculation or glory—in a word, the thousand kinds of happiness adapted to our interests or to our tastes. The word *homeland* recalls to our minds the combination of all these goods, rather than such and such a country in particular. When they have been taken from us at home, we go looking for them elsewhere, and governments have neither the right nor the power to dispute this ability of ours.

# CHAPTER EIGHT ❧ On the Division of Properties

> The small number of owners and the infinite number of non-owners must necessarily have the effect of making subsistence more difficult, and consequently of decreasing population.
>
> BOOK II, CHAPTER 3, P. 226.

A friend of humanity cannot but be struck by the enormous disadvantages arising from the concentration of land ownership. As long as Filangieri concerns himself only with showing these disadvantages, what he says is not very new, but it is very reasonable.

Concentrated land ownership produces two effects: a lack of subsistence and a decrease of population. To these immediate consequences, others slower and less direct are necessarily added: cultivation declines, not only for lack of hands, but also because of the discouragement and disgust of impoverished hirelings. Vast domains are left fallow by the rich man's nonchalance, or used to increase a useless luxury by his pride. The number of proletarians is doubled, and in the end society contains a cause of fermentation and disorder which ought to alarm the friends of power, and yet it is they who complain when properties are divided, so much does their personal interest prevail over their attachment to the principles they profess. These principles are like an offensive weapon for them, but they abjure them as soon as it is a question of applying them.

However, is it not evident that the greater the number of those who have an interest in supporting a government, the greater the zeal with which the government is defended? Thus when we repeat that landowners are the friends of order, should we not conclude from this that to preserve order one should increase its friends' number? Further, it is easy to prove that, even individually, the small proprietor is more interested in preventing disorder than the great.

In fact, an event which barely disturbs a rich man completely destroys the poor man's existence. Look at the history of periods which follow public calamities, invasions, and civil wars. You will see the small proprietor with several years of stubborn work barely manage to gather together a few fragments and make himself a tolerable existence, while the rich man, briefly harmed for a few days or months, has not had his existence disturbed but merely a few of his pleasures interrupted. A burnt cottage, a devastated field, the loss of a few domestic animals or some rude furniture reduces the poor man to beggary. The destruction of a magnificent chateau, the loss of a rich and abundant harvest does not even diminish the other's opulence.

So how can one think the risks are equal between these two men, or, what is more absurd, that one will gamble all his possessions on an upheaval whose odds can never be in his favor, while the other will not risk even a small part of his fortune on a change from which his social position allows him to hope for everything? And if you object that men have illusions about their opportunities and their dangers, we will respond to this objection very briefly: it may apply to the calculations and projects of the one person as much as to the passions of the other. The objection even works in support of our reflections, for there exists a sure instinct which directs man in everything which touches his immediate interest. This instinct always guides the small proprietor, exposed to poverty by a single mistake, while the rich man, more given in all things to speculative ideas, and often looking for his interests further afield, is also often exposed to err with regard to their object.

Sometimes, it is true, the tools of revolutions are found in the ranks of the small landowners, but the leaders of factions always come from those of the large landowners. Destroy the leaders, and disorder will become impossible for that reason alone. The tools are no longer in a position to act. Preserve the leaders, and the tools will not be destroyed. Indeed, you will never destroy them, for if troublemakers can find tools among the small landowners, the proletarians will be even more apt for this employment, having less to lose, more immediate interest in acting, and an equal hope of success. In fact, increasing their number is a strange means of decreasing the strength of those to whom an upheaval might be useful: one wants to decrease the number of their opponents, while accumulating in their hands the objects one thinks will tempt greed.

Another, perhaps stronger, reason also supports those we have developed in favor of the division of land. Industry daily makes immense progress, creates new fortunes, and places newly wealthy people alongside those whom landownership has created. They shine with the same brilliance; the same clientele surrounds them, or rather, since they need more hands to create and maintain their fortune than the landowner, a clientele much more numerous than the landowner's crowds around them daily.

Today, when liquid assets constitute the wealth of individuals, those who live from manual labor must prefer industry to field work, since greater comfort is the result. Furthermore, there is a sort of equality, or rather a sort of homogeneity, between the rich industrialist and the simple laborer which does not exist between the landowner and the hirelings whom he employs. This results in a difference which again is to the advantage of the former.

The industrial worker sees in his boss's fortune the result of work and industry. He hopes to arrive at the same goal by the same path. He is also ready to defend a social position which one day may be his. But condemned in perpetuity to work which enriches another man, unable to ever change his position, the farm laborer is much more aware of the barrier which separates him from the landowner. Is it likely that he will make great efforts to defend him? Is not the rich landowner much more exposed than the rich industrialist?

The army of industry increases daily. Some of the fortunes it creates equal those of the greatest landowners. Intermediate classes of varying wealth, all materially comfortable, take their place between the rich and the common worker. A seamless chain is extended from the poorest day laborer up to the millionaire manufacturer, and its unequal links are connected by the interest of today, the memory of yesterday, and the hope for tomorrow. A powerful body, industry spreads in all its vast ramifications. A homogeneous body, all its parts support and aid each other, because all in their different classes have something to defend, and the fortune of the most modest merchant would not be safe if that of the wealthy banker, acquired by the same means, were shaken. Thus the interest of the masses, the only guarantee for the interest of the wealthy, spontaneously guaranties and props up the industrialists.

How, therefore, in a century when industry has conquered such influence, can landed property preserve its own influence when concentrated in a few hands? All the influence of that property, as long as its holders are few, will necessarily be limited to balancing that of large-scale industry, with this difference, entirely in favor of the latter: the numerous clientele destined to protect industry will not exist for its rival. There is only one means of preserving the influence of landed property, and that is to divide it and create a large number of small landowners between the proletarian and the rich man. Then one could establish relationships between the poor and the rich, give the former an interest in and, as a result, the desire to protect the latter, and effectively balance the interest of the industrial middle class.

Industry will always have, it is true, the advantage that the least hireling sees as his means of advancement the same means which raised his employer, while landed property poses a material barrier between the owner and the one who not being a landowner, farms for others and daily creates a source of wealth from which he cannot profit. But this advantage of industry over land disappears when the latter is extensively divided. Since the small proprietors rise from the proletarian class and live in close contact with them, the proletarians feel the difference less, while it must constantly strike them when their bosses belong to another class, speak another language, and have no relationship with them or any natural cause to bring them together. When the poor man can acquire even one field, class no longer exists, every proletarian hopes by his labor to arrive at the same point, and wealth becomes, in land as in industry, a question of work and effort. In the other case, landed property is a barrier that cannot be crossed.

Almost all governments seem to have ignored these truths, for they have sought to keep the land in the hands of a small number of families. These bizarre and misunderstood efforts have always worked against the government itself, as must be the case. The aim was dangerous, and the means employed to attain it, entails and primogeniture, aggravated its harm. By entails you prevent one person from selling what is useless to him, and you take from another the ability to buy what would be advantageous to him. You decrease the land's real product by consigning it to the hands of an owner who does not know how to use it, and you forbid someone who would know how to employ it usefully to acquire what is unproductive in another's hands.

The right of primogeniture has much more disastrous consequences. It loosens family ties, introduces division in their midst, and weakens natural feelings among the children. By establishing among brothers jealousy on one side, distrust on the other, and hatred everywhere, it destroys the sweetest affections of the soul, the reciprocal tenderness of brothers and filial piety. Let us take England as an example, where the right of primogeniture reigns in full force.

The indifference of children toward their parents and the hatred of the younger for the eldest are things so recognized that they no longer shock even on the theater stage. Dispassionate opinion would never accept certain jokes common in that theater; it would not tolerate being shown either younger sons who wished for their eldest brother's death, nor above all sons congratulating each other on their father's. This is a fate common to all laws which establish a privilege in favor of a few: to see opinion oppose their wish, and through a steady reaction return in hatred or contempt for the privileged class the harm done the other classes on its behalf.

Our century's tendency to divide up landed property is so strong that our arguments, which today could perhaps be accused of being merely paradoxes, will in ten years appear to be commonplaces in no need of proof. Should the truth of our assertion be doubted, we will cite a brochure which shows how widespread these ideas already are in Prussia.

> On 14 September 1814, M. Hardenberg submitted to the king of Prussia a projected law for the redemption of forced labour. The peasants, who were required in return in certain cases to give the nobles half and in other cases a third of the land they possessed, became the real and independent owners of the rest.
>
> Thus was created under the Prussian monarchy the most respectable and irreplaceable class for a country's prosperity, that of farmers, who make fertile an inheritance freed from all servitude, and who are dependent only on the throne and the law. Until then, peasants who owned their land certainly existed in the eastern provinces, but there were very few of them, and the majority of the agricultural class belonged to manorial lands and were part of the lord's property.
>
> The nobles gained from the new law, for it increased the cash value and the annual production of their lands. As soon as the land becomes free, and agriculture is released from all hindrances, the necessary result of this double enfranchisement is the growth of population and wealth. The effect of this increase is the increase in the value of land, and thus greater wealth for those who possess the most considerable lands.

The bourgeois and the peasants gain even more than the nobility. By the new legislation these two classes will be, in the course of a century, the owners of the soil in Prussia as they now are on the banks of the Rhine.[1] Everywhere there are buyers there are sellers, but the best buyers are incontestably those who can pay most for an object, thus those for whom this object has most value and the highest return. But it is for the peasant above all that agriculture is productive, for the peasant who is the first to visit his field in the morning and the last to leave it in the evening. The farmer's sweat is the land's best fertilizer. It is in the nature of man to love property, and as soon as the agricultural class is permitted to acquire property, it finds the means. This class then marries early, because it has no worries about its subsistence. It knows that its labor is its wealth and that its hands are its capital. The cradle is soon placed near the conjugal bed,

1. I realize that this prophecy, which will be fulfilled in France as in Prussia, will hardly please the class which has been deprived of its privileges in opinion and would like to create for itself privileges in property, and which dreams of entailments, *fideicommis*, and properties attached to titles. Its political supremacy attacked, feudalism abandoned its chateaus and lordships two centuries ago and took refuge in the domesticity of the Courts, under the name of nobility. Now it feels the ground of the Courts shaking beneath its feet, and it would like to once again take refuge on its lands by making them inalienable under the name of great estates. But the inalienable large estate is as contrary to the present state of civilization as feudalism. Civilization's effect is to open a wider and freer career to man's moral strength, and to mobilize, if one can express oneself thus, to make available all the means with whose aid he exercises that strength. Landed property today is nothing but one of those means. Thus it tends to be divided in order to more easily circulate. Everything which would oppose this tendency would be fruitless. As soon as some of the land passed into the hands of the third estate, it defeated feudalism. Today industry, which is entirely in the hands of that same third estate, will defeat landed property, will bring it to its own level, will make it mobile, partitioned, circulating to an infinite extent. All efforts by castes to prevent it from taking on this new character will be powerless; it has changed nature. Lands have become in some sense possessions which one trades as soon as one can get a better return on the capital they represent, for it is no longer capital which represents land, it is in some sense land which represents capital. The reason for this is simple. In an industrial system, the best asset is that which requires the least formality to become available, and one then tends to increase as much as possible the availability of all assets.

It must follow that the more progress industry makes, the more all the well-off classes want to have capital at their disposal. In conceding what must be conceded to the habits of the contemporary generation, we can state that in a hundred years the nonagricultural classes will own land only as a luxury, and land, divided and subdivided, will be almost solely in the hands of the laboring classes. Large estates are just about the last link of the chain of which each century detaches and breaks a link.

and the population grows in such a country almost as fast as on the still-virgin soil of North America. Its farmers buy acre after acre. First as tenants, and then as owners, they soon replace that race of agriculturalists who are the heirs and imitators of feudalism and the nobility, who have a tutor for their children, a chambermaid for their wives, a coachmen for their horses, a huntsman for their dogs, a foreman for their workers, and a lady's maid for their servant girls. With the real peasant, the master and mistress of the house fill all these roles in one and the same person.

It matters not to the state in whose hands the land is, provided that it is entrusted to active and hard-working hands. That these working hands might have privileged people for their ancestors is something of little importance. Property and freedom, this is what is needed. Everywhere where these two things exist, man is active and agriculture is flourishing, as the marshes of Holland prove. Where these things do not exist, agriculture declines, and with it the population, as Spain demonstrates, where four-fifths of the land being in the hands of the clergy and the nobility, a population of twenty million has been reduced to ten. Prussia, which at this moment has eleven million inhabitants, should have sixteen by the year 1850, solely due to the new agricultural legislation and the division of lands.

While a Prussian author demonstrates these truths from the depths of Germany, all well-meaning people recognize them in France. With regard to this let us listen to a man whom we have refuted only with regret, and with whom we agree always with joy.

---

To resist this revolution would be useless; to be pained by it is senseless. An almost insoluble problem existed among all the ancient peoples, and among many modern peoples. It has sometimes delayed the establishment, sometimes disturbed the enjoyment of freedom. This difficulty was the limited education of the class devoted to manual labor, and the little interest which this class, composed of proletarians, took in the maintenance of order. Antiquity found a remedy for this curse only in slavery. All the philosophers of Greece declared slavery an inherent and indispensable condition of the social state. Is it not our very good fortune that the division of land delivers today's society from that danger, and that it attaches the majority to stable institutions out of self-interest? The people who deplore this division are precisely those whom it saves by spreading education, ease, and calm in that part of the people which is most dangerous when it is ignorant, poor, and agitated.

Land itself gains in cultivation and value from the division of landed property. You see what a Prussian author says of Prussia; contemplate what has taken place in France since the Revolution; compare our agriculture and its production to the agriculture and production of the last century; finally, meditate on the effect of the multitude of proletarians in England.

"The greatest guarantee that the established order can receive," says M. de Sismondi in his *New Principles of Political Economy*,

> consists in a numerous class of peasant proprietors. Whatever advantage the guarantee of property is to society, it is an abstract idea which those for whom it seems to guarantee nothing but privations find hard to grasp. When ownership of the land is taken from the farmers, and that of the workshops from the workers, all those who create wealth, and who constantly see it passing through their hands, are strangers to all its enjoyments. They form by far the most numerous part of the nation. They say that they are the most useful, and feel themselves disinherited. A permanent jealousy incites them against the rich. We hardly dare discuss political rights in front of them, because we always fear that they will go on from that discussion to one about property rights, and that they will ask for the division of property and of land.
>
> A revolution in such a country is frightful. The entire order of society is subverted, power passes into the hands of the multitude which possesses physical force. This multitude, which has suffered much and which has been kept in ignorance by poverty, is hostile towards any kind of law, any kind of distinction, any kind of property. France experienced a similar revolution, at a time when the great mass of the population was a stranger to property and thus to the benefits of civilization. Amidst a deluge of evils, however, that revolution left several benefits behind it, and perhaps one of the greatest was the guarantee that a similar scourge can never return. The Revolution prodigiously multiplied the class of peasant proprietors. Today, we count more than three million families in France who are absolute masters of the soil they inhabit, which implies more than fifteen million individuals. Thus more than half the nation is interested on its own account in the guarantee of all rights. The multitude and physical force are on the same side as order, and if the government crumbled, the crowd itself would hasten to re-establish one which would protect security and property. This is the great cause of the difference between the revolutions of 1813 and 1814, and that of 1789.

Struck by these serious problems, Filangieri therefore used all the force of his dialectic and called to his aid all the resources of declamation to recommend the division of land. But as a consequence of the error which was habitual with him, he thought that laws could remedy an evil which laws had caused. He surrendered to the most unthinking admiration for all the institutions by which republics tried to limit the accumulation of land. He goes so far as to vaunt the wisdom of agrarian laws, laws which were always the cause of popular convulsions; which, stirring every passion, agitating all souls, putting weapons in every hand, exciting citizens against citizens, could never reach the goal the legislator proposed, soiled as they were with the blood of their most illustrious and generous defenders; and maintain for a few years the illusory benefits that were promised from their establishment.

Among the moderns, the allure of such laws would perhaps still be a source of disturbance, but their result would not be even momentary well-being. If a few extremists can still invoke their name to excite disorder, honest people would dream in vain of their establishment. All passions, all interests, even those of the masses, are opposed to them. It would not be enough to give equal space to all to make everyone happy; it would also be necessary to make them lose the memory of a refined civilization. One would have torn their fortune from the rich without giving ease to the poor. A certain softness has slipped into the poorest classes; other labor has estranged a large number of individuals from field work. The attraction of a mediocre living could never return them to it. Far from seeking to win such a fate at the price of his blood, the proletarian would rather receive a salary from his enemies to fight his defenders, and the Gracchi, victims of their devotion to duty, would perish by the hands of those they defended as well as by the blows of their adversaries.

Filangieri falls into another error which it is hardly necessary to refute because no modern nation would be tempted by it. He approves of the German tribes in which the nation was the sole permanent proprietor and in which portions of land were distributed annually to heads of families. Even if we did not feel the danger of destroying the greatest motivation for our work, the desire to improve an acquired possession, we would at least recognize the impossibility of establishing such a system in our own day, and our refutations would become as superfluous as Filangieri's arguments.

This is not the case with another mistake, which, if not more grave in itself, is at least more dangerous in its effects, since it has been sanctioned by a generally respected assembly and by one of the greatest orators of modern times. By this we mean the abolition of the right to bequeath property as one wishes. This abolition was dictated by circumstances, and even in the circumstances in which it was decreed, it could only be harmful. But the lawgiver was dominated by fear of a class whose yoke had recently weighed on all heads. Above all he wanted to prevent this class's properties remaining in its hands. Abolishing the unjust rights we have highlighted did not seem sufficient to attain this goal, if one left fathers' aristocratic pride the right of concentrating by testament, in the hands of an eldest son, the properties with which the law formerly invested him at his brothers' expense.

Such is the disadvantage of all revolutions. At their birth, certain classes exist, maintained by custom and practice, but which the first political storm must destroy. Disturbed by revolutionary pressures, these classes become agitated, and the individuals who compose them find themselves in a real or presumed state of hostility against the new rulers and the new forms of government. But above all, these individuals are suspected of hostile views by the authors of the political changes. These men are often ardent, enthusiastic, and full of hatred for the fetters which have long held them back. They are sure of the evil which they have suffered at the hands of certain classes, attributing to each of their members the ideas of the whole class, and attributing to them even more ardor to re-conquer their privileges than they themselves had to destroy them.

Thus, in this period of upheaval when people wanted to set up the foundations of a new society and create lasting institutions, the animosity born of circumstances was mixed with general ideas, institutions were disfigured, and men strong in themselves and strong with the consent of the people directed legislation which would regulate the future against the phantoms of the past. Despite the best intentions, such a result is almost inevitable, and yet such a result is a great vice, for there should necessarily exist a great difference between the institutions given a free people by enlightened legislators, and the barriers imposed upon a defeated faction by a victorious party. The freedom of all is diminished in order to suppress the ill will of a few.

It would be better to let time have its effect. What is the need for penalties and threats to abolish an abuse based on habits or prejudices? Time created this abuse, laws have confirmed it. Destroy those laws, and let time regain its empire. Be sure that it will destroy its own work, if it is no longer in harmony with the needs of the century.

To apply this truth to the object which concerns us: If, for a while, old habits, the spirit of resistance, and the pride and approval of a party had influenced the heads of family of the class indirectly attacked, how many natural causes will have sapped their prejudices! How many interests, how many affections will have fought strongly against an unavailing stubbornness! Present interest and unforeseen needs have often led to the sacrifice of decisions taken from pride, and have brought about the division of property.

Individual affections, gradually reviving in hearts hardened by an order of things henceforth impossible, will gradually triumph over habits which no longer receive external support.

When the disposition of property is free, it tends to division. Laws alone can stop this; even then, their attempts to do so are often in vain. Prodigality limiting individuals' existence to the needs of the moment, the spirit of enterprise leaving reality behind for the sake of hope, the love of gain erasing memories—these and a thousand other causes of the same kind must sooner or later produce the division of properties. Let them act: what need is there of coming to their aid? In our century, the aristocracy of wealth has replaced all other aristocracies. Mistress of the most immense fortunes, its real source of prestige and power comes through that alone. Who does not feel that such a state of things doubles the strength of the causes of division we have highlighted, makes them irresistible as soon as laws do not oppose them, and sooner or later even makes them overcome the obstacle of the laws when the laws try to oppose them?

The abolition of the right to bequeath property as one chooses therefore presents a triple disadvantage. It is simultaneously unnecessary, ineffective, and immoral.

This abolition is unnecessary. Is there a need to make laws so that fathers do not leave some of their children in poverty? It is true that prejudices have overcome the inclinations of nature, but these prejudices were the fruit of outmoded institutions. Correct this bizarre and cruel combination: in destroying the cause which gave birth to an unnatural vanity, you will destroy at the same time its deplorable effect. A few exceptions to the general order should not motivate laws which engage the totality of citizens.

This prohibition is ineffective, for nothing is easier to evade than such a law. And we know of no measures which can stop an owner from disposing of his fortune. Gifts to third parties, simulated debts—can they be foreseen and above all repressed?

Finally, this prohibition is immoral. It gives men an interest in evading the law, an interest as corrupting in its effects on men as it is fatal with regard to institutions. In effect, when you give men an interest in evading the law, you create in them the habit of fraud. Furthermore, you destroy the respect they have for laws in general by proving the impotence of some of them. This habit of fraud, which you thereby make them develop to escape from a single torment, becomes familiar to them, they retain it in all their actions, and the most just and most useful laws are disobeyed once men cross the barrier which tormenting institutions have opposed to their interests.

This prohibition is likewise immoral in that it encourages the informing that fraud incites. Informing is introduced into the family. Sometimes in secret, sometimes blatantly, sons feel themselves authorized to exercise an inquisition over those who ought to be the object of their respect. The sanctuary of domestic affections is soiled, and for fear of a brief and not very dangerous inequality, since the nature of things has a remedy for it, you destroy the only salutary inequality nature has consecrated: that which places fathers above their children.

A thought comes to mind. In our period of excessive civilization, relations between fathers and children are only too difficult already. The former live in the past, while the future is the domain of the latter. The present is nothing but a kind of neutral terrain for them, the theater of the great combat, in which one side constantly hastens the fall of what the other side tries to maintain by its efforts. In short, every day the torrent of business, pleasures, and hopes leads the generation which is taking possession of life away from the generation which is leaving it.

This struggle always turns against the old. The result is isolation for the elderly. Distant from them, the new generation looks to create a future for itself, dreams of a rank, a family, a position, of new pleasures. The old have reached their goal or have failed to attain it. But in any case they can no longer enjoy what they have created. The future is closed to them, and every moment demonstrates that they must hasten to profit from the present. Their desires can only tend to preservation and to remaining stationary, for from now on all change would turn against them.

Also, depression is the natural state of the old. For them everything is a great effort. The loss of a moment of happiness seems so much the more cruel as these moments are ever more rare and more brief. At this period of his existence, a man can no longer bear solitude, for illusion alone embellishes solitude, and illusion has become foreign to him. His circle of friends, the cares of friendship, and, for lack of the reality, its appearance, all become precious for beings whom a harsh nature takes pleasure in despoiling every day.

Doubtless, nothing can replace disinterested feelings, and it is sad to think that the tender consolations and attentions dictated by the most delicate feelings can depend on ignoble causes. But we must not create illusions for ourselves. It is good to call interest to the aid of the affections. Perhaps some fortunate exceptions exist, but, in good as in evil, an exception should never motivate a law.

But in the present state of our mores, very few means capable of coming to the aid of paternal authority remain. We recognize it in principle, but it is not and cannot be founded, as among the ancients, on positive laws. Our mores would quickly reject attempts that one might make in this direction. The right of life and death, which the ancients gave to fathers, would disgust us, and those whom one would invest with this terrible right, frightened as much as those who might be struck by it, would recoil from a law made in their interest but whose use would be impossible. Any other despotic power given to heads of families would equally escape them.

Leave fathers therefore their sole remaining means of preserving some power in their family. If interest can still act as a brake, leave them interest as the means of reward and punishment. Give them the disposal of part of their fortune, and let that portion be large enough to accomplish the goals we indicate.

We say a part, for it would be sad to see the opposite abuse establish itself, the unlimited and unrestricted freedom to bequeath property. This freedom would open the door to the seduction of the elderly. It would often tear their wealth from their hands against their real wishes, and it would introduce strangers into families at the expense of the legitimate heirs' interest.

What a remarkable thing! We have destroyed the right to bequeath property out of hatred for the right of primogeniture, and the right of primogeniture is exactly the opposite of the right to bequeath one's property. The right of primogeniture is a limitation, the right to bequeath one's property is a freedom. Thus passion, fixing its eyes on the goal, makes a mistake about the route, and goes astray while thinking it is getting closer.

Finally, we have reason as well as experience on our side. We see in our own time that the right to bequeath one's property does not contain the dangers its enemies thought they saw in it. Fathers of families have the ability to dispose of part of their goods, and very few of them abuse it. The great majority do not make use of it, or use it only moderately and legitimately. The equality of inheritances is not destroyed by this ability, because equality of inheritance lies in men's hearts; because there is no need for laws to make our natural inclinations triumph; and finally because, when a prejudice exists and seems to smother the natural tendency, it is sufficient to destroy the institution to which this prejudice owes its existence in order to see it disappear.

# CHAPTER NINE ❧ On the Grain Trade

> A mistake, born of a false assumption, led governments to believe that the natural movement of trade could make some of what was necessary for a state's internal consumption be exported.
>
> BOOK II, CHAPTER 11, P. 7.

Because of its disastrous consequences, the mistake which Filangieri makes here is one of the most dangerous which has disturbed peoples and led governments astray. It is, however, also one of the most common.

Governments which have made prohibitive laws on the grain trade have made two kinds of such laws. One kind has attempted to ban the export of agricultural products, and thus arise the severe penalties attached to grain export in several countries. The other kind has tried to make trade in these products take place directly between the producer and the consumer without any intervention between them of a class which buys the products of the former to sell to the latter. From this come regulations against hoarders.

Fear that excessive exports will bring about famine has been the motive for laws of the first kind. The motive for laws of the second kind was probably that an intermediary class between the consumer and the producer would tend to raise the price of food because of the need to make a profit, and that this class, cleverly able to profit from difficult circumstances, had the dangerous ability to raise prices to disastrous levels.

In both cases governments' intentions were praiseworthy, but in both cases they chose bad means, and in both cases they failed to attain their goal.

The question of the export of grain is as delicate as it is important. Nothing is easier than to draw a touching picture of the misfortunes of the poor, the hardness of the rich, and an entire people dying of hunger while greedy speculators export grain, the fruit of its sweat and its labor. There is a small drawback to this manner of considering things. It is that everything which is said about the danger of free exportation, which is merely one of the uses of property, could be said with just as much force, and no less foundation, against property itself. Certainly, the nonproprietors are always at the mercy of the proprietors, and if one wishes to imagine that the latter have a powerful interest in crushing, oppressing, and starving the others, the most pathetic pictures would result in abundance from this supposition.

This is so true that the enemies of the freedom to export have always been forced to insult landowners a little in passing. Linguet called them monsters from whom their prey must be torn away without being moved by their screams, and the most enlightened, virtuous, and respectable defenders of the prohibitory system[1] ended up comparing landowners and those who spoke in their defense to crocodiles.

I would like to examine this matter from a perspective which excludes all oratory and, in order to do this, to start from a principle which has been adopted by all interests. Here, if I am not mistaken, is the principle. In order for wheat to be abundant, there must be as much of it as possible; in order for there to be as much of it as possible, production must be encouraged. Everything which encourages the production of wheat favors its abundance; everything which directly or indirectly discourages that production leads to famine.

If you wanted to encourage the production of a product, what would you do? Would you decrease the number of buyers? No, doubtless you would increase it. To the extent that its increase was in his power, the manufacturer who was sure of his sales would increase his production. If, on the contrary, you decreased the number of buyers, the manufacturer would limit his production. He would not want production to exceed the quantity he could dispose of. He would therefore calculate very carefully, and since it would be much worse for him to have too few buyers than too many, he would reduce his production in such a way as to produce too little rather than more than necessary.

What is the country where the most watches are made? The one, I think,

1. M. Necker in his work on grain laws.

from which the most are exported. If you forbade the export of watches, do you think that more would stay in the country? No, but there would be fewer made.[2]

It is the same with the production of grain, as with the production of anything else. The mistake of the prohibitions' apologists is to have considered grain only as an object of consumption, not of production. They said the less one consumes, the more will remain: false reasoning, in that grain is not a preexisting commodity. They should have seen that the more consumption was limited, the more production would be restrained, and that as a result production would soon become insufficient for consumption.

For the production of grain differs from ordinary manufactures in that it does not depend solely on the manufacturer, but also on the weather. However, the producer, forced to limit his production, can only calculate based on his average years. In limiting his production to what is strictly necessary, the consequence is that if the harvest is not in accord with his calculation, the product of his thus limited cultivation will be insufficient. Doubtless most farmers do not deliberately limit their production, but even they are discouraged by the idea that their work, if favored by nature, cannot be useful to them and that their product may remain without buyers and become a burden to them. Even though they do not make deliberate plans as a result of this consideration, they will farm more negligently. In earning less, they have less capital with which to increase what they grow, and in fact production decreases.

In forbidding the export of wheat, you have not ensured that the surplus wheat necessary for a country's subsistence remains in that country; you have rather ensured that the surplus will not be produced. But since this surplus may become necessary as a consequence of the vagaries of nature, you have ensured that what is necessary is lacking.

To forbid exports is to forbid sales, at least beyond a certain point, for when the domestic market is provided for, the surplus production remains without buyers. But to forbid sales is to forbid production, for it is to deprive the producer of the motive which makes him act. Who would think that this is the means we have chosen to make production ever abundant?

I still cannot leave this subject. Hindrances to export injure property. On this everyone agrees. But is it not evident that if grain as property is less

2. Say, *Treatise on Political Economy.*

respected than any other commodity, one would rather have a surplus, that is, an object for sale, of any other commodity rather than grain? That if you alternately permit and prohibit export at will, your permission will never affect anything but the already existing production, and being always susceptible to being revoked, it will not be a sufficient motive to encourage future production?

I will respond to an objection. The increased price of necessary commodities is disastrous for a people, because the price of labor does not increase proportionally. Will it not be said that the export of wheat results in the increased price of that commodity? It will doubtless prevent it from falling to a very low price. But if, on the other hand, the prohibition of export prevents grain from being produced, will not the price increase be much more inevitable and more excessive?

Do you think you can force grain to be produced? You can certainly try to do so. You will forbid landowners to take their land out of wheat production, and this already requires supervision. But will you also watch over their manner of farming? Will you force them to make the advances, to make all the improvements, to purchase all the necessary fertilizers? All this in order to produce a commodity which, if abundant, will be impossible to sell and expensive even to keep. When government wants to have one thing done by authority, it soon finds itself reduced to doing everything.

I have not emphasized other arguments for free export because they have been discussed a thousand times. If wheat is expensive, it will not be exported because for the same price it will be better to sell it on the spot than to export it. It will therefore not be exported except when it will be good that it should be exported. You can imagine a universal shortage, a famine at home, a famine among your neighbors. In such circumstances, unique laws will be required for a unique situation. An earthquake which shifted all lands would demand special laws for a new division of property. Special measures are taken for the distribution of food in a besieged town, but to make permanent laws for a calamity which takes place only once in two centuries is to turn the laws into a permanent catastrophe. Nature is not prodigal with its rigors. If one compared the number of food shortages which have resulted from really bad years with the number of shortages caused by regulation, one would rejoice at how little evil comes from nature, and one would tremble at the evil which comes from men.

I would have liked to take a middle position on this question. There is a certain merit in moderation which it is pleasant to attribute to oneself, and which is not difficult to acquire, provided that one is not very honest. One shows that one has carefully examined both sides of the question, and one presents one's hesitation as a discovery: rather than being right with regard to one opinion, one seems to have been right against both. I would thus have preferred, as the result of my inquiries, to find that we could leave governments the right of allowing or prohibiting exports, but in trying to determine the rules according to which the government should act, I felt that I was plunging myself back into the chaos of prohibitions. How will the government, from a vast distance and at a great interval, judge the circumstances of each province—circumstances which can change before knowledge of them has reached it? How will it repress the corruption of its officers? How will it guarantee itself against the danger of mistaking a momentary problem for a real shortage, or considering a local difficulty a universal disaster? Lasting and general regulations based on passing or partial problems produce the evil one is trying to prevent.[3] The men who most strongly recommend this variable legislation do not know how to go about it when it comes to the means of execution.[4]

If there are drawbacks to everything, leave things alone; in that way, at least the people's suspicions and the government's injustices will not be added to nature's calamities. Of three scourges, you will have two fewer, and you will also have the advantage that you will accustom men not to look to the violation of property as a resource;[5] they will then look for and find others. If, on the contrary, they look to property, they will always go back to it because it is the quickest and easiest. If you use public interest to justify the obligation

3. One can see these difficulties developed to their full extent by Abbé Galiani in his dialogues on the grain trade. I would like to refer the reader to this writer even though he wrote in a tone much too light on such an important matter; as he is the leading and one of the most formidable enemies of the system of freedom, his admission on the problem of administrative intervention in this respect should have great weight.

4. See the work of M. Necker on legislation and the grain trade. He examined with remarkable wisdom all the restrictions, all the regulations, all the measures which compose or could compose grain legislation, and although his purpose was to prove that the continual action of government was necessary, he was forced to condemn all the means which had been tried.

5. See Turgot's letters to Abbé Terray.

imposed on proprietors to sell in a given place, that is, to sell at a loss since they could sell for more elsewhere, you will end up by determining the price of their commodities. One will not be more unjust than the other, and either could easily be represented as equally necessary.

As with any other trade, I therefore accept only a very few exceptions to the complete freedom of the grain trade, and these exceptions are purely circumstantial. The first is the situation of a small state without territory, which is obliged to maintain its independence against powerful neighbors. This small state could establish storehouses so that its neighbors could not conquer it by starvation, and as the government of such a state resembles that of a family, the abuse of these storehouses would in large part be avoided. The second exception is a sudden and general famine, the effect of some unforeseen cause, be it natural or political. I have already spoken of this above.

The third exception is both the most important and the most difficult to accept. Its necessity results from popular prejudices nourished and consecrated by ingrained bad habits. It is certain that in a country where the grain trade has never been free, sudden freedom produces a disastrous upheaval. Opinion rebels, and by its blind and violent action creates the evils it fears. It therefore requires, I admit, considerable accommodation to bring peoples to the principles that are most in conformity with justice and truth. Upheavals are as pernicious along the road to good as on the road to evil, but government, which often creates this good only with regret, does not put much zeal into preventing these upheavals. When enlightened men succeed in dominating the government by the force of ideas, they too often believe in making the government commit itself to hasty measures. They do not recognize that this only furnishes it with specious pretexts for retreat. This is what happened in France in the middle of the last century.

I now move on to laws whose purpose was preventing an intermediary class of merchants from coming between the producer and the consumer in the grain trade. All the advantages of the division of labor are found in the creation of such a class. It has more capital than the producer and greater means of creating stocks. Occupying itself exclusively with this industry, it better studies the needs which it is charged with satisfying. It saves the farmer from giving himself over to financial speculations which absorb his time, divert his funds, carry him off to the cities where his mores are corrupted, and dissipate his savings, a quadruple loss for the farmer. Certainly the cares that this intermediary class takes on must be paid for. However, these same cares, which the farmer himself takes on with less ability and thus at greater expense, since they are not part of his chief industry, must also be paid for. The increased expense falls on the consumer who was supposed to be helped. This intermediary class that we prohibit as the cause of shortages and increased prices is precisely the class that prevents the increase from becoming excessive. It buys wheat in years that are too productive. It thus prevents wheat from falling to a price too low, and consequently it is neither wasted nor thrown away.[6] It takes wheat out of the market when too great an abundance of it would cause a disastrous fall in price for the producer, would discourage him, and would make him neglect or imprudently limit production the following year. When the need is felt, this class puts back on sale what it has stored. So it comes to the aid, sometimes of the cultivator, by supporting the value of his commodity at a reasonable price, and sometimes of the consumer, by reestablishing the abundance of this commodity when its monetary value passes certain limits.[7]

In short, the intermediary class produces the effect that one hopes for from public storehouses created by the state, with the difference that storehouses directed and supervised by individuals who have no other business are not a source of abuses and misappropriations like everything which is publicly administered. The intermediary class doubtless does all this good out of personal interest, but this is because, under the regime of freedom, personal interest is the most enlightened, constant, and useful ally of the general interest.

6. A peasant who cannot sell his wheat profitably tries to have it consumed in order to avoid the expense and loss he would experience in keeping it. He gives more grain to the poultry and animals of all kinds as its price gets lower, but this is so much lost for human subsistence. Consumers do not regret this waste during the year it occurs, but this grain would have filled a gap in some provinces with shortages or in a barren year. It would have saved the lives of entire families, and prevented excessive prices, if the activity of a free commerce, by giving it an outlet that was always open, had given the landowner a great interest to conserve it at the time and not to waste it in uses for which one could employ less precious grain (7th letter from Turgot to Abbé Terray, pp. 62–63).

7. Smith demonstrated admirably that the interest of the merchant who trades in grain domestically, and the interest of the mass of consumers, though opposed in appearance, are exactly the same in years with the highest prices (bk. 4, chap. 5).

One speaks of hoarding, of machinations, of leagues among hoarders. But who does not see that freedom itself offers the remedy for all these evils? This remedy is competition. There will be no more hoarding if everyone has the right to hoard: those who hold on to the commodity in order to get an excessive price for it will be the victims of their absurd and reprehensible calculation, since others will reestablish abundance by contenting themselves with a more moderate profit. Laws serve for nothing, because they are evaded. Competition serves for everything, because personal interest cannot stop competition when the government permits it. But since laws make their authors famous, we always want laws. And since competition is a thing which works by itself and for which no one honors the government, governments despise and fail to recognize the advantages of competition.

If there has been hoarding, and if there have been monopolies, it is because the grain trade has always been loaded with prohibitions and surrounded by fears. Thus it has always been a suspect trade, almost always a clandestine trade. But in matters of trade, everything which is suspect, everything which is clandestine, becomes vicious. Everything which is allowed, everything which is public, becomes honest again. Certainly we hardly have the right to be astonished that an industry forbidden by the government, despised by a mistaken and violent public opinion, threatened with severe punishments by unjust laws, and threatened again with sack and pillage by a deceived populace, has up to now been a trade practiced in the dark only by greedy and vile men who, seeing society armed against them, in critical moments made society pay for the shame and danger with which they were surrounded every time they could. Access to a natural and necessary industry was closed to all businessmen who cared about their honor and safety. How could a premium in favor of thieves and adventurers not result from such a badly understood policy? At the first appearance of shortage, at the government's first suspicion, storehouses were broken into, grain was carried off and sold below its value, and confiscation, fines, and the death penalty were pronounced against the owners.[8] Was it not necessary for the owners to compensate themselves for these chains by pushing to excess all the profits they could grab by fraud amid the hostilities perpetually exercised against them? There was nothing assured

8. Decree of the Parlement of Paris of 11 December 1626.

about their legitimate profits; they had to have recourse to illegitimate gains as compensation. Society had to bear the penalty of its follies and furors.[9]

We have perhaps fought at great length an error which today no longer seems to exist. But errors have a power of resurrection which is always to be feared, and it is precisely when governments throw themselves into one extreme that it is probable that they will sooner or later fall back into the other extreme.

But for some time the contrary error to that we have just unmasked in the preceding pages has won great popularity. As much as one formerly wished to keep the grain one produced at home, so one now fears being flooded with grain grown on foreign soil. An inconceivable terror has seized governments and peoples: great abundance seems a curse to them. By what strange deviation of natural ideas has this opinion been introduced?

We believe it can be assigned two causes. The first is serious: it is overtaxation. It really makes abundance a curse for the farmer, for this overtaxation simultaneously increases his costs of production and decreases his profits.

The second is at bottom much less important but is nevertheless the one which, by tormenting a powerful and vociferous class, causes all the declarations which deafen us. Abundance of foodstuffs hurts the income of landowners who do not farm themselves. Unlike cultivators, they do not see in their lands a means of subsistence for their family. For them abundance does not, as for others, add a little extra to the fruit of ordinary harvests to what is necessary. The sale of their produce, and not the consumption, is what they think about: the costs of production remaining the same in years of abundance and competition causing a decline in the sales price, for them a loss inevitably results.

The remedy to the first of these problems is easy: lower taxes. The cause eliminated, the effects will disappear. As for the second, I do not see much reason to remedy it.

In effect, when agriculture furnishes the country, and chiefly the cultivator, with an abundant subsistence, it has fulfilled its purpose; it matters little that this is at the expense of the large landowners. In pushing all consequences to the extreme, what calamity might we fear from overabundance? The difficul-

9. See, for the following developments, Smith, bk. 4, chap. 5, Morellet, *Declaration to the Magistrates*, 1769.

ties and momentary discomfort of absentee landlords? The landowners will sell their surplus lands, and this change of ownership will be to the benefit of agriculture. More divided, lands will pass entirely into farmers' hardworking hands. The latter, working thereafter on behalf of their personal property, will necessarily tend to the improvement of their property, and the land will be better cultivated.

Let us observe here how many bizarre forms disguise the landowners' selfishness. Abundance is a curse, it is said, because it decreases the price of subsistence, but at the same time, for lack of subsistence, one wants to limit population. But if subsistence is overabundant, are there therefore not enough mouths to consume it? In other words, what do you mean by this word *over-abundance*? Thus let the population grow, and also leave the production of the land alone. Nature will take care of establishing a balance. Those who wish to live from this product without work will sell their lands to the class of farmers. You will soon have a host of families of cultivators which will double the produce of the soil. Abundance will not favor luxury, but it will relieve misery. The population will soon rise to the level of subsistence, and you will attain what seems to be the goal of your search: a large population without shortages, and abundance of food without a glut.

# CHAPTER TEN ❧ On Agriculture as a Source of Wealth

> Any people which renounces the advantages of agriculture, which, blinded by the dazzling profits of the arts and trade, neglects the real profits of the production of its territory, and which prefers, in a word, form to substance, does not recognize its real interests. . . . The cultivator, motivated by the hope of one day enjoying an honor which his hands offer him, and which he is sure of obtaining through merit, will feel his courage reborn.
>
> BOOK II, CHAPTER 10, PP. 4 AND 54.

In reading some writers, one would be tempted to believe that there is nothing more stupid, less enlightened, or more thoughtless than private interest. Sometimes they tell us gravely that if the government did not encourage agriculture, all workers would turn to manufacturing and the countryside would lie fallow, and sometimes that if the government did not encourage manufacturing, all the workers would remain in the countryside, that the production of the land would be well above our needs, and that the nation would languish without trade and industry. They say this as if it were not clear that on the one hand, agriculture will always be in proportion to a people's needs, for the artisans and manufacturers need to have something with which to nourish themselves; and on the other hand, that manufacturing will rise as soon as the products of the land are in sufficient quantity. Private interest will push men to apply themselves to work more lucrative than increasing foodstuffs whose quantity reduces the price. Governments can change nothing in men's physical needs. The increased supply and the price of products, of whatever kind they may be, always conform to the demand for these. It is absurd to believe that in order to make a kind of work widespread it is not enough for it to be useful to those who do it. If there are more hands than necessary to encourage the fertility of the soil, the inhabitants will naturally turn toward other branches of industry. They will realize, without the government warning them about it, that competition beyond a certain point destroys the advantage of work. Private interest, without government encouragement, will be sufficiently aroused by its own nature to look for a more profitable type of occupation. If the nature of the land makes a large number of farmers necessary, artisans and manufacturers will not increase, because survival being a people's first need, a people never neglects its subsistence. Furthermore, being more necessary, the profession of farmer will by that alone be more lucrative than any other. When there is no abusive privilege which inverts the natural order, the advantage of a profession always consists in its absolute utility and its relative scarcity. The real encouragement for all kinds of work is the need people have for it. Freedom alone is sufficient to maintain them all in a healthy and exact proportion.

Production always tends to reach the level needed without the government meddling in it.[1] When a certain kind of product is rare, its price increases. The price increasing, this better-paid product attracts industry and capital. Thus this product becomes more common. This product being more common, its price falls, and with the price falling, some of the industry and capital goes elsewhere. Then, as the product becomes scarcer, the price goes back up and the industry returns until the product and its price reach a perfect equilibrium.

What fools many writers is that they are struck by the languor or malaise that the nation's working classes feel under arbitrary governments. They do not go back to the cause of the evil, but imagine that it can be remedied by direct government action in favor of the suffering classes. Thus, for example, in the case of agriculture, when unjust and oppressive institutions expose farmers to injury from the privileged classes, the countryside soon lies fallow because it depopulates. The agricultural classes flock to the towns as much as they can in order to free themselves from servitude and humiliation. Then some foolish theorists counsel positive and partial encouragements for the farmers; they do not see that everything is interrelated in human societies. The depopulation of the countryside is the result of bad political organization.

1. See Smith, bk. 1, chap. 7; and Say, *Political Economy.*

Help for a few individuals, or any other artificial and momentary palliative, will not remedy it. There is no other resource than freedom and justice. Why are they always chosen as late as possible?

And let us note here that by the very fact that a people is subject to arbitrary legislation, it will no more be commercial than agricultural. Trade will be even less easy for it. Overburdened with taxes, it will not have the capital necessary for its prosperity. Tormented by tyranny, circumscribed in its means of action, tormented by the suspicions of an easily offended authority, and hindered in its course by bureaucrats used to subjecting everyone to their will, it will not have the freedom which alone can create success.

Furthermore, commerce is useful to agriculture: the activity it inspires is the best means of encouraging all the laboring professions. Trade puts a large quantity of capital into circulation, and it opens outlets to agricultural commodities just as to all other commodities; it therefore helps the farmer rather than harms him. It gets men used to working constantly, and to rapidly discovering all opportunities for profit. Thus, as soon as the lack of workers makes itself felt in agriculture, its production becomes more lucrative, and merchants become farmers.

# CHAPTER ELEVEN ❧ On the Protection Given Industry

> Providence, wanting nations, like individuals, to be united by the tie of reciprocal needs, gave each of them something particular to itself, which makes it, so to speak, necessary to the others.
>
> BOOK II, CHAPTER 16, P. 55.

We find the same mistake again here in Filangieri, and though it is naturally deduced from a single principle, a principle whose falsehood we have already shown, it cloaks itself in so many different shapes that we are forced to pursue it under these different forms and fight it again. This mistake comes from the theory that the government can actively interfere in all private relations and make laws to command and encourage virtues and useful things, as well as prohibiting and pursuing violations and harmful things. Applied to industry, this mistake has strange results.

Filangieri seems to believe that governments can make industry blossom and protect it effectively. As a result he advises them to make laws and regulations to encourage industry, as if there were better encouragements than freedom, and thus the absence of laws and regulations.

Filangieri rightly says that in the science of laws everything is relative; he concludes from this that different laws are necessary in the various cases which present themselves in relation to industry. But it is precisely because everything is relative with respect to laws about industry that there should be no laws about industry. In order to adapt the laws to every circumstance, the legislator will make many laws. Or, struck by some large idea, he will make few laws and those laws will be general ones. If he makes a lot of laws, he will torment industry with minute details, and he will interfere with the movement of every cog, obstructing it with his innumerable regulations. Let him not imagine that he can foresee all cases and regulate all circumstances. He can try as he likes to find all the possible combinations, but one will always come along that is unforeseen, produced by causes he did not judge worthy of his attention. Thus he will not gain any advantage from imposing tormenting measures. If, on the contrary, he makes few laws, each general law will have to be applied to different circumstances, and these differences, unperceived by the wisest legislator, can sometimes gravely affect important operations. He will thus obstruct industry by his general laws, and the measures through which he intended to encourage it will, on the contrary, pose hindrances to industry, the object of ill-considered solicitude.

But if laws about industry are not always harmful, they are at the very least always unnecessary. "Not all countries are appropriate for agriculture," says Filangieri; ". . . there are some whose production is infinitely below what is necessary for domestic consumption." Then he concludes "that it is necessary that the laws which direct arts and manufactures in agricultural countries be completely different from those which direct them in barren countries." It would be better to let nature alone. What need is there for laws to support what nature determines irrevocably? In a country whose territory is so small that agriculture is insufficient for domestic consumption, you will never see too many hands devoting themselves to agriculture. The number of farmers is necessarily limited by the extent of the soil, and it is a very childish fear to be concerned that they will go beyond this limit. Filangieri is also afraid that in such a country private industry will be devoted to manufactures which need too many raw materials; let those who share his fears be comforted. To make those fears reasonable, it would first be necessary that they be based on a likely possibility. But is it possible that in a barren country the manufacturers would use too much raw material? From where would they get these raw materials? At their first attempt, they would make them go up in price, and the price increase alone would turn them away from their projects. What need is there for laws to support the very simple action of nature in this instance? One always thinks it is good to create laws to hinder projects that nature forbids absolutely. Nature is stronger than your laws. In vain will you try to destroy an industry which she supports, or establish an industry which she forbids.

Always falling into the same mistake, Filangieri advises governments to encourage the production particular to their countries. What need is there for such encouragement? If the territory contains some product which foreigners do not have, and if foreigners want this product, their demand will increase and industry will necessarily turn toward this product, because it is through this product that it will see the most assured profit. One never produces anything except for sale, and as the facts very quickly teach the producer whether he sells or not, the law has no need to warn him. The only thing which can disturb production is the law's intervention. In encouraging a given product, the law can turn more hands toward it than it needs. At the same time one may harm another industry; the law can be mistaken and sometimes encourage an industry that has little advantage at the expense of another industry which would be more advantageous. Finally, since demand varies and changes its object, the law would harm industry by making it always manufacture the same amount of the product for which demand has considerably decreased. The very word *encouragement* proves the vice of this system. If encouragement is necessary, it is because production has lost money, and clearly it would be harmful to encourage such production. If there is a profit, encouragement is useless, for production brings its own encouragement; laws to substitute for it would be superfluous. In the other case, they would be pernicious. Such laws can have but one effect: to distract the producer's attention through the desire for compensation, and to prevent him from impartially judging the product's profit or loss.

"The arts and crafts therefore have need of secret direction from the laws," says Filangieri. We do not believe that his declarations authorize him to conclude thus. We believe that the reasoning with which we have opposed him authorizes us to come to quite contrary conclusions. No, the arts and crafts do not need the secret influence of the laws, since the influence of nature is enough for them. No, they do not need the secret influence of the laws, for if that influence wants to help the laws of nature, it is superfluous, and if it wants to oppose them, it is disastrous. Filangieri sometimes recognizes this himself. One must first eliminate all the obstacles, he says, and he recognizes that among these obstacles one must first of all place the prodigious number of laws and regulations which tend to trace a path for industry. In this he gives a salutary piece of advice, but this advice is part of our theory, and completely destroys his. This contradiction is strange, and it is still more strange that soon he will tell us that if the government makes genius blossom, it can well protect the arts. Government makes genius blossom! Where did Filangieri get this phrase, which he tells us as a certain fact? Will one cite, as usual, the century of Augustus or that of Louis XIV? But the great men of the century of Augustus all belonged to the Republic. They were, so to speak, the last ray of light that it shed on the world before being forever extinguished. Augustus's successors tried in vain to use their authority to make genius blossom. By the very fact that the government dared to try, the spring of genius dried up and could not be revived. The century of Louis XIV, precursor of the century of freedom, was due to the instinctive need for that noble faculty which was already felt. No one still attributes to Colbert's gold the glory of great men who, for the most part, were already covered with glory before his ministry.[1] These old flatteries are no longer of our time. In truth, there is one justice to render to Filangieri. In his time and his country, he could not have spoken otherwise than he did. He doubtless felt that the influence of governments was harmful, but he did not dare say so explicitly. We also see that when he speaks of the necessity of government interference, he does not go beyond general reflections and vague declarations, while when it is a question of destroying the obstacles laws put in the way of the prosperity of industry, he details the facts and he fights hand-to-hand, so to speak, against every useless regulation. Then his deep conviction lends his style a brilliant color and persuasive warmth which are not usual with him.

1. I have often been tempted to write a work titled "On the obligations of genius to authority." In it, I wouldn't talk at all about politics, the subject of eternal rivalry and combat between power and reason. I would limit myself to particular facts, independent of all theoretical opposition, and resulting simply from the natural and stable relationship which exists between ideas and force, between talent and power. I would show Callisthenes having his nose and ears cut off, imprisoned in an iron cage on Alexander's orders; Plato, called and then chased away by the capricious Dionysus; Augustus, exiling Ovid; later, Tasso imprisoned at Ferrara; Richelieu, persecuting *Le Cid* at Paris; Milton, poor and constantly in danger under Charles II; Louis XIV, making Racine die of sorrow, and annoyed by Fénelon; finally, in our day, M. de Chateaubriand threatened and Mme. de Staël proscribed by Bonaparte. These examples balance out a little, it seems to me, the favors given adulatory poets and unfaithful historians.

# CHAPTER TWELVE ✤ A New Proof of Filangieri's Fundamental Mistake

> Such was the fate of the Indies and of China, of Persia and Egypt.
>
> BOOK 2, CHAPTER 16, P. 55.

In Filangieri we always find this admiration, which we have already been forced to combat, for ancient peoples and distant countries. The sentence which serves as the text for this chapter is perhaps one of the most incredible examples of it.

What people has ever suffered from a despotism more degrading than one subjected to foreign leaders, with the aid of the shameful torture of the bastinado?[1] A despotism more absolute than a people governed in the name of the gods by priestly castes? Finally, a despotism more brutal and more extravagant than a people dragged over foreign lands by a ridiculous tyrant, chastising the elements by its master's orders because they were the sole obstacles opposed to his will![2]

To say that along with the treasures of nature, China and Egypt possessed the most brilliant inventions of the arts: is this not to explicitly deny not only all historical tradition, but also our own eyes? No, these peoples, whose whole existence was regulated in advance by the will of their priests, did not possess the most brilliant inventions of the arts. They did not even have the power to leave their father's profession for a profession closer to their tastes. How could they have made noble and useful discoveries? No, these peoples who

1. Beating with a stick or cane, typically on the soles of the feet.—Trans.

2. The reference is to the Persian ruler Xerxes (fifth century B.C.) who, according to Herodotus, ordered the sea whipped for disobedience.—Trans.

have no moral existence do not possess the most brilliant inventions of the arts. They do not even know the arts in the noble sense of the word, since, limiting their desires to physical life, they are equally incapable of enthusiasm and intellectual enjoyment.

On the contrary, never have the arts, that astonishing creation of the divine in our nature, whose impact on us defies analysis, the arts—not those which tend toward the physical preservation of our existence, but those which raise our soul to the knowledge of the beautiful, and offer it as pleasure solely the idea of perfection, without material utility—never have the arts made less progress, and remained in a more imperfect state, than in Egypt and China.

It is true that the Egyptians attained an elevated stage in the discoveries necessary to the preservation or improvement of our physical life fairly quickly. They were always mediocre and coarse in the arts proper. Even in work of common utility, they were soon stopped by priestly despotism.

How could a people make progress in the arts and sciences when the priests took them over as a monopoly? They were barely allowed to be the instrument of the priests' discoveries. All other claim was forbidden them. The people were simply made into machines, and if they were sometimes given some skill, it was still the perfection of a machine, since skill can coexist with a complete lack of knowledge. The worker accustomed by daily routine work to polish steel, or to make it into chains, hooks, or wheels, would be as much a stranger to the admirable mechanism of the watch as the individual springs made by his hands were, if the art which assembles them was hidden from him, and if one made a severe law that he must always work at this task without thinking about its purpose.

This was to some extent the organization of the working classes in Egypt, and they also never made any really important discoveries. Today we recognize competition as one of the greatest causes of improvement. We rightly fight against masterships, guilds, and other weak hindrances to competition, and yet we emphatically praise the insurmountable obstacles that priestly jealousy opposed to the inventive genius of the Egyptians, so much do declarations acquire force in passing from mouth to mouth across the centuries.

As for China, which has so absurdly been proposed as a model, and which Montesquieu alone had the good sense to condemn amid the general praise, it is difficult to explain the singularity which has made it an object of admiration. A remarkable thing! Some friends of freedom have pronounced elegies to a people insensible to the most odious and disgusting oppression. Some men full of enthusiasm for the arts and sciences have wished for us, in the name of reason, the fate of a people among whom the absence of all religious feeling and all generous ideas, combined with the mechanism that has been called civilization, smothers the germ of enthusiasm in our nature—in other words, the germ of all success in the arts and sciences, as in everything that is not a vain form. The philanthropic Filangieri takes as the text for his panegyrics institutions which degrade man and destroy what makes his excellence.

What great qualities thus redeem such degradation? What important discoveries of this nation demand our admiration? Would it be a physical industry which no more belongs to human nature than to that of some animal, to bees or beavers? Would we regard this sad advantage as compensation for the loss of all that is moral in man? Would one elevate the mechanism of our senses above the perfection of our soul?

China's religion is nothing but a form: people admit this, and people are in ecstasies when they see that this form still commands some respect. We agree that it is no longer based on belief, and we are assured that it is a guarantee of mores. A bizarre error! For if religion is no longer founded on belief, only the influence of fear or habit delays its fall, and then it would be just as worthwhile to rely on that influence and let it act directly on mores, rather than to create yet another useless intermediary. Belief makes men better, not by fear of torture, not by the habit of arbitrary rites, but by the noble relationship it establishes between man and superior powers, more perfect as well as stronger than he. A religion in which one no longer believes is never useful. On the contrary, the respect given to it is in a certain way a symptom of degradation. It announces either the triumph of habit over intelligence, or a dangerous and guilty hypocrisy. But let us examine what mores these peoples have, of whom it is claimed that religion guarantees their mores.

Like religion, mores and virtues are only external forms among them. None of their relationships has a moral basis: they content themselves with appearances, and that is what we call order. If someone departs from this order, torture makes them return to it. Creating a more elevated influence is scorned. It is true that the uniformity of the government, solidly based on the brutalization of this people, resembles order, because the people are deprived of movement. It is true that everything moves at a single gesture, the emanation of the will of a single individual. It is true that in the midst of revolutions and conquests, this people, molded for passive obedience, is ready to offer obedience to whoever demands it, and that its character thus does not change, but this is because it does not make any progress. Finally, it is true that such an order of things must seem marvelous to the tyrants who profit from it, but we cannot conceive how it could have attracted the elegies of enlightened and independent philosophers. If such is the perfection that is proposed to us, the coarseness of primitive ages would perhaps be better, or even the absolute absence of civilization.

# CHAPTER THIRTEEN ❧ On Guilds and Masters

> The greatest obstacles opposed to the progress of the arts are all the establishments, all the laws which tend to decrease the competition of workers. . . . Such are above all the rights of masters and guilds.
>
> BOOK II, CHAPTER 16, P. 61.[1]

Too many writers before us have risen up against guilds, masterships, and apprenticeships for us to go into the subject in lengthy detail. Apprenticeships prevent individuals from exercising such and such a trade; the masterships and guilds are associations which determine the number of their own members and the conditions for admission. These institutions are privileges of the most absurd and iniquitous kind, the most iniquitous, since one individual is not permitted the work which preserves him from crime except at the good pleasure of another. Since one of the conditions of apprenticeships is to pay for being received into a trade, those who most need to work are driven away from work. These institutions are absurd since, under the pretext of the perfection of the trades, obstacles are placed in the way of competition, the most certain motivation for perfection. Since the number of men exercising each profession is fixed, it is likely that this number will not be proportional to consumers' needs. In effect, there may be either too many of them or too few. If there are too many, the men of this profession, being unable to adopt

1. Constant took the first two paragraphs of this chapter from the *Principles of Politics Applicable to All Governments*, book 12, chap. 1. See Benjamin Constant, *Principles of Politics Applicable to All Governments*, trans. Dennis O'Keeffe (Indianapolis: Liberty Fund, 2003), pp. 231–32.—Trans.

another, work at a loss or do not work, and fall into poverty. If there are too few, the price of labor increases according to the greed of these workers.

The interest of the buyers is a much more certain guaranty of bountiful production than arbitrary regulations which, coming from an authority which necessarily confuses all goals, does not distinguish among the various trades and prescribes an equally long apprenticeship for the easiest as for the most difficult. It is bizarre to imagine that the public is a bad judge of the workers it employs, and that the government, which has so many other concerns, will know better what precautions must be taken to appreciate their merit. The government can only give its confidence to men who, since they are a separate group within the state, have a different interest than the mass of the people. Such a group works on the one hand to decrease the number of producers, and on the other hand to increase the price of the product, and makes products simultaneously worse and more costly. Apprenticeships are oppressive for consumers, for in decreasing the number of workers they increase the cost of labor. They thus harm the poor and overcharge the rich.

However, from our observations on the complete freedom of trade we except professions which concern public safety: architects, because a house's lack of solidity threatens all citizens; doctors and pharmacists, whose advice and merchandise can save citizens' lives; notaries, etc. As for other professions, experience has everywhere pronounced against this regulatory mania. The English towns where industry is most active, which have experienced the greatest growth in a short period of time, and where the work has been brought to the highest peak of perfection are those which have no charters[2] and where no guilds exist.[3]

Despite its system of prohibition, England has always tended to liberate in-

2. Birmingham, Manchester, V. Baert.

3. The most sacred and most inviolable of all properties is that of one's own industry, because it is the usual source of all other property. The poor man's inheritance is in the strength and dexterity of his hands, and to prevent him from employing this strength and dexterity in the manner which he judges most convenient, as long as it does no harm to anyone, is a manifest violation of this most basic property. It is a flagrant usurpation of legitimate freedom, as much that of the worker himself as of those who would be inclined to give him work. It is simultaneously to forbid someone from working at what he thinks appropriate, and someone else from employing whomever seems good to him. One might well confidently trust in the prudence of the person who hires a worker to judge if that worker merits employment, since he does so in his own interest. The solicitude which the legislator affects for preventing the

dustry. Apprenticeships have been limited to trades which existed at the time when Elizabeth's statute established them, and the courts have welcomed the most subtle distinctions tending to withdraw as many trades as possible from these statutes. It is necessary, for example, to have been apprenticed to make wagons, but not to make carriages.

Let us observe here how freedom, how the simple absence of law brings order to everything. Associations of individuals exercising trades are ordinarily a league against the public. Will we conclude that these associations should be forbidden by prohibitive laws? Absolutely not. In forbidding them, government would condemn itself to injuries, surveillance, and punishments, which would have serious inconveniences. But let government not sanction these associations; let it not recognize their right of limiting the number of men in such and such a trade to themselves. By this very action, such associations will no longer have a purpose. If twenty individuals in a given trade want to combine to raise the price of their work too high, others will present themselves to do the work at a better price, and the interest of the first will force them to give way.

I would not add anything to these arguments if I did not know that the motives publicly alleged in favor of abuses were usually nothing but attempts to fool and disarm opinion. The refutation of these arguments, whose weakness is recognized even by those who employ them, is of very little use. It is the secret calculations which must be attacked, the hidden interests which must be reassured.

In the present situation, the defenders of masterships, guilds, and apprenticeships fundamentally do not care in the least about the improvement of trades, and the consumers' interests which they claim to preserve from fraudulent or faulty manufactures concern them very little. What attaches them to these outdated institutions is that they think they will find in them the means of policing and watching over the working class, a class always feared because it is always more or less unhappy. In order to respond to these people, and basing myself on the very fears which shape their logic and blind their egoism to the truth, I will cite a writer who occupies a distinguished rank among those who have most deeply studied questions of political economy:

---

employment of incompetent persons is evidently as absurd as it is oppressive. See Adam Smith. See also Bentham, *Principles of the Civil Code*, part 3, chap. 1.

> Do we not know that if masters to whom the local police are subordinated can keep workers in order, they can also excite them to uprising and sedition, when that is in their interest or in accord with their opinions? How many times have masters opposed effective resistance to the views of the best-intentioned and most enlightened governments! How many seditions have owed their origin to the masters' seduction and corruption! Governments which know well their strength and their power should no longer base themselves on the fickle and varying interests of the working class. The general interest of the nation, always certain, always constant, offers them a more solid and unshakeable support. (Ganilh, *On Systems of Political Economy* I, pp. 233–34)

A persecution still more outrageous, because it is more direct and less disguised, is the fixed price of a day's work.[4] This fixing, says Smith, is the sacrifice of the majority to the minority. We will add that it is the sacrifice of the poor to the rich, of the workers to the at least comparatively well-off, of those who are already suffering from society's harsh laws to those whom fate and institutions have favored. One cannot describe this struggle of poverty against greed without pity. Here the poor man, who is already pressed by his needs and those of his family, who has no hope except in his work and is unable to wait an instant without his very life and those of his family being threatened, meets the rich man. The rich man is not only strong in his opulence, and in his ability to overcome his adversary by refusing him the work which is his sole resource, but is armed still further with harmful laws which fix salaries without regard to circumstances, ability, or the worker's zeal. And let us not believe that this fixing is necessary to repress exorbitant claims and overpriced hands; poverty is humble in its requests. Does not the worker have behind him a hunger which presses, which leaves him barely an instant in which to debate his rights, and which only too strongly disposes him to sell his time and strength beneath their value? Does not competition keep the price of labor at the lowest level compatible with physical subsistence? Among the Athenians, as among us, the salary of a worker was equivalent to food for four persons. Why have regulations when the nature of things makes law without doing harm or violence?

Fixing the price of a day's work, so injurious to the individual, is not at all

4. On the efforts of the masters to lower the price of a day's work, and those of the workers to raise it, and on the uselessness of government intervention in this regard, see Smith, I, pp. 132–59, Garnier's translation.

to the public's advantage. Between the public and the worker a pitiless class arises: that of masters. It pays the least and asks the most possible, and thus alone profits both from the needs of the working class and the needs of the wealthy class. What a strange complication of social institutions! An eternal cause of equilibrium exists between the price and the value of work, a cause which acts without constraint and in such a way as to make all calculations reasonable and all interests content. This cause is competition, but today we reject it. We create obstacles to competition by unjust regulations, and then we want to reestablish equilibrium by other, no less injurious regulations which must be maintained by punishments and harsh controls.

# CHAPTER FOURTEEN ❧ On Privileges for Industry[1]

> The misfortunes the India Company has undergone in this century are well known.
>
> BOOK II, CHAPTER 21, P. 101.

What is a privilege for an industry? It is the use of force on the social body, so as to divert for the profit of a few men the advantages which it is the purpose of society to guarantee for all. This is what England did when, before the union of Ireland with that kingdom, she forbade the Irish almost all forms of foreign trade. This is what England does today when she forbids all the English from trading with the Indies independently of the company which has seized that vast monopoly. It is what the citizens of Zurich did before the Swiss Revolution, by forcing the inhabitants of the countryside to sell almost all the agricultural products and all the objects they made to them alone.

This is manifestly unjust in principle. Is there utility in the application? If privilege is the share of a small number, there is doubtless utility for that small number, but this utility is of the kind which accompanies all robbery. That is not what we propose, or at least what we admit to proposing. Is there national utility? No, doubtless, for in the first place the great majority of the nation is excluded from the profit. For the majority there is thus loss without compensation. In the second place, the branch of industry or trade which is the object of the privilege is exploited more negligently and in a less efficient manner by individuals whose profits are assured purely by the effects of monopoly, which would not be the case if competition obliged all rivals to continually outdo

1. This chapter is also found in Constant, *Principles of Politics*, trans. O'Keeffe, pp. 229–31.

one another through skill and energy. Therefore the national wealth does not draw from this activity all the gain which it might. There is thus a relative loss for the nation as a whole. Finally, the means which the government must use to maintain privileges and beat off the competition of unprivileged individuals are inevitably oppressive and harmful. For the nation as a whole there is therefore once again a loss of freedom. Thus, there are three real losses brought about by this kind of prohibition, and compensation for these losses is reserved for only a handful of privileged persons.

The usual excuse for privileges is the inadequacy of individual means and the utility of encouraging the associations which replace them. But this inadequacy is greatly exaggerated, and the necessity no less exaggerated.[2] If individual means are insufficient, perhaps some individuals will bankrupt themselves, but a few examples will be sufficient to enlighten all citizens, and a few individual misfortunes are much preferable to the incalculable mass of misfortunes and public corruption that privileges introduce. If the state wanted to supervise individuals in all the operations in which they might harm themselves, it would soon become their tyrant. If associations are necessary for a branch of industry or long-distance trade, associations will form themselves, and individuals will not struggle against them but will try to join them to share the advantages. If the existing associations refuse to accept them, you will see new associations born, and the rival industry will be more energetic as a result. Let the government intervene only to maintain both associations and individuals in their respective rights and within the limits of justice; freedom will take care of the rest and will take care of it successfully.

Furthermore, one is mistaken when one looks at trade companies as something advantageous by their very nature. Any powerful company, even when it only trades in competition with individuals, observes an author versed in this question, first bankrupts them by lowering the price of merchandise. After the individuals are bankrupted, this company, conducting trade alone or almost alone, bankrupts the nation by raising prices. Then, its excessive profits leading its agents into negligence, it bankrupts itself. We see in Smith, book 5, chapter 1, through numerous and incontestable examples, that the

2. It has always been said that the India trade could only be carried on by a company, but for more than a century the Portuguese carried on this trade without a company with more success than any other people. Say, book I, chap. 27, p. 183.

more exclusive, the more invested with important privileges, and the more rich and powerful the English companies have been, the more problems they have had while they lasted, and the worse they have ended. The only ones which have succeeded or endured are the companies limited to a modest capital, composed of a small number of individuals, and employing only a few agents—that is, those as similar as possible in their administration and their means to what associations of individuals could be. In 1780, Abbé Morellet counted fifty-five companies, established since 1600 in different European countries and adorned with exclusive privileges, which had all ended in bankruptcy. It is the same with companies that are too powerful as with all powers that are too great: like states that are too great, they begin by devouring their neighbors, then their subjects, and finally they destroy themselves.

The sole circumstance which renders a company acceptable is when individuals associate themselves in order to establish, at their own risk and peril, a new branch of trade with faraway and barbarous peoples. As compensation for the danger they brave, the state may give them a monopoly for a few years. But when the term has expired, the monopoly must be eliminated so that trade can again become free.

One can cite some isolated facts in favor of privileges, and these facts seem all the more convincing because we never see what would have happened if these privileges had not existed. But in the first place, I affirm that in including time among the elements which one vainly attempts to overlook, and in not surrendering to childish impatience, freedom will always end up by producing, without any evil mixed in, the same good that one tries to extract through privileges at the price of many evils. And I declare, secondly, that if a branch of industry existed which could not be exploited except by the introduction of privileges, the inconveniences for the morals and freedom of a nation are such that no advantage compensates for them.

# CHAPTER FIFTEEN ❧ On Taxation

> Everywhere society exists, a government must exist which governs it domestically and defends it externally. This administration and this protection require expenses which must be paid by the society to which they are useful.
>
> BOOK II, CHAPTER 27, P. 140.

The government, having to provide for the domestic defense and external security of the state, has the right to ask individuals for the sacrifice of a portion of their property in order to provide for the expenses which the fulfillment of these duties requires.

On their side the governed have the right to require of the government that the sum of taxes does not exceed that which is necessary in order to attain the goal. This condition can be fulfilled only by a political organization which limits the demands, and therefore the greed and extravagance, of rulers. We find traces of this organization in the institutions of the least-limited monarchies, such as the majority of the German principalities or the hereditary lands of the house of Austria, and the principle is solemnly recognized by the French constitution.

The details of this organization are not within our subject. One observation, it seems to me, must not be omitted. The right to consent to taxes can be considered from two perspectives: as a limit on power and as a means of economy. It has been said a thousand times that since a government is unable to wage war, or even exist domestically, if one does not pay for its necessary expenses, the refusal of taxes is an effective weapon in the hands of the people or their representatives, and that in courageously employing it, they could force the government not only to remain at peace with its neighbors, but also to respect the freedom of the governed. In reasoning thus, one forgets that what at first glance seems decisive in theory is often impossible in practice. When a government has begun a war, even an unjust one, to deny it the means of sustaining the war would be not to punish it alone, but also the nation, innocent of its faults. It is the same with refusing taxes for misgovernment or domestic injuries. The government commits arbitrary actions. The legislative body intends to disarm it by not voting any taxes. But imagining, with difficulty, that in this extreme crisis everything happens constitutionally, who will bear the burden of this struggle? The executive power will find temporary resources in its influence, in the funds previously put at its disposal; in advances from those who, enjoying its favors or even its injustices, do not want them changed; and also from those who, believing in its triumph, will speculate on its needs of the moment. The first victims will be low-ranking employees, entrepreneurs of all kinds, the state's creditors, and, as a result, the creditors of all those individuals of these different classes. Before the government succumbs or gives way, all private fortunes will be disturbed. A universal hatred against the representatives of the nation will result. The government will blame them for all the citizens' personal privations. The latter will not pay any attention to the motivation for resistance, and without concerning themselves with questions of right and theory, amid their sufferings, they will blame the legislature for their lacks and misfortunes.

The right to refuse taxes is therefore not in itself a sufficient guarantee to prevent the excesses of executive power. One can consider this right as an administrative means for improving taxes or as a means of economy for decreasing their total, but many other prerogatives are needed for representative assemblies to be able to protect freedom. A nation can have so-called representatives invested with this illusory right and at the same time tremble in the most complete slavery. If the body charged with this function does not enjoy great respect and great independence, it will become the executive power's agent, and its assent will be only a vain and illusory formula. For the freedom of voting the taxes to be anything other than a frivolous ceremony, political freedom must exist in its entirety, just as in the human body it is necessary for all the parts to be healthy and well-constituted for any one of them to function fully and regularly.

A second right of the governed relative to taxes is that their nature and the way in which they are collected should be the least burdensome possible for the taxpayers, should tend neither to harm nor corrupt them, and should not give rise to the creation of new taxes through useless expenses. From this right it follows that the governed have the right to demand that taxes weigh equally on all proportionally to their wealth; that they have nothing uncertain or arbitrary in quantity or in the means of collection; that they do not make any land or industry sterile; that to raise them costs only what is absolutely necessary; and finally, that there is a certain stability in their basis.

The establishment of a new tax always produces an upheaval which is communicated from the branches which are taxed to those which are not. Many workers and much capital flow toward the latter to escape the tax which strikes the others; the profits of the one decrease because of the tax, the profits of the latter because of the competition. Equilibrium is only slowly reestablished. Any change is thus harmful for a certain time.

It is in applying these rules to various forms of taxation that we can judge which are acceptable and which are not. It is not part of our subject to examine them all. We will choose only a few examples in order to give an idea of the way of thinking which seems best to us.

Some enlightened men of the last century recommended the land tax as the most natural, most simple, and most just. They even wanted to make it the sole tax. To tax the land is indeed a very seductive thing which immediately comes to mind, and which seems to be based on an incontestable truth. The land is the most obvious and most durable source of wealth; why look for artificial, indirect, and complicated means instead of going straight to the source?

If this doctrine has not been put into practice, it is much less because people thought they had found flaws in the land tax than because it was felt that, even by raising it to the highest level, one could not draw from it all the money one wanted to take from the people. Other taxes have been combined with it, but in most European countries it has not ceased to be the largest tax of all, and to some extent the basis of the financial system.

As a result, while the principle was rejected, not all its consequences were, as should have been done. In order to reconcile the contradiction of this conduct, one has had recourse to a theory whose result was almost the same as that of the land tax's apologists. The latter claimed that in the final analysis all taxes fell on land; some of their adversaries have claimed that in the final analysis all taxes were paid by the consumer. As the former affirmed that the taxes passed, so to speak, through the consumers in order to reach the land, and concluded from this that one should spare them this detour from the beginning and make them weigh directly on the land, so the latter, imagining that by a reverse process taxes on land rose to the consumers, thought that it was useless to relieve the land of a burden that it did not really bear.

If we apply to the land tax the rules we have established, we will be led to very different conclusions. On the one hand, it is false that all taxes on consumption fall on the land. The tax on postage is certainly not borne by landowners in their capacity as landowners. A landowner who uses neither tea nor tobacco does not pay any part of the taxes put on these commodities at the moment of their import, their transport, or their sale. Taxes on consumption do not weigh at all on classes which do not produce or consume the thing taxed.

It is equally false that the land tax influences the price of the commodity and falls on the consumer who buys it. What determines the price of a commodity is not always what it costs to produce, but the demand for it. When there is more demand than production, the commodity increases in price; it declines when there is more production than demand. But when the land tax decreases production it bankrupts the producer, and when it does not decrease production, it does not increase demand at all. Here is the proof: When a tax bears on land, one of two things happens. Either it takes all the net produce, that is, the production of a commodity costs more than it brings in, and then cultivation is necessarily abandoned, but the producer who abandons cultivation does not profit at all from the disequilibrium that abandonment might cause between the amount of demand and that of the commodity he no longer produces. Or, the tax does not take the whole net product, and thus the sale of the commodity still brings in more after taxes than the cost of production. Then the landowner continues to farm. But in this case, the quantity of production being just as abundant after the tax as before, the relationship between production and consumption remains the same, and the price cannot increase.

Despite what has been said, the land tax therefore weighs and will always continue to weigh on the landowner. The consumer pays no part of it unless, as a result of the gradual impoverishment of the farmer, the product of the land declines to the point of creating a shortage, but this calamity cannot be an element of calculation in a tax system. The land tax, such as it exists in many countries, is therefore not at all in conformity with the first rule we stated. It does not weigh equally on all, but particularly on one class.

In the second place, this tax, whatever its amount, always blights a certain portion of a country's lands. There are lands which because of the soil or the climate bring in nothing and as a result remain uncultivated. There are other lands which bring in the smallest imaginable production above nothing. This progression continues in increasing amounts until one reaches lands that have the greatest possible production. Calculate this progression as a series of numbers between 1 and 100, where 1 represents the smallest possible indivisible amount of production. The land tax takes away a portion of the product of each of these lands. In imagining it to be as low as is conceivable, the tax will not be below 1; as a result all the lands which bring in only 1, and which without the tax would have been farmed, are reduced to the rank of unproductive lands, and go back into the category of uncultivated lands. If the tax rises to 2, all the lands which do not bring in more than 2 will suffer the same fate, and so on, so that if the tax rises to 50, all the lands which produce up to 50 inclusive will remain uncultivated. It is therefore clear that when the tax rises, it takes out of cultivation a portion of land proportionate to the increase, and that when it goes down, it returns to cultivation a part proportionate to its fall. If one responds that the land tax is not fixed, but proportional, this would not resolve our objection. The proportional tax weighs on the gross product. This always means that if you fix the tax at an eighth of the gross product, the land which costs 9 to cultivate to produce 10 will become barren as a result of the tax. If you fix the tax at 25 percent, lands which cost 8 to produce 10 will become likewise, and so on.

That taxes have this effect is proved by governments' own precautions. The most enlightened, like England and Holland, have exempted from all tax lands rented beneath a certain value.[1] The most violent have declared forfeit lands left uncultivated by their owners. But what landowner would leave his land uncultivated if he could profit by farming it? None. For the rich man himself would rent it or sell it to a poor man. Lands only remain uncultivated for one of the reasons described above: either because they cannot produce anything, or because taxes take away the production they are capable of producing. Thus governments punish individuals for the evil which they

1. In Holland, thirty shillings; in England, twenty pounds sterling.

themselves have committed. This law of confiscation, as odious as it is unjust, is also as absurd as it is useless, for into whatever hands the government gives the confiscated lands, if these lands bring in less than their cultivation costs, someone may well try to farm them, but he will certainly not continue. In this second case, the land tax becomes still further removed from one of the necessary conditions for an acceptable tax, for it makes landownership in private hands sterile.

In the third place, the payment of the tax depends on the foresight of the farmer, who in order to be in a position to pay it must save fairly large sums in advance. But the working class is not gifted with this foresight; it cannot constantly struggle against the temptations of the moment. He who would pay daily, in small sums, and almost despite himself, a portion of his taxes, if they were combined with his usual consumption, will never in the course of a year save the sum necessary to pay them all at once. The collection of the land tax, although simple, is therefore not at all easy. The means of constraint which must be employed make it very costly. From this latter perspective, the land tax is harmful because it gives rise to expenses in raising it that a different form of taxation might spare.

I do not in the least conclude from this that the land tax should be eliminated. Since there are consumption taxes which landowners can avoid, it is just that they bear a portion of the public burden in their capacity as landowners. But since other classes of society do not bear the land tax at all, this tax must not exceed the proportion which ought to fall on the landowners. There is therefore no justification for making the land tax the sole tax, or even the chief tax.

We just said that the land tax, increased to a certain point, makes land sterile in its possessors' hands. The tax on business permits and premises[2] makes industry barren. It takes away the freedom to work, and this is a pretty ridiculous vicious circle. One can't pay anything if one doesn't work, and the government forbids individuals to do the work they are capable of if they have not first paid. This tax is thus harmful to the rights of individuals. It doesn't only take from them part of their profits; it also dries up their source, unless they previously possess the means necessary to pay the tax, a supposition for which we have no grounds.

2. *Patente.*—Trans.

This tax nevertheless can be tolerated if it is limited to professions which, in themselves, imply a certain previous financial comfort. It is then an advance which the individual makes to the government, and for which he reimburses himself through the profits of his industry, like the merchant who pays taxes on the commodity which he trades, later including them in the price of that commodity and making consumers bear them. Directed at the professions to which the poor might devote themselves, however, the tax on business premises is a revolting iniquity.

Indirect taxes or taxes on consumption are mingled with pleasures. The consumer who pays them in buying what he needs or what gives him pleasure does not distinguish the repugnance that paying taxes inspires from the feeling of satisfaction he obtains. He pays the tax when it is convenient to him. These taxes adapt themselves to the times, circumstances, abilities, and tastes of each individual. They are so small as to be imperceptible. The same weight we bear easily when spread out over the whole of our body would be unbearable if it bore on a single part. The distribution of indirect taxes is made, so to speak, by itself, for it is made by voluntary consumption. Considered from this point of view, indirect taxes do not at all violate the rule we have established, but they have three serious problems. The first is that they are susceptible to being multiplied to infinity in an almost imperceptible manner. Second, their collection is difficult, harmful, and often corrupting in several respects. Third, they create an artificial crime, smuggling.

The first problem is solved by the authority which votes the taxes. If you assume that this authority is independent, it will know how to block their useless increase. If you do not assume it is independent, don't hope to limit the sacrifices that will be required of the people, regardless of the nature of the tax. They will be defenseless in this regard as in all others.

The second problem is more difficult to prevent. I nevertheless find in the first problem a proof that the second can be prevented, for if one of the flaws of indirect taxes is that they can be increased beyond measure in an almost imperceptible manner, it must be the case that their collection can be so organized that they are not unbearable.

As for the third problem, I am less inclined than anyone to minimize it. I have said more than once that artificial duties tend to lead men to shrug off their real duties. Those who violate the laws relating to smuggling soon violate those relating to theft and murder. They don't run any extra danger, and their conscience has gotten used to revolting against society. However, if one considers the question well, one will see that the real cause of smuggling is less indirect taxes than the prohibitive system. Governments sometimes disguise their prohibitions in the form of taxes.

Taxes become contrary to individuals' rights when they necessarily authorize harm against citizens. Such is the *alcabala* of Spain, which subjects all property, both movable and real, to sales tax every time something passes from one hand to another. Taxes again become contrary to individuals' rights when they bear on objects which are easy to hide from the knowledge of the authority charged with collecting them. In directing taxes against objects that are easy to hide, you necessitate inspections and inquisitions. You are led to demand from the citizens mutual spying and informing. You reward these shameful actions, and your tax falls into the class of those which are unacceptable because their collection is immoral.

It is the same with taxes collected in ways that invite fraud. The greater or lesser probability of hiding an object from the government's knowledge is determined by the material ease of concealment, and by the interest found in hiding it. When the profit is considerable, it can be divided among more hands, and the cooperation of a larger number of agents in the fraud compensates for the physical difficulty on which the treasury may have counted. When the object taxed is not capable of being hidden in this way, taxes sooner or later destroy the branch of trade or the kind of transaction on which they weigh. They must be rejected then as contrary to the rights of property or industry.

Obviously, individuals have the right to limit their consumption according to their means or according to their will, and to abstain from objects that they don't want or can't consume. Thus indirect taxes become unjust when instead of being based on voluntary consumption, they are based on forced consumption. What was odious about the gabelle,[3] which people have so ridiculously wanted to identify with the salt tax, is that it required citizens to consume a fixed quantity of that commodity.

3. A tax imposed in most of France before the French Revolution in which consumers were required to buy a fixed quantity of salt at an artificially high price from the government or its agents.—Trans.

In order to tax a commodity, one should never forbid industry or private owners to produce this commodity, as was formerly done in some parts of France with regard to salt and as is done in several parts of Europe with regard to tobacco. This is clearly to violate private property, and to unjustly harm industry. One needs severe penalties to enforce obedience to these prohibitions, and these penalties are then revolting both in their harshness and their iniquity.

Indirect taxes should bear as little as possible on absolutely necessary commodities; otherwise, all their advantages disappear. The consumption of these commodities is not voluntary, it no longer changes according to the situation, and it is no longer proportional to the wealth of the consumer. It is not at all true, as is too often said, that since taxes on absolutely necessary commodities make these commodities more expensive, they produce a rise in wages. On the contrary, the more expensive commodities necessary for subsistence are, the more the need to work increases. The competition of those who offer their labor goes beyond that of those who offer work, and labor falls to a lower price, just when it ought to be at a higher price for the workers to be able to live. Taxes on absolutely necessary commodities produce the effects of barren years and shortages.

However, there are taxes whose collection is very easy which should be rejected, because their direct tendency is to corrupt and pervert men. No tax, for example, is paid with as much pleasure as lotteries. The government needs no coercive force to bring in this tax, but lotteries offer a means to wealth which has nothing to do with industry, work, or prudence; they throw the most dangerous kind of confusion into the calculations of the people. The multiplicity of chances creates an illusion about the probability of success, and the small sum of the bet invites repeated attempts. Disorder, embarrassment, bankruptcy, and crimes result from this. The lower classes of society, victims of the seductive dreams which intoxicate them, strike at the property which lies within their reach, flattering themselves that a favorable draw will allow them to hide their fault by repairing it. No fiscal consideration can justify institutions which bring about such consequences.

From the fact that individuals have the right to demand that the manner of collecting taxes be the least onerous possible for taxpayers, it follows that governments should not adopt a form of administration in this respect which is essentially oppressive and tyrannical. I am speaking of the custom of farming out the taxes. This is to put the governed at the mercy of a few individuals who don't even have the same interest the government does to spare them. It is to create a class of men who, clothed in the armor of the law and favored by a government whose cause they seem to defend, daily invent new injuries and demand the bloodiest measures. Tax farmers in all countries are, so to speak, the born representatives of injustice and oppression.

Whatever the taxes adopted by a country may be, they should bear on incomes and never touch capital; that is, they should take only a portion of the annual production and never touch the assets previously accumulated. These assets are the sole means of reproducing capital, the sole food of work, and the sole sources of fertility. This principle, unknown to all governments and many writers, can be proved from the evidence.

If taxes bear on capital instead of weighing solely on income, capital decreases every year by a sum equal to the amount raised in taxes. As a result annual production is struck by a decline proportionate to the annual decline in capital. With this decrease in production decreasing income and the tax remaining the same, every year a larger proportion of capital is taken away, and as a result, every year a smaller sum of income is produced. This double progression is always growing.

Imagine a landowner who cultivates his property. Three things are necessary to him: his land, his labor, and his capital. If he had no land, his capital and his labor would be useless.[4] If he had no labor, his capital and his land would remain unproductive. If he had no capital, his work would be in vain and his land barren, for he could not provide the advances necessary for its production. He would not have any tools for plowing, or seed, or animals: these are the things which make up his capital. Whichever one of these three objects you touch, you will equally impoverish the taxpayer. If, instead of taking from him every year a portion of his capital, you take away from him a portion of his land equivalent to a given sum, what would happen? The next year, in taking away from him the same portion of land, you would take a relatively greater portion of his property from him, and so on, until he

4. For the simplicity of the example I assume that he cannot employ his capital and his labor elsewhere. If he can, the reasoning would bear on the raw material on which he would employ his capital and labor.

found himself entirely despoiled. The same thing takes place when you tax his capital. The effect is less obvious, but no less inevitable.

Whatever his profession, capital is for every individual what a plow is for the farmer. Now if you take from the farmer a sack of wheat which he has just harvested, he goes back to work and will produce another next year, but if you take away his plow, he can no longer produce wheat.

Let no one think that private savings can solve this problem by creating new capital. By taxing capital, one diminishes individuals' incomes, because one takes away from them the means that produce this income. From what income do you want them to save? Let no one say either that capital reproduces itself. Capital is nothing but accumulated value, taken gradually from income, but the more the capital is touched, the more the income decreases; the less accumulation can take place, the less capital can reproduce itself.

The state which taxes capital therefore prepares the bankruptcy of individuals. It gradually takes their property from them. But the guarantee of this property being one of the state's duties, it is obvious that individuals have the right to demand this guarantee against a tax system whose result would be contrary to this purpose.

Let us now prove that the interest of the state is in accord with the rights of individuals in the matter of taxes. Unfortunately, it is not sufficient to show what is just; one must also convince the government that what is just is not less useful.

We have shown the iniquity of the land tax when it goes beyond the rate necessary to make landowners bear their proportional part in the payment of taxes. The same tax hurts the government, both by the expense of its collection and by its bad effects on agriculture. It keeps the majority of the agricultural class in poverty. It keeps in useless activity a mass of workers who are only employed to collect it. It absorbs capital which, producing nothing, is taken from private wealth and lost to the public wealth. Our costs of enforcement, our innumerable sheriffs,[5] and the armed force spread over the countryside to recover taxes in arrears should have convinced us of these truths. It has been stated that raising 250 million in taxes of this kind brings about 50 million in enforcement costs. As a result, the nation most famous

5. "Sheriff" here translates *garnisaire*, an agent sent by the government to live in the house of a refractory taxpayer, at his expense, until the taxes were paid.—Trans.

for the skill of its financial administration, far from taking the land tax as the base of its income, does not raise it to beyond the twelfth part of the totality of taxes.[6]

We have condemned, as an affront to the sacred rights of work, the tax on business permits and premises when directed at trades which the poor man could exercise. This tax organized in this way is one of the hardest to collect, and one of those which bring about the most nonpayment, that is to say the greatest losses for the public treasury.

We have said that taxes become contrary to the rights of individuals when they authorize tormenting searches. We cited the *alcabala* of Spain, a tax which subjects to a payment every sale, of whatever kind of object. Don Ustaritz considers it the cause of the decline of the Spanish economy.

We have rejected the taxes which lead to fraud. Is it necessary to prove how harmful this struggle between the government and the citizens is? And does one not see at a glance that it is ruinous even from a financial perspective? We have added that when taxes, by their excess, destroy a branch of commerce, it is a blow against industry. Spain has been punished by such a blow. Several of its mines in Peru remain unworked because the tax due to the king absorbed the owners' entire production. This was a double damage, both for the treasury and for the individuals.

We have criticized lotteries, even though they are easy to collect, because their effect is to corrupt people, but governments themselves bear the burden of this corruption. First of all, the harm lotteries cause to industry diminishes production, and thus the national wealth. Secondly, putting aside all moral considerations, the crimes they lead the working class to commit are a public expense. Third, lower-ranking agents let themselves be seduced by the lotteries' lure, and this is at the expense of governments. In a single year under the Directory there were bankruptcies by tax collectors that cost twelve million, and it was confirmed that the lottery had ruined two-thirds of these collectors. Finally, the collection of such a tax, while it is easy, is nonetheless expensive. In order for lotteries to be profitable, one must multiply temptations, and in order to multiply temptations, lottery offices must be multiplied, and from this come the high costs of collection. In M. Necker's time, the revenue from the lottery was 11,500,000 francs, and the costs of collection

6. As the text makes clear later, Constant is referring to England.—Trans.

2,400,000 francs, or 21 percent, so that the most immoral tax is at the same time the costliest to the state.

Finally, we have established that taxes should only bear on income. When they affect capital, individuals are bankrupted first, but the government is bankrupted next. The reason for this is simple. All men who have any notion of political economy know that consumption can be divided into two classes, productive and unproductive. The first kind is consumption which creates value; the second is consumption which creates nothing. A forest which is cut down to build ships or a town is just as much consumed as one devoured by fire, but in the first case the fleet or the city that has been built advantageously replaces the forest which has disappeared. In the second case, only ashes remain.

Unproductive consumption can be necessary. Each individual devotes a portion of his income to his nourishment. This is an unproductive but indispensable consumption. A state at war with its neighbors consumes a portion of the public wealth in order to provide for the armies' subsistence and to furnish them with offensive and defensive munitions. This is not useless consumption, even though it is unproductive consumption. But if unproductive consumption is often necessary to the existence or security of individuals and nations, it is only productive consumption which can add to the wealth of the one and the other. That which is unproductively consumed is always an excusable and legitimate loss when need requires it, senseless and inexcusable when need does not require it.

Money, which producers use as a medium of exchange, has served to spread some obscurity over this question. Since money is consumed without being destroyed, it has been believed that however it is employed, the thing remains the same. One ought to have realized that the money could be used productively or it could be used without producing anything. If a government spends ten millions to make an army march in different directions, or to give magnificent parties, spectacles, illuminations, dances, and fireworks, the ten millions thus employed are not destroyed. The nation is not impoverished by these ten millions, but these ten millions have not produced anything. From this employment of capital the state is left with only the ten millions which it employed originally. If, on the contrary, these ten millions had been employed to construct factories or buildings for any kind of industry, to improve lands, in short to produce any kind of commodity, the nation would have had on the one hand the ten million consumed in this way, and on the other the value that these ten millions would have produced.

I would like to continue with this important subject, for there is no more disastrous view than the one which describes all employment of capital as equal. This opinion is favored by all those who profit from government extravagance, and by all those too who repeat on faith principles that they don't understand. Money, the sign of wealth, in all cases undoubtedly only passes from one hand to another, but when it is employed in productive consumption, instead of one value there are two; when its consumption is unproductive, instead of two values there is only one. Moreover, since in order to be wasted in unproductive consumption it is torn from the class which would have employed it productively, if the nation is not impoverished in its money it is impoverished by all the production which did not take place. It retains the symbol, but it loses the reality, and the example of Spain teaches us well enough that the possession of symbolic money is anything but real wealth. It is therefore certain that the sole means of prosperity for a nation is the employment of its capital in productive consumption.

But even the wisest governments cannot employ the funds taken from individuals in anything but unproductive consumption. The payment of the salaries due public officials of all kinds, the expenses for law enforcement, justice, war, and for all administration, are expenses of this kind. When the state uses only a portion of income for this consumption, the capital which remains in the hands of private individuals serves for the necessary production. But if the state diverts capital from its destination, production declines, and since it is then necessary, as we have shown above, to take a larger proportion of the capital every year, production will eventually cease entirely and the state as well as individuals will find itself bankrupt. M. Ganilh, in his *History of Public Revenue* (vol. 2, p. 289), says that just as the spendthrift who spends beyond his income decreases his property by the amount by which he exceeds his income and soon sees both property and income disappear, the state which taxes properties and consumes their production like income marches to a certain and rapid decline.

Thus it is that in matters of taxation as with all other things, the laws of equity are the best ones to follow, even if they are only considered from the perspective of utility. The government which violates justice in the hope of a miserable profit pays dearly for that violation, and the rights of individuals ought to be respected by governments even when these governments have only their own interests in view.

In thus indicating in a necessarily very abbreviated fashion some of the rules relative to taxation, we propose to suggest to the reader ideas which he can extend, rather than to develop any ourselves. This work has led us far beyond the bounds which we have set. An incontestable axiom which no sophism can hide is that all taxation, of whatever kind, always has a more or less harmful influence. If the use of a tax sometimes produces a good, raising the tax always produces an evil. It may be a necessary evil, but like all necessary evils, it should be made as small as possible; the more means one leaves at the disposal of individual industry, the more a state prospers. Because it takes away a portion of these means, taxation is inevitably harmful. The more money one takes from nations, says M. de Vauban in *The Royal Tenth*, the more money one takes from trade. The best-employed money in the kingdom is that which remains in the hands of private individuals, where it is never useless or idle.

J. J. Rousseau, who was ignorant with regard to finance, followed many others in repeating that in monarchical countries the ruler had to consume the excess of the subjects' surplus through luxury, because it was better for this excess to be absorbed by the government than wasted by private individuals. In this doctrine we perceive an absurd mixture of royalist prejudices and republican opinions. The ruler's luxury, far from discouraging that of individuals, serves them as an encouragement and example. One should not believe that in despoiling them he reforms them. He may plunge them into poverty, but he cannot bring them back to simplicity. However, the poverty of some is combined with the luxury of others, and of all combinations this is the most deplorable.

Some thinkers no less illogical have concluded that because the most-taxed countries, like England and Holland, were the richest, they were richer because they paid more taxes; they took the effect for the cause. One is not rich because one pays: one pays because one is rich.

Everything which exceeds real needs, says a writer whose authority we will not contest on this matter, ceases to be legitimate.[7] There is no difference between the usurpations of private individuals and those of the sovereign,

7. M. Necker.

other than that the injustice of the former is in accord with simple ideas which everyone can easily recognize, while the other is linked to schemes whose extent is as vast as it is complicated, and no one can judge them other than by conjecture.

Wherever the constitution of the state does not pose an obstacle to the arbitrary multiplication of taxes, and wherever the government's ever increasing demands are neither contested nor halted by insurmountable barriers, neither justice nor morality nor individual freedom can be respected. Neither the authority which takes from the working classes their laboriously acquired subsistence, nor those oppressed classes who see that subsistence torn from their hands to enrich their greedy masters, can remain faithful to the laws of equity in this scandalous struggle of weakness against violence, poverty against greed, and need against spoliation. Every useless tax is a theft, which the force which it accompanies does not make more legitimate than any other theft of this kind. It is a theft still more odious in that it is executed with all the formalities of law, still more culpable in that the rich exercise it against the poor, and still more cowardly since it is committed by an armed government against disarmed individuals. The government itself is soon punished for it. The peoples in the Roman provinces, says Hume, were so oppressed by the tax collectors that they joyfully threw themselves into the arms of the barbarians, happy that coarse and unluxurious masters offered a domination less greedy and less despoiling than that of the Romans.

One would be wrong again in supposing that the inconvenience of excessive taxes is limited to the poverty and privations of the people. A greater evil results from it, an evil which does not seem to me to have been sufficiently noted up to now, which I discussed in another work. There I said that the possession of a very great fortune inspires in individuals desires, caprices, and disordered fantasies that they would never have had in a more modest and more restrained situation. It is the same with governments. Excessive opulence makes them as drunk as excessive strength, because opulence is a strength, and of all strengths the most real. From this derive chimerical plans, unbridled ambitions, and gigantic projects that a government which possessed only the necessary means would never have conceived. Thus the population is not poor only because it pays beyond its means, but it is poor again through the use the government makes of what it pays. Its sacrifices are turned against it. It doesn't pay more taxes in order to have peace assured by a good system of defense—it pays for war, because the government, proud of its immense treasury, invents a thousand pretexts to spend the taxes, as it says, gloriously. The people pay not for the maintenance of domestic order, but on the contrary so that a few favorites, enriched with their spoils, can trouble the public order with their unpunished misdemeanors. Thus a nation which has no guarantee against the increase of taxes pays with privations, misfortunes, troubles, and dangers. In this state of things, the government is corrupted because of its wealth, and the people because of its poverty.

# *Part Three*

## CHAPTER ONE ☙ On Criminal Prosecution Confided Exclusively to a Magistrate

> Among very many nations . . . [T]he common interest all members of society have in the preservation of public order, and consequently in seeing the law obeyed, decreasing crime, and frightening evil people has led the most enlightened legislators to believe that one could not refuse one citizen the right of prosecuting another.
>
> BOOK III, CHAPTER 2, P. 232.

Criminal prosecution by individual citizens is impossible among the moderns. The gentleness of our mores, the complication of social relations, the need for rest, and finally a certain delicacy or softness of mores which do not permit one man to harm another when there is no direct interest in doing so, or when he is not required to do so by his job (for among the moderns jobs explain and excuse everything): these various causes make prosecution entrusted to the citizen completely illusory. In certain cases an austere virtue—or what is much more common, personal hatred—may lead someone beyond the usual attitude, but these cases are so rare that they cannot be taken into account. Their result would be so harmful to those who imposed this painful duty on themselves, and the social animosity against what would seem like disinterested malice (for what we pardon least, in a time of egoism, is the appearance of disinterestedness, in evil as in good) would pursue them so much, that a single example would be enough to divert people permanently from such a dangerous course. Despite what Filangieri, who always admires whatever he finds established among the ancients, says, it is therefore necessary to have a public person created by law to pursue the guilty and demand their punishment.

It is not that this institution does not present serious problems. Give a man a job, and you inspire in him the desire to do it, because that is the only way he can prove that this job is necessary. Soldiers feel obliged to fight for all causes. While admitting that a war is unjust, they wage it to the best of their ability. This is natural. Furthermore, as a general rule it is good that this is natural, for without wishing to challenge a man's right to question, for which I have great respect, I concede that if in all cases everyone questioned what he was ordered to do by superior authority in the course of his functions, there would be anarchy and confusion. But in the same way that soldiers would like to fight as often as possible, men made into prosecutors will want to prosecute as soon as there is a plausible pretext. If ten years passed without any crime being committed, what would happen to the importance of those who have no importance except in the pursuit of crimes? In supposing them, as I do, to be the most humane and honest of men, a hidden discontent would arise in their souls when they saw themselves reduced to a level of inaction which deprived them of all means of fame and celebrity.

It follows from this that prosecuting magistrates will multiply prosecutions and charges, perhaps without explaining their own motives. The most trivial circumstances and the most improbable evidence will take on a seriousness in their eyes which it would not have in the eyes of men disinterested in the question. If the ancients' system, transferred to us, tends to no one prosecuting because everyone can prosecute, the modern system must tend to the individual who is specially charged with making accusations prosecuting often, because it is his prerogative.

This danger, which would always exist to a certain extent in the most peaceful times when it is only a question of ordinary crimes, becomes much more pressing when violent agitation has sown trouble and dissension in society. When a country is so unfortunate that there can be political crimes in it, one can be sure that prosecutions for political crimes will multiply infinitely. Dependent on the government, prosecutors do not wish to overlook anything that seems to them, from near or far, in appearance or in reality, to threaten authority. By letting an opportunity for prosecution escape, they would make themselves suspect of negligence. By prosecuting frivolously, they will incur no other reproach than that of showing too much zeal, and this is a fault people pardon.

It will be objected that almost everywhere the magistrate charged with prosecution is not invested with the right to prosecute in the first instance. He submits evidence to judges more independent than he, and the prosecution is their work;[1] but one should reflect on the fact that the protective forms in force once the prosecution is accepted are eliminated when it is only a question of the appropriateness of the prosecution. Prosecution is decided on in the absence of the accused. Magistrates, who live on close terms with the man who presents the accusation, pronounce on the fate of an unknown person without hearing him, and with the thought in the back of their minds that if he is innocent he will be acquitted. This thought inclines them to be more lax. When one can say to oneself that what one does is not irrevocable, one is much more inclined to weakness, or at least to being compliant.

If, as I think, it is nevertheless necessary today to make prosecution a special duty and, in a certain sense, a monopoly, it is desirable to eliminate or to mitigate the problems that this course of action presents. Some persons would like the minister charged with prosecuting to be independent of the government. This independence could be acquired only if he was not removable from office. But would this irremovability be effective, and would it not have other very harmful consequences beyond its ineffectiveness?

In the first place, it would not be effective. Irremovability, which seems at first glance a very reassuring guarantee, is at bottom anything but that. Position, personal relationships, habitual dealings, and secret favors destroy its effects in ways all the more harmful in that they are hidden from view. Secondly, if we reject any idea of hidden influences and guilty connivance, as soon as there is a possibility of promotion, irremovability is an illusory guarantee. Finally, from the fact that we want to preserve individuals from imprudent actions by the magistrates created to prosecute them, it does not follow that we want to expose society to the sad results of those magistrates' negligence, and if these magistrates were irremovable, what recourse would remain to society against their inertia and inaction?

In my opinion, the sole means of resolving all these problems is to subject the question of whether citizens will be indicted to the sole power which is equally reassuring for the security of all and the tranquility of each. The public prosecutor then will do his duty and fulfill his functions with a zeal

1. In the French legal system, an official presents evidence for a prosecution to a judge or panel of judges who decide on whether the prosecution will go forward.—Trans.

whose very exaggeration will be harmless. The idea is certainly not new, since it is what existed in France, what exists in England, and what despotism has destroyed.

Without a grand jury, unfounded or frivolous prosecutions will constantly threaten citizens. The public prosecutor and the judges charged with examining his allegations, being taken from a different class than the accused, will often think, as I have already said, that since a final judgment will have to be made later, innocence will be recognized at that point. They will not think about the consequences of a prosecution even when it is followed by an acquittal. The members of a grand jury, being in the same position as the one who is the object of the lawsuit and subject to exposure to the same danger, will feel that prosecution alone—bringing with it imprisonment, interruption of business, disruption of credit, bankruptcy perhaps, or at least a great reversal of fortune, and these evils being in no way repaired by a tardy absolution—is itself a punishment to which the imperfection of human knowledge sometimes forces people to condemn an innocent person, but which one should not inflict on anyone without the greatest precautions and the greatest scruples.

In general, when you want a job carried out zealously and energetically, specialize it, and give it to a man whose entire existence will be dependent on that function. But when you want a question to be examined with impartiality, calm, and candor, charge men with examining it whose usual profession it is not, and who lose none of their importance but rather gain in security if they decide it negatively.

Let me summarize. To look for all the circumstances which may call for severe and exact investigation, a professional prosecutor is useful. To sweep aside all those frivolous or misleading appearances which would lead to unfounded prosecutions, a grand jury is indispensable.

## CHAPTER TWO ❧ On Secret Indictments

> This operation takes place in secret. . . . The citizen on whom falls either the accusation of an individual, or the report of an informer, or the suspicion of the judge, is ignorant of all that is being concocted against him, and if he is innocent, he cannot defend himself against this storm which threatens his head.
>
> BOOK III, CHAPTER 3, P. 249.

This entire chapter is excellent. Some of the abuses which Filangieri eloquently points out have been mitigated since his book was published. We no longer allow, or at least we are not supposed to allow prisoners to be left for weeks or months without questioning them, and without informing them of the suspicion which led to their imprisonment. But several, and the most important, of the vices against which the Italian author directs his complaints still persist, and often the remedies applied to the others are evaded, sometimes by culpable negligence, sometimes by calculations and considerations still more criminal than negligence.

When, in order to give the appearance of satisfying the law, one questions a prisoner in the period of time determined, after which if no interrogation had taken place his detention would become illegal, and, having questioned him once, he is allowed to rot in a cell without any prosecution beginning, it is clear that the performance of a vain formality changes nothing in the iniquity of which this prisoner, guilty or not, is victim. Society has the right to deprive of their liberty those of its members it supposes to be the authors or accomplices of a crime. This is a terrible right that necessity forces us to give society, but this right is inseparable from one condition which is clearly required in order to make it legitimate. This condition is that the detention will last only for the time necessary to find out what is needed for the discovery of the truth. The causes which influence this length of time should not include either other business which prevents the judges from taking care of the case, or the convenience of those judges, or in short anything which is not part of the matter itself—nothing which is foreign to the accusation and the accused. It is for society to take measures so that a man is judged as soon as all the evidence acquired to convince the judges is assembled. If society keeps him behind bars one day more without bringing him to trial, it is guilty of injustice and arbitrariness toward him. It is up to society to organize the courts in such a way that there are always judges available when there are men in prison.

Above all, this principle will seem incontestable if one reflects that society, in claiming for itself the right to arrest those it suspects, does not think it has the obligation to compensate those whom it has suspected unjustly. Certainly, in thus freeing itself from what all equitable men would consider a duty, the least it could do is refrain from prolonging the anguish and suffering of the innocent person it has harmed, a harm it does not wish to take into account.

From these thoughts, directed against an abuse the laws have recognized but which they have repressed only in a way that is ineffective and unfortunately too easy to evade, let us pass to vices that the laws have not perceived, and that as a result they consecrate. I confess that it is impossible for me to conceive what reasoning one can follow to prove that it is just that the prosecution of a man be determined in that man's absence. How can one not see that one word from him may clear up a circumstance that all the evidence of the investigation cannot put in its true light if he is absent? The prosecutor interrogates him. He responds, but he cannot divine what inferences will be drawn from his responses. These responses may be incomplete. He does not foresee what doubts they will give birth to, the new suspicions they may suggest. He would clear up these doubts and dissipate these suspicions if he were allowed to see the report according to which the indictment might be brought, and it is precisely in this most important moment of all for him that he is forbidden to be present at the decision which decides his fate.

It cannot be repeated too often: to be indicted is already a punishment; to accuse a man without hearing him, based on a summary of his responses made by one who himself has an interest in supporting the accusation he initiated, is to pronounce judgment without observing the forms prescribed by human reason and by the principles of judgment engraved at the bottom of our hearts.

One very true remark by Filangieri, of the utmost importance, is that according to the jurisprudence established among almost all peoples, the situation of a guilty person is almost more favorable than that of an innocent man. The guilty person knows what he might be accused of, he knows all the circumstances of his crime, and he calculates everything he should say to hide the evidence that these circumstances could bring against him. He is in some sense on the same level as the judge. The one and the other both know what it is all about. By contrast the innocent person debates with himself in darkness. He is not able to foresee what charge the most innocent response may credit against him, he has no idea of the combination of facts which are alleged against him, and he responds haphazardly, while the guilty person knows what is most useful to say to parry the blows intended for him.

Let us take an example. A man is accused of a murder. Proof of an alibi would get him acquitted, but the crime was committed three months ago. He is asked to remember where he was on the day of the crime.

Certainly the guilty man will remember without difficulty. The day is too important in his life for each minute and the use of each minute not to be imprinted in his memory. Therefore if he can prove, by bringing forward or putting back the time necessary, that he was then somewhere else, and he has been able to take precautions to facilitate this proof, he will evade the rigor of the laws, and he will evade them precisely because he is guilty.

Conversely, the innocent person, having no foresight of the accusation which will make it so important for him to give an account of his conduct and the place he was on such and such a day of such and such a month, can easily have forgotten everything he did at the time. Forced to respond precisely to the questions addressed to him, it is possible, even probable, that he will make a mistake in some details. If he confesses that he does not remember what is asked of him, his forgetfulness will be imputed to crime. If he makes an effort and is wrong, his mistake will rebound on him as an evident proof of his guilt, and he will be condemned precisely because of his innocence.

In general, the role played by the prosecutor and the consequences he draws from the contradictions of the accused have always seemed to me a major flaw in our procedures. One can always bet that it is the innocent person who contradicts himself and the guilty person whose answers are always consistent, because the latter knows, while the former does not know; and between a man who knows and a man who does not know, the odds are that the former arranges his answers and gives them the appearance of coherence.

By all that precedes this I do not mean to say that in my opinion the guilty escape and only the innocent are ever condemned. But if this misfortune does not happen constantly, it is not because of the laws, but because of human nature. Providence has willed that an invincible disturbance accompany crime, and that this disturbance be still more irresistible as the crime is more odious. Whoever reads criminal trials carefully will see that the discovery of murderers is almost never due to the vigilance of the magistrates or the wisdom of the laws but to the imprudence of the guilty, and the sort of delirium which seizes them. As a result, the law should take much more care that the innocent not be condemned than that the crime not go unpunished. For, sad to say, if disturbance is ordinarily associated with crime, as if destined by heaven to betray it, there is no more completely false assumption than the one so lightly accepted: that calm is the companion of innocence. Being accused of a crime of which one is incapable is just as likely to cause fright as to arouse indignation. To require that an unfortunate should remain impassive, when on false pretenses society raises itself up in all its power with its threatening machinery against him, is to ask something beyond human strength. The effort is possible when it is a question of crimes with which an opinion is associated, and when pity, sympathy, or sometimes admiration compensate the victim and turn punishment into a triumphal parade. But when it is a question of ignoble or ferocious crimes against which one and all rise up, of which the mere suspicion places a barrier between the accused and his fellow citizens, and which offer only the prospect of contempt, reprobation, and the scaffold, the person accused of such a crime is already struck to the core by the idea that he could have been misunderstood to such a degree. His pain is natural, his terror excusable. Far from concluding anything to his disadvantage from this, perhaps we ought to draw the opposite conclusion. Far from increasing his terror, he ought to be reassured; far from interpreting his contradictions as evidence against him, we should look for how he might have contradicted himself without being guilty.

# CHAPTER THREE ❧ On Denunciation

> In order to be persuaded of the injustice of the legislation in this regard (the restriction of the right to prosecute), it is sufficient to observe that at the same time as we have abolished the freedom to prosecute, we have established the freedom to inform.
>
> BOOK III, CHAPTER 3, P. 263.

Everything which Filangieri says here about the problems with informing is perfectly well-founded; however, there is, it seems to me, vagueness in some of his expressions. To criticize the laws for establishing the freedom to inform seems to me absurd. It is a freedom one could not forbid. Will you punish the man who, knowing of a crime, goes to a magistrate to reveal it? You will turn all the citizens into a nation of the voluntarily deaf and dumb. One would be as afraid of the chance that brought a crime to light as of the crime itself. Will you claim that if denunciation cannot be punished, it ought to be rejected? That means you will require the magistrate charged with investigating crimes to close his eyes to those of which he will often have the most precise and positive knowledge. Will you require the informer to be the prosecutor? The same reasons by which I showed that in our day the right to prosecute will not be exercised will easily show that having to prosecute after having denounced a crime would impose silence on all members of a society who only aspire to rest and to the peaceful exercise of all their faculties. No one is disposed to run risks or to submit to interruptions to his work or pleasure—in a word, no one is willing to disturb his well-arranged, commodious, and pleasant life for something which concerns only the public interest. Public interest no longer has almost any link with individual interest, thanks to the individual independence and resources created by civilization.

Doubtless the freedom to inform has problems which can be extremely serious. Hatred, envy, and all the base or malevolent passions will use that freedom. Innocence can be slandered. The most irreproachable citizens will find themselves at the mercy of a hidden enemy. But it is up to the prudence of the magistrate to whom the denunciation is addressed to decrease the number of these problems. It is up to him to appraise the value of the evidence submitted to his wisdom. It is for him to reflect that it is rarely because of zeal and disinterest that men bring themselves to take measures that have something odious about them and that, of a hundred denunciations, it is probable that barely one will have been dictated by the love of justice or the hatred of crime.

Note further that in the modern system, which specially charges a magistrate as a matter of routine to pursue the crimes that are committed, the duty of that magistrate is to gather everything which might lead him to knowledge of those crimes. If he finds a body in the road, he concludes that there is a possibility of murder, and he uses his vigilance to discover if, in fact, a murder has taken place and who is guilty of it. A denunciation is nothing but an encounter of the same kind. It does not establish anything, nor does it prove anything; it only warns that there is something to be examined. The magistrate who, based on a secret denunciation, would have the denounced man thrown into irons, commits an unjust and inexcusable act; but one who receives a denunciation and seeks to discover what might be its degree of probability and accuracy acquits himself of the obligation imposed on him.

Filangieri was misled by the aversion naturally inspired in every noble soul by denunciations and informers. In our present social state, an informer, even when the fact he reveals is true and when the crime he unveils is serious, deserves neither esteem nor moral approval. Society is sufficiently provided with instruments devoted to this rigorous profession for citizens to rely on the zeal of those who are dedicated to it. Let us suppose that the informer is not inspired by any interest derived from passion, hatred, or jealousy; he always has a vicious interest, an indiscreet and unattractive ardor to involve himself in something that is not his business. There is a need to make himself known, a hope perhaps of creating for himself some right to the favor of the government which he claims to have served by his officious revelations.

But from the fact that an informer, however disinterested and however useful, is always more or less contemptible, it does not follow that the law can forbid the freedom to inform, or even surround this freedom with procedures that would render it entirely illusory. What Filangieri should have attacked with the most energetic criticism is, on the one hand, rewards designed to encourage informing and, on the other hand, threats employed to bring forth denunciations.

Rewards thus promised sow corruption throughout society. The man who denounces or surrenders his fellow in order to obtain a financial reward commits an action more vile, and at least as odious, through this prize awarded to infamy than whatever crime whose discovery one wished to facilitate. No interest of public safety or present danger gives society the right to pervert and degrade its members. Individuals pay dearly enough for society. They invest it with rights strong enough for it to do its job without doing damage to feelings that it should respect, those feelings of pity which unite man to man and which make him recoil from the idea that he would voluntarily drag a fellow citizen to the scaffold. To smother that instinct in our nature by arming greed or destitution against it is to weaken the basis of all virtues in order to obtain one more means of discovering a few crimes; it is to sacrifice the primary and permanent interest of the human species to a secondary and fleeting interest.

It is still worse when the social power attempts to force denunciations by threats, punishments, or assumptions of complicity. Then, after having tried to corrupt us, it punishes us for having resisted corruption. It groups us with the jailors and executioners it bribes, with the sole difference that it wants to get from us by fear what it gets from them with money. Governments have tools to watch over, denounce, arrest, and pursue; it is not permissible for them to impose any of these painful functions on anyone who has not undertaken them voluntarily. No one can be justly forced to engage in cruel acts whose justice he cannot judge. I know of an action which seems to me to be a crime, but am I certain that my knowledge of it is really correct? Can I judge an action which is only partly known to me, and of whose most important circumstances—those which decide whether it should be considered guilty or innocent—I am ignorant? Based on mere appearances, which I do not have the means to go beyond, I would be required to make inaccurate disclosures to the legal authorities which could bring down on the head of an innocent man captivity, bankruptcy, the humiliation of a public trial, and all the uncertain chances which always accompany the exercise of human justice.

This applies to all legal provisions which require denunciation, no matter what the crime. But this reasoning acquires even more force when it is a question of crimes which are to some extent fictitious, that is to say, crimes which are only considered such because they go against a dominant opinion. I have sometimes asked myself what I would do if I found myself shut up in a town where it was forbidden on penalty of death to give refuge to men suspected of political crimes, or where I was required to inform on them. My response has been that if I wanted to save my life I would make myself a prisoner for as long as that measure remained in force.

# CHAPTER FOUR ❧ New Thoughts on the Idea of Giving Each Citizen the Right to Prosecute

> The first object of a reform of criminal procedure should therefore be to return the right to prosecute to the citizen while making it difficult to abuse.
>
> BOOK III, CHAPTER 4, P. 266.

Since Filangieri still insists on the necessity of giving citizens the right to prosecute, we must continue to examine his reasons and refute them. I said that one of the problems with this right, when brought into modern times, would be that citizens would be reluctant to use it. Filangieri responds with a sentence from Machiavelli. "The right to prosecute," says this writer (*Discourses on the First Ten Books of Livy*, bk. 1, chap. 7), creates an "outlet for the bad feelings which are born in a town against every citizen."

It is obvious that in expressing himself thus Machiavelli had in mind the ancient republics, or the Italian republics such as they existed in the Middle Ages. There, discontent could in fact arise against eminent citizens. The right to prosecute, a recourse of the weak against the strong, could be a consolation, a calming influence, a compensation for a people envious of its superiors.

Moreover it is clear that in the sentence cited by Filangieri, Machiavelli was not thinking of prosecutions brought against private crimes. He was thinking solely of political prosecutions. Assuredly, in questions of theft or murder, it was not a question of bad feelings which arose against a citizen in a town. Our writer has thus mixed up two questions which have nothing to do with one another.[1]

1. In truth Filangieri in another place distinguishes—or rather promises to distinguish—between public crimes, for which every citizen may become the accuser, and private crimes, which only the offended party has the right to pursue. But so much incoherence reigns in his

Modern states are not, and cannot be, popular states—for there is nothing less popular, nothing which less mobilizes the mass of the people than representative government, which only gives the people a right of election exercised over a few days and always followed by a fairly long period of inaction. Modern states not being and incapable of being popular states, the discontent of which Machiavelli speaks cannot be born in the mass of the nation. Today in ordinary circumstances it is very rare for a citizen to become so important that people pay attention to him for very long. This becomes more rare every day. The progress of industry, offering everyone the means to material well-being through his own will and his work, creates for everyone a sphere in which all his interests are concentrated and outside which he only occasionally casts his attention. Only leisured societies regard individuals as the object of their enthusiasm or their hatred, however well known the individuals may be. Other societies criticize or approve of them in hours of leisure. But with all social energy being employed in private enterprise and speculation, and in some sense dispersed, the discontents for which the right of prosecution would be an outlet have no need of this outlet, because they do not exist.

But if Machiavelli's sentence describes a problem which has become imaginary and proposes a remedy for that problem which is thus superfluous, this passage is good for showing us a danger which escaped Filangieri and which would make the right he wants to revive particularly harmful. Animosity against citizens will not arise among the people, but these bad feelings might very well arise against them in Courts. When a ruler's wisdom or a government's needs have put a wise minister in charge of affairs—an enemy of inequalities and arbitrary power, and above all one who is frugal—do we not see what a wave of paid accusers the courtiers can conjure up? When the people's choice has raised to representative office an incorruptible citizen, an orator made eloquent by his talent and his conscience, the same wave of accusers will surround him and reduce him to constantly defending his life, his reputation, or his fortune before the law courts. Do you think that in a corrupt society there would not be found enough lost souls who, sure of pay if not of impunity, would bring the most injurious and least founded prosecutions?

ideas that here he praises the Egyptians for having required every witness of a murder to become an accuser, and the Franks for having imposed the same duty on whoever had knowledge of a theft.

What greed and hatred now do by slander would be done by prosecutions. One would steal the right of contempt from the innocent. Instead of being able, as is the case today, to oppose calumny which has no official or legal character with silence, the honest minister and the courageous deputy would be forced to devote to their own court cases the time and strength they would like to devote to their country. Who doubts that Turgot and Malesherbes, Necker and Mirabeau would have been constantly torn from the council of ministers or the national tribune by insolent accusations and lawsuits, which scandal would crown with a sort of success?

This would not be all. In a large association, which has arrived at an excessive civilization, everything becomes a trade. If prosecution was permitted to every citizen, doubtless a profession of accusers would soon be created. In Rome, every ambitious young man's debut was a public prosecution. He chose a person to be accused as the stepping-stone of his future glory, whose loss would give him as much fame as his victim had. It was in some sense a sacrifice that he offered to fate at the beginning of his career.

It is in vain that Filangieri piles up precautions against unjust prosecutions. The punishments do not frighten, and they are those sorts of punishments which would only make the situation worse. But as I have already said, no respectable man who wished to cultivate honorable society would profit from the ability to prosecute. Only men already rejected by society would take it up; the punishments would not scare them. What do fines matter to someone who does not have enough money to provide for his daily subsistence? What does prison matter to someone who, except for prison, has no home?

Filangieri thinks that by restricting the right to prosecute he is bringing an effective remedy to bear on this problem. He bases his argument on the example of the Romans, who refused this right to women, freedmen, and people of bad reputation, but then my first objection would regain all its force. You want only worthy citizens to prosecute; the worthy citizens will not prosecute. You reject men whose character and intentions seem suspect to you, but these men are the only ones who, in our modern times, can consent to fill the role of prosecutor.

# CHAPTER FIVE ❧ On the Right to Prosecute Given to Servants, When It Is a Question of Crimes against Society

> Among the number of persons who were deprived of this freedom (that of prosecution), were counted a class of men who fortunately do not exist today; these were slaves. We have in truth a class of individuals who have all the vices of servitude, although they enjoy the rights of citizens, who sell for an indeterminate period of time their personal freedom while retaining their civil freedom, and who thus are not worthy of the law's confidence, although they have the right to its protection: this class is that of our paid servants. They should be deprived of the right to prosecute, except in the case of a personal offense or of crimes committed against society.
>
> BOOK III, CHAPTER 4, P. 268.

The error into which Filangieri falls at the beginning of this chapter is unfortunately almost universal. All political writers have simultaneously accepted two propositions that the simplest common sense shows to be irreconcilable. One is that in all ordinary and usual circumstances one should deprive of the right to prosecute, and often even to testify, a class of men brought into contempt by their voluntary abjection. The other is that one can accept these same men as accusers or witnesses when it is a question of the crime that is easiest to allege and most rigorously punished. This unusual contradiction has its origin in an opinion which, were it well founded, would hardly prove favorable to the social order established in all modern nations, it must be admitted. This opinion is that society is constantly threatened by men whose only desire is to overthrow and destroy it.

Fortunately, nothing is less just or more exaggerated than this supposition. The human species is naturally inclined to order. Its inclinations, its interests, and its habits center around what exists. When an abuse has lasted a long time, it loses the appearance of an abuse in the eyes of those who suffer from it, almost as much as in the eyes of those who profit from it. The reason for this is simple. Each generation and each individual enters into existing institutions as into a building where it is important to find lodging. However deplorable certain parts of this edifice are, however dark and unhealthy are the dungeons inhabited by a large portion of its residents, one shelters there, gets comfortable, and grows accustomed to it.

How many centuries went by under the most abusive governments without those governments having to complain of a single attempt to overthrow them! And if one carefully examines the attempts at overthrow that interrupted this long line of resignation, one will see that most of the time it was governments which gave the signal. When this signal is given, the shocks are undoubtedly strong and the calamities sometimes frightful, but these are exceptions to the usual rule, and it is not for exceptions that one should make laws.

Let us therefore consider from this perspective Filangieri's acceptance of admitting as prosecutors, in the case of crimes committed against society, men whom he himself declares tainted by all the vices of servitude. Certainly, of all the classes in society, that of mercenaries who subject their personal liberty to the fantasies of a master is least interested in the maintenance of the established order. This order is entirely directed against them: it weighs on them more than on any other class. The peasant has his field. The tenant farmer who lives on someone else's field is guaranteed by the law of more or less lasting possession of what a contract has assured him. The artisan has his industry. Even the day laborer has his hands. Paid servants have nothing of value to offer except their willingness to serve or to anticipate someone's caprices and the patience to bear the insolence of a master. It has often been rightly noted that the more a man has to do with things, the more his moral character improves, while when he chiefly has to do with his fellows, his character experiences a clear deterioration. This is because in relations with things all vices become useless. Ruse, calculation, and baseness cannot be elements of success; the farmer has only one means of making the land productive—to plow it. The courtier has a thousand means of obtaining the ruler's favor and almost all are based on corruption, presuppose it, or produce it. Domestic servants are the petty courtiers of those who pay them, and since their profession is not surrounded by the prestige which raises courtiers in their own eyes, which is always a salutary thing for morality, the class condemned to domestic service becomes the most abject of all.

Add to this that this class is also the most irritated by the social inequality that causes its abjection, and that it is in perpetual contact with superiors who offend and humiliate it every minute of the day. What good might remain in its soul turns into hatred. The spectacle of vices which they learn of by necessity or indiscretion, the obligation to be their instrument, the thought that people are much more grateful to them for their zeal in this regard than for any virtues they might display: all the thoughts that these deplorable relations must suggest to this class mingle contempt with hatred.

As I said above, Filangieri feels this, for he rejects the testimony of these servants in ordinary cases. But when it comes to what he calls political crimes, he not only accepts their testimony, he encourages them to inform. Just a moment previously they were not allowed to say what it was public knowledge that they knew, and now they are called upon to be informers or prosecutors, to tell what they could just as well have invented as discovered. It is thus that the prestige of the phrase *public security* blinds the best minds. They authorize perverse men to take it over. Let us remember what slaves and freedmen were in Rome, who were allowed to denounce and prosecute their masters. Let us think what that same class, with a few honorable exceptions, was during the Revolution. It is already a social flaw to degrade certain classes, but when society has degraded them, it should disarm them, and when one does wrong, it is certainly the least one can do to take precautions against that wrong.

# CHAPTER SIX ❧ That the Prosecuting Magistrate Should Be Responsible, If Not for the Truth, at Least for the Legitimacy of the Accusation

> If there is in the state a single person who can freely slander, my freedom is in danger: the laws' protection is no longer sufficient to defend it.
>
> BOOK III, CHAPTER 4, P. 272.

I think there is no one who does not feel the justice of Filangieri's observation. Freed from all responsibility, the prosecuting ministry would be a dictatorship more threatening than any political dictatorship, because it would simultaneously strike the honor and the freedom of those who were the objects of its vengeance or hatred. Plunged into dungeons and deprived of the capacity to defend themselves, they would see hovering over them the suspicions which accompany unjust captivity, and their captivity would take away from them all means of dissipating those suspicions. Public opinion, already so inattentive and so disposed to forgetfulness when troubles become prolonged, would find in the oppressor's slander a pretext for losing interest in the victim. Egoism would call itself respect for the law or for the court's judgment, and the dishonest magistrate would launch from the height of his tribunal inviolable thunderbolts against an innocence accused and reduced to silence.

Such is the state of affairs, however, that the legislator permits in most civilized countries, if not in fact, at least in law. I like to believe that magistrates do not frequently abuse these terrible prerogatives. But it is sufficient for abuse to be possible for it to be urgent to prevent it, and the rights most dear to the citizen must find their guarantee in the laws, and not depend on chance or the honesty of men, whose very virtues are nothing but fortunate accidents.

Society, in whose name the magistrate brings charges against an innocent person, owes to that person compensation proportionate to the harm. When the charge brought is not justified by sufficient evidence and probability, the magistrate himself should be responsible for the frivolousness of the accusation.

It will be objected that in subjecting the men charged with prosecuting crimes in the state's name to such a dangerous responsibility, one will discourage their zeal. Surrounded by dangers and risking punishment for a mistake committed with the purest intentions, they will fulfill their severe duty only while trembling, and their uncertain and cautious step will multiply the number of the guilty, by multiplying the odds of impunity.

This objection is not without some force. In order to resolve it, one must distinguish between the truth and the legitimacy of an accusation. An accusation can be simultaneously false and legitimate. That is, unfortunate circumstances may have surrounded the person suspected of a crime with probabilities great enough for common sense, which the organs of society must follow, to be impressed by these resemblances and demand a scrupulous investigation.

The magistrate who proceeds with this investigation, by beginning a prosecution and taking the suspect individual into custody, doubtless commits an error if the individual is not guilty, but it is an error which is impossible for him not to commit. The victim of this error has a right to compensation because his suffering was unjust, but he does not have the right to attack the magistrate who is the innocent and irreproachable author of the mistake from which he has suffered. But if, on the contrary, the accusation is not supported by any probability, if it is clear that the magistrate did not have any commonsense reasons for beginning the prosecution, if he cannot plead anything but excessive zeal and haste to act, it is no longer simple compensation that society owes the accused person. It owes him the exemplary punishment of the magistrate who was too superficial, too credulous, or too zealous. And let no one think that the principle we establish here does not have any practical application. If one goes through the registers of all countries' courts of justice, one will see countless examples of individuals pursued, detained, or ruined because it has pleased magistrates to accuse them of crimes from which the simplest common sense would have been enough to absolve them.

But, it will be said, how can one judicially establish the legitimacy of a prosecution? How can we decide if the magistrate who brought it was not really convinced that it was well founded? Here, I admit, the question is purely moral. It is impossible for the law to fix the basis. Also I would not want to submit this question to a tribunal required to pronounce according to the letter of a law. Every time a moral question must be resolved, it falls within the competence of the only judges who can listen to their conscience alone, and who have no other guide but their conviction: by this I mean juries. It is before them that such cases should be brought. They will pronounce whether the magistrate brought before their bar had sufficient reason to begin a prosecution and to expose a citizen to shame, damages, pain, and all the inevitable results of prosecution, even one washed away by an absolution which is always belated.

## CHAPTER SEVEN ❧ On Prisons

> Cast an eye on these prisons, where thousands of your subjects languish through the vices of your laws and the negligence of your ministers; consider these sad monuments to the misery of men and the harshness of those who govern them; approach these terrible walls, where freedom is surrounded by chains, and where innocence is mingled with crime.
>
> BOOK III, CHAPTER 6, P. 290.

It would be impossible to add anything to this pathetic and unfortunately all too accurate description of the sufferings of those whom the imperfections of our social state and the insensitivity of those in power condemn to languish in prisons. But in recognizing the frightening accuracy of the picture, it is painful to have to tell oneself that of all the improvements humanity demands, those which concern the fate of prisoners are the most difficult to put into practice. Man is struck by a unique lack of foresight, which seems to be attached to his egoism in order to somehow prepare his own punishment. As long as he enjoys his freedom, he feels sheltered from the blows of fate. One would think that those who tremble at the bottom of dungeons were of a different species from his own. It is only after events have tossed him among the proscribed race that his prideful illusions disappear, and then it is too late to fix what he disdained to prevent.

Nevertheless, the progress of civilization has this advantage: that the equality which necessarily results from this progress subjects a greater number of individuals to uniform penalties. Despite the exceptions which survive, thanks to the tradition of privilege, prison in our day is open to classes which formerly never crossed its threshold. Subject to hardships which astonish them and make them indignant, they learn to feel compassion for evils which they used to be ignorant of because they had not suffered them.

Thus some principles of justice or pity gain ground in theory. This is important, for whatever people say, practice always follows theory, even though it is with a slow and halting pace. Already it is a recognized truth that those imprisoned for different reasons should be separated from one another and treated differently. This truth, which seems obvious, would perhaps never have triumphed if some upper-class men had not found themselves mixed up with criminals whose coarseness scandalized them more than their crime. The pride of social position corroborated the impression of physical disgust, and humanity gained from the demands of wounded vanity.

Soon people will feel likewise that if prison is necessary to hold individuals accused of a crime or violators of a promise, since this severe measure is only a precaution (for I am not speaking about imprisonment as a legal punishment here), it should be limited to what is indispensable to attaining the proposed purpose. Everything which exceeds the limits of the strictest necessity is an injustice; everything which can improve the prisoners' lot without encouraging their escape is a sacred duty.

When one wants a duty to be fulfilled, one must attach punishments to its violation. However, there is no country in which jailors who exceed their legitimate powers or violate the laws of humanity are threatened with sufficient punishment. Society seems to be afraid of discouraging these instruments of rigor. It arms them with almost discretionary authority and creates obstacles of all kinds to asking them to account for the use they make of that authority. It is a singular tendency of the human mind to reason falsely when it comes to directing reason against power. The more powerful a man is, the more people believe it necessary to declare him inviolable; nevertheless, it is obvious that the more powerful he is, the further the abuses of his power may extend and diversify. This does not apply to royalty, because a monarch transmits power and does not exercise it, but for all subordinate functions, from the minister down to the jailor or the policeman, the responsibility must be all the more severe since arbitrariness is mingled with the exercise of that function.

But inside a prison, because of the force of circumstances, because of the necessity of maintaining order among men who are all unhappy with their captivity, and because of the disproportion between their number and that of their guards, a jailor finds himself invested with almost unlimited power.

Therefore, put in the seriousness of the punishment the preservative that you cannot introduce by limiting authority. You are forced to surrender the defenseless prisoner to a man whose character is rightly suspected of insensitivity and greed, for who would want to be a jailor, if he didn't have a heart of stone and a greedy soul? Therefore, put yourself between the prisoner and this man. You are responsible for all the injustices he may suffer, for you have tied him up, you have made it impossible for him to defend himself against injustice, and you have closed off all means of physical escape. Thus open all outlets for his complaints and demands, and above all do not limit yourself to procedures which are only a cruel joke, and to formal visits which are only traps, since the unfortunate captive who has complained will find himself once again under the yoke of the master whom he has just annoyed.

It is not for the government, always biased toward its agents, to pronounce on the crimes of those agents whom it protects. It is always a party in this kind of matter. However frivolous the prisoner's grievance may be, it is up to the courts and the jury to examine it. They should examine it with all the more scrupulousness as the plaintiff is in a situation which deprives him of some of his strength, and in which it is more in his interest to seek the favor of a man on whom he is continually dependent, and who can harm him in a thousand ways while avoiding the commission of any formal crime. If he braves the dangers inseparable from such an unequal struggle, it is because he is forced to do so by a painful and irresistible need. In this case, and in this case alone, all the presumptive evidence is in favor of the accuser and against the accused.

# CHAPTER EIGHT ❧ On the Shortening of Legal Procedures

> It is easy to see how absurd the rule of criminal law is, and how unjust the laws of the majority of Europe are, which dispense with rigorous proof when it is a matter of heinous crimes.
>
> BOOK III, CHAPTER 9, P. 319.

The reader will readily think that on this point I am in complete agreement with Filangieri. For the past thirty years I have not stopped saying and publishing that it was by the strangest sort of illogic that in certain cases we cut short formalities, under the pretext of the crime's atrocity or the security of the state.

Certainly legal forms have no other purpose but to lead judges to knowledge of the truth. If they did not attain this goal, they would be useless. In that case, why introduce them? Why keep them in ordinary trials? In the matter of legal proceedings, everything which is not indispensable is harmful. Every delay is an inconvenience which is excusable only by necessity, and if the facts could be ascertained and crime or innocence recognized with as much certainty by the summary justice of the Turks as by our multiple precautions, the summary justice of the Turks would be preferable to the multitude of our precautions.

But if the truth can be discovered only by scrupulous adherence to the forms, how can it be that when this discovery affects life or honor you eliminate protective formalities? Should a shameful penalty involving the loss of civil rights or capital punishment, and which entirely negates a citizen's existence and removes him from among the living; or a punishment which allots him only chains, isolation, and a shame staining those dear to him, seem to you to require less investigation, fewer scruples and delays in application, than a light fine or a few days in prison? From looking at the dispositions of almost all law codes, and all governments' consistent practice, one would say that legislators had reasoned in this fashion.

A man is accused of a simple theft, a fraud, some encroachment on someone else's property or rights, or an act of violence—a homicide dictated by jealousy, vengeance, or poverty. You surround him with all the safeguards; you leave him the benefit of his natural judges; you do not take from him the protective resource of the jury, nor the helpful services of a counsel for the defense; you do not hasten, shorten, or hurry anything. This same man is accused of a more serious crime, against which the law is more severe and the punishment more harsh. He is charged with a plot to murder a ruler, or a conspiracy that threatens the safety of the state. Immediately you refuse him all the guaranties which protect him if he is innocent. No more jury, often no more counsel for the defense, abbreviated legal forms, extraordinary courts, summary judgments! Would one not say that the more terrible an accusation is, the more unnecessary it is to examine it carefully?

And note well that this absurdity in your proceedings is only the first. You combine it with others as soon as you are launched on this path, and every step you take is a contradiction and an injustice. You punish a man in advance, and it is only after he has been punished that you look to see if he is guilty. For either the legal forms are safeguards, or they are only pointless superfluities. If they are safeguards, to deprive an accused of them is to inflict a punishment on him: it is to put him in a position more unfavorable than other members of society before conviction. But if you are certain that the accused deserves punishment, why do you treat him in other regards as if you admit that he could be innocent?

Will you respond to me that the punishment, if there is one, which he incurs from the shortening of some legal forms is not comparable to that which he will be subjected to if he is found guilty? Fine, I agree. But it is still a punishment. If he is innocent, he has not deserved it, and as long as you do not know that he is not innocent, by what right do you subject him to it?

This is similar to the way in which men allow themselves to be perpetually fooled by artful legal formulations. We say in the law codes that those guilty of such and such crimes will be judged according to such or such form of legal proceedings, and as a result we find it perfectly natural that those accused of these crimes be so judged. However, this is as if the law code said: It will be up to the first-comer to take away from whomever he chooses the benefit of protective forms, provided that he also chooses the crime of which it pleases him to accuse that person. A man may well not conspire, nor murder, but he cannot prevent any other man from accusing him of murder or conspiracy, and such is the weakness of the human mind that the logical error obviously made by this code passes unnoticed in all its hatefulness, thanks to a slight change of language.

Listen to the speakers and writers who defend summary judgments, special courts, commissions—in short, the suppression of the usual guaranties—in some particular cases. They reproach those who demand these guaranties with being the defenders of thieves, conspirators, or murderers. But before we know that these are murderers, conspirators, or thieves, don't we need to ascertain the facts? But what are legal forms if not the best means for arriving at the facts? If you think you are able to do without them, or substitute for them more rapid and less painstaking examination, I consent to this; but then follow the same path for all trials. Is it not foolish to claim that for certain acts, and precisely the least revolting and the least serious, one must be constrained by slow legal forms, whereas for other acts, and precisely the most serious and most horrible, one can decide quickly? Have the modesty to be consistent. If haste is without inconvenience, eliminate slow proceedings, for they are superfluous; if slow procedures are not superfluous, abstain from haste, for it is dangerous.

If nature had wished us to be able to distinguish the innocent from the guilty by infallible and visible signs, the sophisms that are always put forward to cut short legal forms would have an excuse or a pretext, but then it would not only be the legal forms which needed to be cut short, it would be the trials themselves that would need to be eliminated as useless. Against known criminals enforcement of the law is enough. But these signs do not exist. The legal forms are the sole means of distinguishing guilt from innocence. To shorten them, to limit them, to change the smallest part of the safeguard they represent is to declare that one cares little about making this distinction, and that provided one strikes, one will take few pains to strike only criminals.

I have seen the principle postulated a hundred times that the nature of the court should be determined by the nature of the crime postulated. This sententious phrase only serves to combine pedantry with iniquity. Once again, one should say it is not the nature of the crime; it is the nature of the charge. To change the court by virtue of the charge is to put the accused at the mercy of the accuser; it is to treat the suspect as guilty; it is to presume conviction before examination and make the punishment precede the crime. For I repeat, to deprive a citizen of his natural judges is to inflict a very strong punishment on him indeed.

# CHAPTER NINE ❧ On Defense Witnesses

> The witness who testifies in favor of the accused will be listened to in the same way as those who testify against him. The accuser and the accused will be present at their deposition. In the same way as the accused has the right to examine the witness produced by the accuser, the latter will have the right to examine the witness produced by the other. All other things being equal, evidence in favor of the accused will invalidate the evidence presented against him.
>
> BOOK III, CHAPTER 16, P. 385.

All the rules that Filangieri establishes in this chapter are in perfect conformity with the laws of humanity and justice. However, it is unfortunate that in certain countries they are continually infringed, and that in others the legislator's eagerness to secure convictions has been such that he has never even thought about these essential precautions. One would say that in the eyes of more than one prosecutor, the position of defense witnesses is not very different from that of the accused. The one shares in the disfavor which surrounds the other, and to give testimony in favor of a man who is suspected of a crime is an act of complicity, or at least a semi-criminal act.

While we encourage prosecution witnesses, warn them of the contradictions into which they fall so that they can make them disappear or reconcile them, suggest explanations to them, and praise them, defense witnesses are threatened, interrupted, and even frequently accused of lying. The public prosecutor or the judges warn them against false testimony in the middle of the debate, and as a result the sword of Damocles is suspended over men sworn to tell the truth, to whom one points out by voice and gesture the bench for the accused waiting for them if they do not lie. I know nothing so scandalous, so criminal as this conduct, and between the accused and the prosecutor who acts in this way, the most serious guilt seems to me to be on the prosecutor's side.

It would be entirely fair to make a fundamental and inviolable rule which obliged the accuser or the prosecutor, if they accused a defense witness of perjury, to prove their assertion during the trial and before sentence was rendered against the accused. The contrary practice ought to strike any enlightened mind as problematic. The testimony of a witness accused of lying is necessarily tainted in the jury's mind. It loses its weight and even becomes new presumptive evidence damaging to the accused, who is suspected of one more crime beyond the one for which he is standing trial—the crime of having suborned witnesses and having urged them to commit perjury. It is with this warning that the jury pronounces its verdict. Prejudiced by this idea, circumstances which would have determined it in favor of the accused turn against him. The alibi attested by the witness becomes suspect. That alibi, which otherwise would be proof of innocence, is transformed into an additional charge, a probability of new crimes. When the principal verdict has been pronounced, when the executioner has seized the victim, when blood has reddened the scaffold, when afterwards a belated inquiry clears the witness whom an impassioned accuser or an implacable prosecutor cast suspicion upon, what does it matter to the unfortunate whom the ax has struck, and whose last moments were made worse by shame?

To reach the height of iniquity and absurdity, it should be noted that in almost all the countries of the world the present mode of procedure entirely separates the witness's case from the case of the accused, and that even when the truthfulness of the former is recognized, one does not draw any conclusion from it in favor of the latter. Is it not clear, however, that if the testimony of the witness whose evidence had been challenged is declared true, the situation of the accused is completely different? If, for example, a witness had attested the presence of the accused in a place far away from the scene of the crime, and after the honesty of his story was questioned it was accepted as incontestable by a solemn verdict, does it not follow from this that the question of the alibi would be decided in favor of the accused? And would it not be contrary to all reason to persist in the condemnation pronounced against him, despite the verdict which accepted as proven a circumstance by which the impossibility of the crime would be demonstrated?

And yet this is what happened in a well-known trial. A man accused of armed rebellion produced three witnesses who testified in favor of his alibi for the time when that rebellion had taken place. The public prosecutor interrupted these witnesses, threatened them, accused them of perjury, and brought charges against them. Meanwhile the trial continued, and the accused was condemned. When the sentence was pronounced, and even, I think, after it was executed, the trial for perjury took place, and the witnesses were acquitted. Therefore their testimony was not false and the alibi that they had testified to was real. Is it not manifest that if the latter question had been resolved before sentence was pronounced against the principal accused, the jury's view would have been different, and its verdict different as well?

# CHAPTER TEN ❧ On Judgment by Juries

> The examination of facts was (among the Romans) reserved to judges named by lot, along with the parties' consent. . . . 450 citizens, of recognized probity, were named each year. . . . The Praetor . . . threw their names in an urn. . . . The judge drew the lots . . . for the number of names prescribed by law. . . . The accuser and the accused then rejected those which seemed suspect to them. . . . Other names drawn from the urn as previously were substituted for them. . . . As long as names remained in the urn . . . each party had the right to look for another judge by lot. . . .
>
> BOOK III, CHAPTER 16, P. 396.

We see that Filangieri does not imagine that jurors can be named otherwise than by lot. In France, however, for many years this nomination has been confided to a government or lesser official. This practice, subversive of all principles, was bequeathed to us by a man from whom we have inherited all the bad traditions which disfigure or denature our constitutional regime.

However, one cannot disguise the fact that an official instituted, salaried, and revocable by the executive branch of government is less capable than any other person of proceeding in a safe manner to choose the man who decides in the final instance about the honor and life of all citizens. The rule of conduct of every dependent functionary is the order he is given. His zeal is his greatest merit; submission is his first duty. By contrast a juror should decide only according to his conscience. He does not recognize any superiors, and in him submission would be the blackest of crimes.

Jurors nominated by the government are commissioners. And as the corruption of what is good is the worst of all things, jurors thus drawn for a purpose are limited by fewer restraints, have less shame, and shed all moral responsibility more easily than permanent judges who, because they are permanently exposed to public view, may at least refuse to bear the odium of iniquitous verdicts and dictated sentences. By contrast jurors, returning to the crowd, merge with it again. After the most scandalous conduct they flatter themselves with being forgotten or living in obscurity.

It is objected that not all men are gifted with education or possess enough perspicacity to decide questions that are often complicated. I respond that most of the time these questions are only so difficult because they have been complicated on purpose. Intelligence is not so unequally divided among men as those who would like to establish an intellectual oligarchy, in order to support and perpetuate a social and political oligarchy, like to suppose. There is almost no one who does not have a mind just enough and honest enough, when passion or interest do not corrupt it, to judge honestly and easily a case clearly described, supported or challenged by testimony which is informed and balanced, and presented from all perspectives by the respective sides of the accused and the accuser.

But while it is true that lack of intelligence leads from time to time to minor difficulties, I ask whether these difficulties are comparable to those which accompany the dependence, the servility, and even, setting aside the annoying suspicion of more guilty motives, that severe and hostile attitude which government agents in all countries bring to their contact with citizens—an attitude which is an unfortunate but natural and inevitable effect of a position different from others? Certainly, if it were proposed to me to be judged either by twelve ignorant artisans who do not know how to read or write but who are chosen by lot and not given any orders except by their conscience, or by twelve academicians of the greatest elegance—twelve men of letters with the greatest expertise in matters of style but named by the government, which would hold suspended over their head decorations, titles, and rewards—I would prefer the twelve artisans.

And if one said to me that these ignorant and coarse jurors have only too often shown, in the Revolutionary tribunals, what innocence might expect from them, I would reply that doubtless in those execrable Revolutionary tribunals there were all the excesses of ignorance combined with the excess of ferocity. But those vulgar and atrocious men were only the tools of a more enlightened class. They had members of those upper classes in their ranks as advisors and guides, and the jury which condemned the Girondins was presided over by a marquis of the old regime. The educated class furthermore is not so small that it does not offer the means to choose by lot among men gifted with education. You have two dangers to fear: partiality and ignorance. Steer clear of the proletarians, who are ignorant; steer clear of the government agents, who will be servile; and let chance decide among the others. Chance is impartial, because it is blind. It does not distinguish between ordinary trials and extraordinary trials, or between private cases and political cases; it is not moved by the word *conspiracy*, and it alone can give you real jurors and not creatures of the government.

It has not seemed necessary to enter into the general question of juries here. However, among the accusations with which this salutary institution is periodically targeted, there is one which is evidently such an aberration of logic, and which nevertheless is sometimes clothed in such attractive forms, that I think it is useful to refute it in passing; or, to put it better, to briefly repeat an already-published refutation. It has been said that if jurors find a law too severe they will absolve the accused and declare the case not consistent with their conscience. Thus, when the punishment seems excessive, they will pronounce contrary to their conviction. The author imagines the case where a man will be accused of giving asylum to his brother, and will have by that action incurred the death penalty. Who does not see that here it is not the jury but the law which is being severely criticized?

Man has a certain respect for the written law. He needs to have very powerful motives to overcome it. When these motives exist, it is the fault of the laws. If the punishments seem excessive to the jurors, it is because they are. They have no interest in finding them such.

In extreme cases, when jurors are placed between an irresistible feeling of justice and humanity and the letter of the law, it is not a bad thing if they set the law aside. There ought not to exist a law which revolts the humanity of ordinary men such that jurors drawn from the midst of a nation cannot make up their minds to agree to the application of that law. The institution of permanent judges, whom habit would reconcile with this barbarous law, far from being an advantage would be a scourge.

In my view the example chosen by the jury's opponent gives it the greatest praise. He proves that this institution creates an obstacle to the execution of laws contrary to humanity, justice, and morality. One is a man before being a juror. Thus, far from blaming the one who, in this case, would fail in his duty as a juror, I would praise him for fulfilling his duty as a man, and for running, by all the means in his power, to the aid of an accused about to be punished for an action which far from being a crime is a virtue. This example does not prove that there should not be juries. It proves that there should not be laws which pronounce the death penalty against someone who gives asylum to his brother.[1]

1. *Course of Constitutional Politics*, vol. 1, pp. 114–15.

# CHAPTER ELEVEN ❧ On the Death Penalty

> From the principles from which we have deduced the right to punish derive the right to pronounce the death penalty.
>
> BOOK III, CHAPTER 5, P. 16.

Independently of Filangieri's metaphysical reasons, many practical considerations require us not to reject the death penalty, against which the most estimable philosophers of the last century arose too hastily and without distinguishing among the nature of the crimes. Assuredly nothing is more horrible than the barbarism with which our present law codes pronounce this penalty against a mass of crimes which the legislator ought to consider with indulgence and pity, given the laws of nature and justice, the flaws of our social organization, and the poverty of the classes which this organization disinherits. My first concern will therefore be to show carefully how few crimes ought to incur this punishment.

Property is doubtless a sacred thing. Society owes it all the guarantees which are necessary. Society owes property these guarantees from the very fact that society accepts it. Since to abolish property is impossible, to only partly tolerate it would be absurd. The more primitive equality may revolt against an unequal division whose origin goes back to the right of the stronger, the more this inequality, once recognized as inevitable, must be defended against the ever-renewed protests of the portion of the population it despoils.

However, it does not follow from this that society may legitimately direct all kinds of punishment against this kind of crime. Violations of social conventions, however respectable they are, are never as criminal as violation of the eternal laws stamped in all hearts. From the sole fact that the death penalty is the most severe, it is unjust to apply it indiscriminately both to theft and premeditated murder. No circumstance excuses someone who deliberately takes the life of his fellow. A thousand reasons may make someone take a piece of property which the law denies him, and he may be led to do this by motives which, without absolving him, mitigate his offense.

Certainly the more progress civilization makes, the more work offers resources to the class which has only that means of existence. But we have not yet arrived at the point where work will always be available for the whole of that class. And by a deplorable complication, this resource usually becomes more insufficient when unfortunates have more need of it. The more poor there are for whom work is necessary, the more obstacles they encounter in obtaining it, and the lower their salary is. Now, can we imagine them tormented by anguish and by their family's struggle against death, and thus subject to the reproach of letting perish from poverty and hunger beings to whom, by giving them birth, they have implicitly promised aid and protection? Can we mentally follow them into the miserable hovels where all manner of sufferings besiege them, and imagine that before deciding to brave the law, they dragged themselves on their knees to the rich man, perhaps a hundred times, to ask him not for a gift but for any kind of job? Then perhaps we will judge less harshly crimes which, far from presuming an absence or forgetfulness of natural feelings, like murder, can in this extreme and terrible situation be the result of the power of those very feelings themselves. These crimes must be punished, doubtless. We are condemned to do so by our social state. But to make the man who stole because he saw his wife dying of hunger and the one who murdered his wife mount the same scaffold is an atrocity so stupid that one is astonished to find it in the law code of more than one well regulated nation today.

And here a reflection strikes me which is not, it seems to me, without importance. The miserable situation of a large part of the human species is not the necessary result of the existence of property. Whenever there is peace and freedom in a country, the poor laborer finds his subsistence there. But when a government undertakes useless wars or imposes capricious hindrances on citizens, the resources of the poor disappear. Agricultural, industrial, and commercial enterprises perish, fail, or are at least suspended by the speculators' worries, and the temptation to commit a crime becomes the inevitable consequence of the impossibility the poor man encounters of feeding himself honestly.

It is therefore not the poor man, who is not consulted about the fate which is imposed on him and for which he cannot bear any responsibility, but rather the ambitious or arbitrary government which burdens him, that we should in all fairness blame if laws are broken and property threatened. Yet it is this government which punishes with pitiless severity the disorder of which it is the real and sole author!

One could say that the more needs are pressing, anguish heartbreaking, evil without remedy, the more the government thinks it is right to increase its severity. See what discontent manifests itself among the wealthy classes at the slightest decrease or interruption in their ease. When the stock market goes down or when commercial calculations are upset, how many grumbles, how many threats even are there against the government whose mistaken measures have brought about this state of crisis! And yet those who grumble, those who threaten, are harmed only in a few of their pleasures! They have time to wait for more favorable circumstances. They will not perish along with their families before those circumstances present themselves. And one demands less impatience, more resignation, more scruple from the poor man who does not have time on his side—the poor man whom hunger presses, whose meager resources it devours, whose children it harvests!

No, the death penalty can never be directed with justice against simple violations of property. The law must be armed to maintain the current basis of human society, but it should not confuse all degrees of guilt; it should not strike with the same sword the ferocious murderer who has shown himself pitiless and the unfortunate person who has perhaps been led by pity for suffering beings whose cries rent his soul and overturned his reason.

I would say the same about political crimes. These crimes, presuming the government is not organized in such a way as to throw peoples into despair, show an absence of reason which must be put in a position where it cannot do harm and cause disorders which must be repressed. But these crimes often do not reveal any real perversity, and sometimes they are compatible with lofty private or public virtues.

The death penalty is all the more unjust against these kinds of crimes, when they do not involve murder and armed assault, in that this penalty has little sway over souls sufficiently exalted to conceive the project of establishing what appears to them to be freedom, or ambitious enough to meditate the conquest of power. The value of a successful revolution is always, for the one who leads it, far above the risks that it entails. It is therefore only as a security, and to rid themselves of dangerous enemies, that governments apply capital punishment to political crimes. But in our day this calculation is very dubious, and it is useless.

It is dubious because in a country where opinion is sufficiently critical of the government's actions for conspiracies to be dangerous, a government thus criticized escapes the fate which threatens it only for a necessarily very short period of time. Scaffolds are built, blood is shed, but opinion swims through it, finds other means, and returns to the charge, stronger than before because of its experience, and it triumphs.

When, on the contrary, conspiracies are nothing but the result of personal ambition, it is pointless to punish with death guilty persons one has disarmed. Without roots in the mass of the people, they cease to be dangerous. Exile or prison can do justice to them without danger to society. Exile is the natural punishment which is justified by the very nature of the crime and which, by separating all cause of irritation from the guilty person, puts him back, so to speak, in a state of innocence and gives him the ability to stay there. A writer of our own time, M. Guizot, has shown very well that the influence of individuals has been next to nothing in our century. The masses alone are to be feared, and since we cannot condemn them to death, we must work to satisfy them.

Several law codes punish with death the intention to commit a crime, which they equate with its execution. This disposition reveals a great ignorance of human nature. Long after a man has become used to the idea of a criminal act, he may recoil from that act. The need which torments him and the passion which agitates him have suggested to him the frightful project of a murder, but who can tell if he would never have let the steel drop in the presence of his victim? The legislator has recognized this possibility, since he reduces the punishment when it is proven that circumstances dependent on the will of the accused prevented the carrying out of his murder. But when unforeseen obstacles, independent of his will, have produced this result, nothing proves that if these obstacles had not presented themselves, the conscience would not have awoken. The unfortunate who, in his guilty exaltation, encourages himself to the crime and believes he is strong enough to commit it, feels agitation, terror, and remorse because of this deplorable resolution, whose effects one cannot calculate. Until the last moment, he may give up a project which throws his soul into disorder and makes him hateful in his own eyes. Not to recognize this possible change of heart is to think too poorly of the human species. Not to have regard for it in law is to exclude all consideration of justice and all feeling for equity from the writing of the laws.

When these various rules are accepted, the death penalty seems acceptable to me. To deny society the right to inflict it and to claim that in doing so it exceeds its jurisdiction would be to establish a principle which would lead us farther than can be foreseen. Pain, imprisonment, forced labor, deportation, and even exile—all moral or physical suffering—shorten life, and if the state has no right over the life of its members, it is no more authorized to shorten it than to put an end to it.

Furthermore, the death penalty is the only one which dispenses government from infinitely multiplying a class of men professionally devoted to odious functions, which, when filled voluntarily and zealously carried out, are proof of perversity and corruption. I have said elsewhere that I prefer a few executioners to a lot of jailors, policemen, and police thugs. I prefer that a small number of despised agents should turn themselves into machines of death, surrounded by public horror, than that we see everywhere men reduced to the level of intelligent watchdogs for a miserable salary, and who, paid enemies of their fellows, exercise a prickly and ferocious surveillance over the unfortunates delivered to their mercy.

# CHAPTER TWELVE ❧ On Convict Labor

> Condemnation to public works is a punishment which brings society two kinds of advantages. It offers an example of the evils attached to crime, and it makes socially profitable the occupations of those who have offended society.
>
> BOOK III, PART 2, CHAPTER 9, P. 58.

In opposing Filangieri's opinion about convict labor I do not conceal from myself that I am putting myself in opposition to ideas much vaunted by many writers who were friends of humanity. In my opinion, however, there are grave objections to be raised against both the principle on which these ideas rest and against their practical application.

What is society's right against individuals who violate its laws and sow trouble and disorder within it? It is the right to put them in a situation where they cannot do harm. As we have seen above, this right can extend to the deprivation of life. But from the fact that in my legitimate defense I have a right to kill a man, do I have the right to force him to work, to reduce him to the condition of a slave? A principle which seems to me incontestable, and without which the slavery abolished by religion and the progress of ideas would be on the verge of being reborn daily, is that man cannot alienate his person and his faculties except for a limited time and by an act of his own will. If the use he makes of them is harmful, take their use away from him. If the evil of which he is the author is such that the public security requires that he be deprived of them forever, condemn him to death. But to turn his faculties to your profit, to use him like a beast of burden, is to return to the most barbarous epochs. It is to consecrate servitude and to degrade the human condition.

And let us not be fooled by false appearances of philanthropy. Either the work imposed on the condemned is different from that which necessity imposes on the innocent laboring classes of society, or it is not different from it either in its excess or its nature. In the first case, it amounts to a slower and more painful death. We see, and we saw above all under Joseph II, half-naked prisoners, their bodies half underwater, painfully dragging ships on the Danube. The unfortunate perishing on the scaffold was certainly subject to less frightful and less prolonged suffering.

In the other case, transforming moderate work into punishment in my opinion sets a dangerous example. The organization of our present societies obliges a fairly large class to labors that are often beyond human strength. It is imprudent to portray the position in which it finds itself placed, without having committed any crime or even fault, as a punishment for the most shameful disorders or the most guilty actions.

In several regions in Germany and in Switzerland those condemned to convict labor are treated gently. Their subsistence is assured, their illnesses cared for. They are physically more fortunate than the poor. They soon overcome the shame which surrounds them, the only real evil of their situation. They work no more or less than they did in freedom, and we see them simultaneously happy and degraded, debased and satisfied, without worry for the future, and consoling themselves with that security for the opprobrium of the present. Must not such a sight corrupt the working class, whose innocence only serves to make its existence more uncertain and not less painful?

# CHAPTER THIRTEEN ❧ On Deportation

> If the experience of all antiquity, and above all the examples of a large number of Greek colonies, did not testify that the outcasts of one nation can become an excellent political society, if the history of our modern times did not offer us a similar spectacle, reason alone would make us feel that it is possible to make a good man out of a dishonest one by taking him far away from the scene of his crimes, his shame, and his condemnation.
>
> BOOK III, PART 2, CHAPTER 9, P. 62.

There is no one who, descending to the depths of his soul and looking over the whole of his life, has not found that most of the time his faults—above all those which, committed at the beginning of a still uncertain career, decisively influence the future—had their origin purely in the opposition between man's original nature and the institutions which society has imposed on him. This is not at all said in disapproval of or hatred for those institutions. There are some which are necessary which are not, however, engraved on the heart or indicated by instinct. These are conventions which have become sacred because good order is based on them, but which nevertheless are essentially artificial. From this it follows that the inexperience of youth is often led to cross barriers of which it is scarcely aware, despite the warnings given to it, warnings that it hardly has time to listen to, amid the impressions which make it tremble and the passions which lead it on. Youth sins sometimes by ignorance, sometimes by impetuosity. Then youth, while excusable in the eyes of moral justice, is not less guilty before positive law, or, if it does not go so far as to provoke the laws' severity, it is pursued by that of opinion, which judges inattentively and stigmatizes without examination.

There arises an opposition and hostility between those struck by this sad fate and society, a hostility which grows from the very feelings it produces. Its forms vary, but we find them in individuals of all classes. For individuals from the lower ranks, whom one does not even deign to instruct in the laws which rule them, and who only learn these laws when they are punished by them, this opposition, this hostility, becomes the source of many crimes. Punished with a severity which is always accompanied by a greater or lesser amount of shame, these crimes immediately create a chasm beneath the criminal which makes impossible any return to virtue, to a peaceful life, or to an innocent and harmless existence. The belief that everything is irreparable is an obstacle to any attempt at reform, and from this it frequently results that a single mistake precipitates an individual destined for a better fate into a series of ever more serious crimes.

To tear away from this deplorable situation those whom ignorance, a moment of passion, or the anguish of need have cast there despite themselves is the greatest good that society, which is perhaps not entirely above reproach in their regard, can give them. In tearing them away from the pressure of institutions they have disobeyed and relationships they have permanently damaged, one gives them back a calm, a security, and a kind of anticipated innocence which will reestablish order and harmony in their moral being. I say this with deep conviction: If by a miracle one could put a man who has just stained himself with a crime back to the moment which preceded this fateful act, there is hardly one in a thousand who would persist in committing it.

Deportation or colonization has this advantage: it represents, so to speak, a new birth, a new era, where a man freed from troublesome memories has the choice between good and evil again. Experience has shown how salutary this regeneration is. Have we not seen, in the colony of Botany Bay, criminals covered with shame in Europe begin social life anew and, no longer believing themselves at war with society, become useful members of it?

Everything which Filangieri says on this point is therefore perfectly just, but he should have added that in order for the benefits of colonization to be all that they can be, on the one hand the criminals who are returned to the state of innocence must forget their sense of shame and their previous crimes; and on the other hand society, to the extent that public safety allows, should cover this sad past with the same forgetfulness. Doubtless some precautions are allowed against men one is unsure of, but the less tormenting these precautions are, the more rapid and easy improvement will be. The first condition required for a man to raise himself from a degradation which only corrupts him more and more is for him to relearn self-esteem. Therefore, in order to encourage him, begin by showing him that it is possible for him to regain your esteem. If you torment him with the specter of your distrust and reprobation in the new hemisphere where you have transported him, he will soon tire of keeping to the straight and narrow, and he will become guilty again in the present, because you have let him see too clearly that you remember he was guilty in the past.

European governments too often lose sight of this principle. The arbitrary authority exercised over the deported, the contempt showered upon them, the useless hindrances which offend them, the humiliating punishments inflicted on them, and the conviction shown them that one believes them capable of anything for which chance may make them suspect, are all commemorations of infamy which prudence as much as humanity should forbid. You have given these unfortunates a new sky, a new land. Let them contemplate this sky and cultivate this land by showing them that the ocean which separates them from their former homeland also separates them from their mistakes, and that it is truly a new future which is presented to them.

# *Part Four*

# CHAPTER ONE ❧ On Education

> If children's ears were insensitive to error, truth would easily penetrate their souls. Only an education regulated by the magistrate and the law can produce this effect in the people. Such an education can only be a political education.
>
> BOOK IV, PART 1, CHAPTER 2, PP. 15–16.

Filangieri's whole book on education is stamped with his admiration for antiquity, and as a result marked with the same flaw that I have too often had occasion to bring up. I will therefore not speak any more of it here. I will even recognize that Filangieri sometimes dares to criticize some of the institutions he finds among the ancients, and that he furthermore indicates some particular measures that might be useful. The fundamental error exists nonetheless. Despite this he wants to confide the almost exclusive direction of education to the government. It is this error that it is above all important to refute.

Education can be considered from two points of view. In the first place, one can look at it as a means of transmitting to the rising generation the knowledge of all kinds acquired by preceding generations. From this perspective, it falls within the competence of government. The preservation and increase of all knowledge is a positive good. The government should guarantee us its enjoyment.

But one can also see education as the means of seizing control of men's opinions in order to mold them to adopt a certain number of ideas, whether they be religious, moral, philosophical, or political. It is above all for leading to this goal that writers of past centuries have praised education.

First of all, without questioning the facts which serve as the basis for this theory, we could deny that these facts are applicable to our present societies. Education's empire and the omnipotence attributed to it—accepting that they existed among the ancients—are for us a memory rather than a contemporary fact. One misunderstands the times, the nations, and the periods if one applies to the moderns what was practicable only in another era of the human mind.

Among peoples who, as Condorcet says,[1] had no notion of personal freedom, and where men were but machines whose springs were regulated and all of whose movements were directed by the law, government action could have a more effective influence over education because this uniform and constant action was not opposed by anything. But today all society would rise up against government pressure, and the individual independence that men have reconquered would react strongly against the education of the children. The second education, that of the world and of circumstances, would quickly undo the work of the first.[2]

Further, it is possible that we have taken for historical fact the fictions of a few philosophers, imbued with the same prejudices as those who have adopted their principles today. If so, this system, rather than having been in the past at least a practical truth, would only be a mistake perpetuated from age to age.

Where in fact do we see this marvelous power of education? In Athens? But there public education, sanctioned by the government, was confined to the lower schools, which limited themselves to basic instruction. Elsewhere there was complete liberty of education. In Lacedaemon? The uniform and monastic spirit of the Spartans came from an ensemble of institutions of which education was only a part, and this whole, I think, would be neither easy nor desirable to renew among us. On Crete? But the Cretans were the most ferocious, most restless, most corrupt people of Greece. People separate institutions from their effects, and admire them according to what they were intended to produce without considering what they produced in reality.

People cite to us the Persians and the Egyptians, but our traditions about

1. Mémoires sur l'instruction publique.

2. Helvétius, *De l'homme*.

Persian and Egyptian institutions are sometimes proved false solely by the obvious impossibility of the facts they contain, and are almost always rendered very doubtful by irreconcilable contradictions. What we know for certain is that the Persians and Egyptians were governed despotically, and that cowardice, corruption, and degradation—the eternal consequences of despotism—were the lot of those miserable nations. Our philosophers agree with this in the very pages where they cite them to us as examples with regard to education: a bizarre weakness of the human mind, which because it sees objects only in detail, lets itself be so dominated by a favorite idea that the clearest results do not enlighten it about the impotence of the causes whose power it wants to magnify. These historical proofs mostly resemble the one which M. de Montesquieu presented in favor of gymnastics. The exercise of wrestling, he says, made the Thebans win the battle of Leuctra. But over whom did the Thebans win that battle? Over the Lacedaemonians who had practiced gymnastics for over four hundred years.

The system which puts education in the government's hands is based on two or three errors of logic. First of all it presupposes that the government will be the kind we want. It always sees the government as an ally, without thinking that it could become an enemy. It does not recognize that the sacrifices imposed on individuals may not turn out to profit the institution that one thinks perfect, but any institution whatsoever.

This consideration is of equal weight to the supporters of all opinions. You regard absolute government, the order it maintains, and the peace which, according to you, it makes as the supreme good. But if the government seizes for itself the right to take over education, it will seize it not only during the peace and quiet of despotism, but also amid the violence and furor of factions. Then the result will be altogether different than the one you hope for. Education subject to the government will no longer inspire the coming generation with those peaceful habits, those principles of obedience, that respect for religion, and that submission to visible and invisible powers that you consider the basis of happiness and social peace. Once it has become their tool, the factions will make education serve to spread in the souls of youth exaggerated opinions, savage principles, contempt for religious ideas that appear to them as enemy doctrines, a love of bloodshed, and a hatred of pity.

This reasoning will have no less force if we address it to the friends of a wise and moderate liberty. We will say to them: You wish that public authority should control education in a free government in order to form the citizens from the most tender age in the knowledge and maintenance of their rights, in order to teach them to stand up to despotism, to resist unjust power, to defend innocence against oppression. But despotism will use education to bend its docile slaves beneath its yoke, to break every noble and courageous feeling in the heart, to overturn all notions of justice, to throw into obscurity all the most self-evident truths, and to push back into the shadows or scourge with ridicule everything which has to do with the most sacred and inviolable rights of the human species.

In all these hypotheses, what one wants the government to do for good, the government can do for evil. Thus hopes can be disappointed, and the authority that one extends infinitely, on the basis of unfounded assumptions, can tend in the opposite direction of the goal for which it was created.

Education provided by the government should be limited solely to instruction. The government can multiply the channels and means of instruction, but it should not direct them. Let it guarantee citizens equal means of instructing themselves, let it procure for the various professions instruction in the positive knowledge which facilitates their exercise, let it trace a path for individuals to arrive at all the known truths of fact[3] and at the point where their intelligence can soar spontaneously toward new discoveries. Let the government assemble for the use of all inquiring minds the monuments of every opinion, the inventions of every century, and the discoveries of all methods. Finally let it organize instruction in such a manner that each person can devote to it the time which accords with his interest or his desire, and perfect himself in the trade, art, or science to which his tastes or his destiny call him. Let it never appoint the teachers. Let it only grant them a salary which, assuring them of the necessities of life, nevertheless makes the arrival of students desirable to them. Let it provide for their needs when age or infirmity puts an end to their active career. Let it be that it cannot remove them without serious cause, and without the agreement of men independent from it,[4] for teachers subject to the government will be simultaneously negligent

3. One can teach facts uncritically, but never reasoning.

4. For the details of the organization of public instruction, which are not within the scope of this work, I refer the reader to Condorcet's *Mémoires,* where all questions that relate to this matter are examined.

and servile; their servility will make their negligence pardonable. Subject to opinion alone, they will be simultaneously active and independent.[5]

In directing education, the government arrogates to itself the right and imposes on itself the task of maintaining a body of doctrine. This phrase alone shows the means which it will be obliged to use. If we grant that it would first choose the gentlest means, it is at any rate certain that it will not allow any but the opinions it prefers to be taught in its schools.[6] There will thus be a rivalry between public education and private education. Public education will be salaried: there will thus be opinions invested with a privilege. But if this privilege is not sufficient to make the favored opinions dominant, do you believe that authority, jealous by nature, will not have recourse to other means? Do you not see a more or less disguised form of persecution, the constant companion of all superfluous action by the government, as the final result?

Governments which appear not to hinder private education at all nevertheless always favor the establishments they have founded by requiring of all candidates for positions relating to public education a form of apprenticeship in these establishments. Thus, talent which has followed an independent road, and whose solitary labor has perhaps allowed it to acquire more knowledge and probably more originality than it would have done in routine instruction, finds its natural career, that in which it can be communicated and reproduce itself, suddenly closed.[7]

All things being equal, it is not that I do not prefer public education to private education. The former gives the rising generation an apprenticeship in human life more useful than all the lessons of pure theory, which never more than imperfectly substitute for reality and experience. Public education is beneficial in free countries above all. Men brought together at whatever age, and above all in their youth, contract by a natural effect of their mutual relations a feeling of justice and the habits of equality, which prepare them to become courageous citizens and enemies of arbitrary power. Even under des-

5. Smith, *Wealth of Nations*.

6. Condorcet, first *Mémoire*, p. 55.

7. Everything which requires or commits a certain number of students to remain at a college or a university independently of the merit or reputation of the teachers, such as the necessity of taking certain degrees which can only be conferred in certain places, or scholarships and assistance given to studious poverty, has the effect of diminishing the zeal and making less necessary the knowledge of the teachers thus privileged in any form. Smith, V, 1.

potism, we have seen schools dependent on the government generate, despite it, the germs of freedom which it tried in vain to smother.

But I think that this advantage can be obtained without constraint. That which is good never needs privileges, and privileges always deform what is good. Furthermore, it matters that if the system of education which the government favors is or seems to be imperfect to some individuals, they can have recourse to private education or institutions without any relationship to the government. Society should respect individual rights, and among these rights are included the rights of fathers over their children.[8] If society's action injures them, resistance will rise up which will make the government tyrannical and which will corrupt individuals by forcing them to evade it. To the respect we demand government have for the rights of fathers, people will perhaps object that the lower classes of the people, reduced by their poverty to profiting from their children as soon as the latter are capable of helping them in their work, would not have them taught the most necessary knowledge, even if instruction were free, if the government was not authorized to force them to do so. But this objection is based on the hypothesis of such an extreme poverty among the people that with this level of poverty nothing good could exist. What is necessary is that this poverty should not exist. As soon as the people enjoy the ease they are due, far from keeping children in ignorance, they will hasten to give them an education. They will put their pride where they feel their interest. The most natural tendency of fathers is to raise children above their own rank. This is what we see in England and what we saw in France during the Revolution. That period was unsettled and the people suffered much from their government, yet by the very fact that they acquired more wealth, education made astonishing progress among that class. Everywhere the people's education is in proportion to its wealth.

I said at the beginning of this chapter that the Athenians subjected only the lower schools to the magistrates' supervision. Schools of philosophy always remained absolutely independent, and this enlightened people transmitted to us a memorable example on this subject. When the demagogue Sophocles proposed subjecting the teaching of the philosophers to the authority of the government, all these men who, despite their numerous errors, should forever serve as models both of love of truth and respect for toleration, resigned from

8. Condorcet, first *Mémoire*, p. 44.

their positions. The assembled people declared them formally free from all inspection by the magistrates, and condemned their absurd adversary to pay a fine of five talents.[9]

But, it will be said, if there was an educational establishment based on principles contrary to morality, would you deny the government the right to repress this abuse? Doubtless not, no more than one would refuse it the right to act against all writings and actions which disturbed public order. But repression is different from direction, and it is direction I forbid the government. Furthermore, we forget that in order for an educational establishment to be created or to subsist, it needs students. In order for it to have students, their parents have to put them there. Setting aside the morality of the parents, which is nevertheless completely unreasonable, it will never be in the parents' interest to have the judgment misled and heart perverted of those with whom they have the most important and most intimate relationships throughout their lives. The practice of injustice and depravity can be useful temporarily and in particular circumstances, but its theory can never be of any advantage. The theory will be professed only by lunatics, which will immediately repulse general opinion without the government even getting involved. The government will never need to suppress educational establishments where lessons in vice and crime are given, because there will never be such establishments, and if there were, they would hardly be dangerous, for the teachers would remain all alone. But for lack of plausible objections, people rely on absurd conjectures, and this calculation is not without cleverness: if there is a danger in not responding to these conjectures, there seems likewise to be foolishness in refuting them.

I have greater hope for the perfection of the human species from private educational establishments than from the best-organized public instruction by the government. Who can limit the development of the passion for education in a free country? You imagine that governments possess a love of education? Without examining here to what point this tendency is in their interest, we ask you only why you do not imagine that the same love exists in individuals of the cultivated class, in enlightened minds, in generous souls? Everywhere the government does not weigh on men, everywhere it does not corrupt wealth by conspiring with it against justice, there literature, inquiry,

9. Diogenes Laertius, *Life of Theophrastes*.

the sciences, and the increase and exercise of the intellectual faculties are the favorite enjoyments of society's affluent classes. See how in England they act, come together, rush from all sides; contemplate the museums, the libraries, the independent associations, the scholars devoted solely to the search for truth, the travelers braving every danger to advance human knowledge a single step.

In education, as in everything, let the government observe and preserve, but let it remain neutral. Let it remove obstacles, let it smooth the road; one can leave it to individuals to march down the road to success.

# CHAPTER TWO ❧ On Religion

The part of Filangieri's work which is going to concern us now is the most imperfect of all. Its flaws do not come solely from the fact that a premature death prevented the author from putting the finishing touches to it, but from the fact that the author wrote at a period less inclined than any other to adopt impartial views or just ideas about religion. Dogma and unbelief divided the countries of Europe—dogma armed with the crude, harmful, and always inadequate means of the law, unbelief strong in resources and suppleness of mind and encouraged by the indignation that intellectual oppression produces in men. Thus the part of society that either chance or tradition had invested with power saw in reason only sedition or rebellion, and the majority of the governed, betrayed by the use that the government made of belief, wished to see in religion only an enemy of freedom. At the same time, intolerance, while threatening enough to arouse irritation, was no longer sufficiently dangerous to inspire fear. This caused all kinds of moral disorder in people's heads. Hypocrisy claimed to command submission, but it betrayed itself, because whenever unbelief is the general rule, individual vanity, even in those who fight the irreligious tendency, likes to let doubt show. Philosophical hostility, on the other hand, violent and passionate, condemned examination as weakness, and even impartiality as betrayal.

No writer of the eighteenth century could cross this chaos with a firm step; some rushed headlong into a dogmatic irreligion as absurd as the positive beliefs of the least enlightened tribes. Others only avoided this excess by throwing themselves into the most obvious contradictions, one after another. Voltaire was very attached to the legislative and, so to speak, penal part of religion because he had become a member of society's upper class, and he feared for the delights of the wealthy from the atheism of the poor. He did not pour any less contempt and irony, not only on this or that religion in particular, but on the ideas and the emotions without which any religion cannot subsist. Rousseau, dominated by his soul while Voltaire was dominated only by his mind, destroyed with alacrity what he raised up with enthusiasm. Montesquieu appears to avoid the difficulty only through his extreme moderation, his subtle mockery, his calculated laconicism, and the distance he deliberately puts between opposite assertions.

What was impossible for the leading men of this period had to be even more impossible for Filangieri, who entered the lists with a pure heart, the most praiseworthy intentions, an uncritical erudition, and a mediocre intelligence. So we see him, ignorant of the implications of the principles he proclaims, constantly recoil from their consequences. From philosophy he borrows degrading hypotheses, fortunately false, about the original source of religious ideas. Having thus debased religion from the beginning, he then rejoins the party of the devout, or rather of the politicians, who want to impose devotion on unbelieving nations so as to imitate erroneous theories about the application of belief to positive legislation.

To reconcile Filangieri's contradictions, his prejudices alternately philosophical and religious, his assertions based on his word alone, and his numerous mistakes when discussing antiquity; and to replace the confused compilation he has bequeathed us with a clear doctrine—one that begins with human nature and is corroborated by facts—would be to undertake a volume longer than his. Such is not the task of a commentator. I have furthermore made an effort to accomplish the latter part of this task in another work, of which the first volume has already appeared.[1] What I can attempt here is to reveal each error of detail in a few words by indicating the truth with which, in my opinion, Filangieri should have replaced it.

"Religion," he says, "in the savage man is nothing but the worship of fear which he renders to the object of his vague terrors." In this phrase the Italian author merely repeats the trivial axiom on which the unbelievers of all centuries have built their systems. Superficial observers and prejudiced judges, they saw that the savage was afraid of what he adored, and they concluded from this that he adored only what he feared. But by thus attributing the savage's religious ideas solely to fear, they ignored what is precisely the fundamental

1. *De la Religion, de sa source, de ses formes, et de ses développements*, vol. 1.

question. They did not try to find out at all why man was the only creature affected by terror of hidden powers which acted on him, and they did not take into account in the slightest the need only he feels of discovering and adoring these hidden powers.

If religion was only a result of man's fears, the animals over which these fears have still more sway should not be completely alien to religious ideas. For note that the philosophers always suppose that man differs from the animals only because he possesses in a superior degree faculties with which they too are endowed. But, if his intelligence is of the same nature as theirs, if it is only more developed and extended, everything which intelligence produces in him it ought to produce in them, in an inferior degree doubtless, yet nonetheless in some sort of degree.

From this you have a choice of two things: if man has faculties, instincts, and feelings to which animals cannot attain, then one must look for the cause of what he experiences in faculties, feelings, and instincts which are peculiar to him. Or if he has only a relative preeminence over the animals, then the closer the animals come to that preeminence, the more we should find in them everything which we perceive in man. If religion has no other origin than fear, and since fear is an emotion common to man and animals, religion should not be completely alien to the latter. If it remains alien to them, it is because it has its source in a feeling exclusively reserved to man, and this feeling is not fear.

Indeed, examine the objects that the savage adores: they are not only those which he fears, but all those he meets. That he is subsequently afraid of them afterwards, because he believes them to be filled with a divine nature stronger than he, is foolish: but his terror is a result of his adoration. It is its result and not its principle. This adoration has another cause which cannot be fleeting, accidental or exterior, for such a cause would not change the permanent and interior nature of man, nor would it give him another nature.

This cause is internal to him; it is an instinct proper to him. This instinct manifests itself in the most primitive as well as the most civilized condition, amid the most profound ignorance as well as the most developed education. It develops itself according to the degree of that education. It is proportionate to the degree of ignorance, but it never ceases to act, and in the very periods when it seems to be most smothered by the dominant opinion, it still survives, struggles, and triumphs.

"In barbarian societies," Filangieri continues, "religion is the principle of that authority whose exercise by men would not be tolerated, but which one puts into the hands of the gods with more confidence." In expressing himself in such a general way, Filangieri seems to have misunderstood the essential differences which distinguish from each other the barbarian societies of which we have retained some recollection. Among these societies, several doubtless owed their civilization only to priests. But the most remarkable—those which we know best, from which we take our philosophical doctrines, and which serve us as a guide and model in the career of genius and the arts (one will guess that I mean the Greeks)—did not place in the gods' hands the authority they did not wish to confide to men. When they left the savage state to pass into barbarism, the first step on the social ladder, they always accorded the temporal power an uncontested preeminence over the priestly power. In the ages described by Homer, no one was more subordinate than the priests. It was only with trembling, and after having invoked the protection of Achilles, that Calchas dared to resist Agamemnon's will. "I am only an ordinary man," he says, "and I cannot confront a king's anger." It is the political leaders who preside customarily and by right at religious ceremonies. The priests often do not take any part in them whatsoever, and when they are called, it is because of some sudden terror, some unforeseen calamity, which throws peoples back into an unaccustomed superstition. Homer also puts the priests in the category of mercenaries, living on the kindness and liberality of the public, along with singers, cooks, and other equally precarious and subordinate professions.[2]

There is thus already one barbarian society to which the rule established by Filangieri does not apply. This is not the place to examine if the Greeks were subject to priestly domination before the heroic centuries. Some traditions are favorable to this hypothesis, but it is nonetheless true that barbarian Greece did not make religion the basis of social power. This purely military social power found its support in the attractions which warlike hordes found in expeditions which satisfied their thirst for pillage. Religion and the priesthood certainly exercised much influence, but this influence was accidental and occasional. Greek religion could accelerate civilization by consecrating truces, sanctuary, and common ceremonies, but nothing ever existed in

2. I will develop this truth further in the second volume of my work on religion.

Greece like that theocracy whose principle is suggested by the Neapolitan author, and which he describes as a necessary passage between the savage state and the ordered state in the following sentence: "Under the auspices of this theocracy, religion follows by preparing and effectuating by degrees the difficult, slow and progressive passage from the state of natural independence to social dependence." Nothing is more false. Under the auspices of theocracy, passage from the savage state to the social state is not in the least slow and gradual. On the contrary, there is nothing gradual about that transition when it happens under the empire of theocracy; then it is sudden. The savage enters the social state as if dominated by an exterior force, but he stops at the lowest rung. The same force which makes him take the indispensable steps to assure his physical subsistence and his material security against the scourges of nature forbids him all later improvement, and strikes him with a sort of immobility. It is only when he arrives at civilization by causes independent of theocracy, by the natural progress of intelligence, or what is more frequent, by the communication of peoples among each other that his march is slow and gradual. Compare Greece and Egypt, and you will have proof of what I affirm. Examine the constitution of the priesthood in Egypt and in Greece, and you will have the explanation of that for which the facts offer you the proof.

## CHAPTER THREE ❧ Of the Growth of Polytheism

> Man, penetrated by the fear which the terrible phenomena of nature excite in him . . . must have supposed a power, a strength which produced them. . . . He must have addressed invocations to it as the only weapons he could employ against it. Such is the first step that the human mind, left to itself . . . must have made towards religion, and which in fact it did make. . . . This is . . . the period when the unknown force which agitated nature and terrified men was the sole object of the wishes and worship dictated to the first humans by terror. . . . But soon . . . men, contemplating the sort of war that the various forces of natures seemed to wage against each other, and being unable to explain it except by supposing several intelligences charged with presiding over these forces and these various powers . . . personified them, gave them a life and senses, invoked them, adored them as more powerful than themselves. Such is, such was, and such will always be the first origin of polytheism. . . . It is the second period of religion, in which the unknown force alone ceased to receive the wishes and homage of mortals . . . and had to share them with several powers of the same nature. . . . Error has a progressive march like truth. . . . Once the human mind has taken the first step towards polytheism, it must necessarily arrive at the god Crepitus and the god Sternutius.
>
> BOOK V, CHAPTER 4, PP. 62–73.

It is impossible to invert all our ideas more completely and attribute to human intelligence a route more different than reason indicates and the facts demonstrate. What! Men began by exclusively worshipping a single force, unknown and general in nature, before rendering homage to various powers which seem to mutually oppose and combat each other! And from where therefore would the notion have come to the savage of that mysterious unity, when everything which struck his senses and his observation suggested to him on the contrary division, opposition, and struggle? It is much in vain that our author wishes to rely upon the traditions Hesiod put together in a completely arbitrary order, or rather without any order whatsoever. I cannot enter here into the developments which would be necessary in order to explain how the *Theogony* was apparently compiled, and what in reality this confused and bizarre poem is.[1] It is enough for me to say (which I think would not be denied by any of those who have studied Greek mythology elsewhere than in the systematic works of our French writers) that while Homer offers us an exact picture of the religion of the early period of Greece when she was departing the savage state, Hesiod presents us with a very incoherent collection of all the traditions brought from the colonies, edited without criticism or discernment and imprinted with the priestly spirit of the countries where those colonies originated, and thus without any relation to either the Greek national spirit or their native beliefs. Of the ten parts or periods composing the *Theogony*, nine are foreign to the popular religion, and it is only in the last one, in the reign of Jupiter, that the polytheism professed in the heroic age finally appears. This arrangement is very natural in a compiler who was more curious than enlightened and who gathered together all the reminiscences, travelers' tales, and legends of the priests, wanderers, and missionaries of the

1. In the third part of my work on religion I will treat the formation of Greek polytheism. I will show that the inhabitants of Greece, preserved by fortunate circumstances, or freed by some now-forgotten revolution from all priestly influence, passed from fetishism to Homeric polytheism solely because of the permanent relationship between that polytheism and their political and moral progress. I will show that that Hesiod, who, despite what has been said, came later than the author or authors of the *Iliad* and the *Odyssey*, did no more than assemble some traditions and dogmas, which were for the most part foreign. These dogmas and traditions were never part of the public belief, and if we find many traces of them in the mysteries, it is because the mysteries were in some sense the depository of all that Egyptian, Thracian, and Phoenician emigrants were able to introduce into the national religion. In consequence, one should consider Homer alone the poet of the popular religion, and regard Hesiod as that of the occult religion which the Greek genius always rejected. But all this would take me too far in the *Commentary*. Thus I can only very strongly encourage my readers to see in my present assertions only fragments of a larger whole, fragments which necessarily lose much of their probability in not being supported by all the proofs and accompanied by all the explanations necessary to surround them with the evidence proper to them.

priestly guilds of Egypt, Phoenicia, and Thrace in order to sing mysterious doctrines to barbarous tribes. It has fooled the studious but credulous troop of our ordinary scholars. They thought that because Hesiod placed a kind of cosmogonic unity before the gods of Olympus, from the mutilation of which these gods were descended, that that abstract and obscure unity had in fact been the first object of adoration. They did not see that this conception was obviously borrowed from Phoenicia and other lands subject to the priests, in whose language the mutilation of the gods served as an emblem of the cessation of creative power. These dogmas belonged to the scientific systems of the great guilds of physicists and astronomers, melded with the priestly guild, which claimed the monopoly of all sciences. They had nothing in common with Greek religion, free from all guilds and the common property of the people as a whole, who without noticing it or perceiving the changes, fashioned it, bent it, modified it, and improved it according to the progress of their intelligence and the softening of their mores.[2]

This fundamental error led these scholars into all the mistakes which diminish, if not the utility of their research, at least the merit of their results. They had to find explanations for an inexplicable phenomenon, and to make plausible the hypothesis of the human species passing from the religion of the whole to the religion of the parts when, on the contrary, it has always passed from the religion of the parts to that of the whole. First came individual gods, fetishes, without any fixed number, like their worshippers. Next came more generic gods, in lesser number; then an assembly of a limited number of gods, which could normally not increase; and then one god, the head of that assembly, with all the others under his rule. Later, this god alone was believed to be truly divine, and the rest inferior spirits. This is the real march of the

2. All this, I feel, would demand many explanations, and the gaps which despite myself I leave behind unfilled will furnish pretexts for more or less plausible objections. In favor of the existence of priestly corporations in Greece, there will be alleged, for example, the Eumolpids, the Branchides, and many other families in which the priesthood was transmitted as an inheritance, and who presided alone either at the mysteries or even at ceremonies of public worship. People will try to prove the powerful influence of the Greek priesthood by the persecutions it carried out, and the names of Socrates, of Prodicus, of Diagoras will hasten to range themselves beneath my opponents' pens. I am annoyed by this, but I cannot say everything at once, nor above all in this book. Those who will oppose me for the sole pleasure of opposing me are masters of profiting from the advantage I give them. Those who search for the truth are invited, before judging me, to look at the work I indicated in the first note attached to this chapter.

mind, a progress that is troubled and interrupted—sometimes by the internal resistance of superstition, sometimes by the effect of external calamities—but nevertheless followed or returned to, and finally leading man to the notion of theism.

Like many others, Filangieri was fooled by an appearance which, however, should not have created an illusion for any but a very superficial observer. During the decline of polytheism he saw the gods multiply infinitely, and he imagined that this progression was an effect of the religious progression of ideas, when it was only the result of unbelief. When the discredit of beliefs is complete, poets use them and play with these beliefs. They invent gods whom no one disputes, because everyone knows that no one is trying to impose the worship of these imaginary gods. In what period did Filangieri find the god Percutius and the goddesses Prema, Pertunda, and Perfica?[3] In the period when polytheism was about to cease to exist, when no one worshipped Jupiter the very great and very good any more, everyone was allowed to imagine ridiculous gods. If in a previous century, a century still serious and religious, under the republic of Cincinnatus and Camillus, someone had spoken of the god Crepitus,[4] he would have provoked a scandal. In the time of the emperors, he created laughter: this was because religion was defeated. Rats and reptiles slide into ruined buildings, but one should not conclude from this that they are admitted when the buildings are standing and inhabited by men.

There is almost no single sentence of Filangieri's which is not mistaken. He cites Porphyry on the primitive worship of the Greeks. But everyone knows that Porphyry worked purely in order to reconcile his contemporaries not to the dogmas of the old worship, but to its forms, by attributing to them a purity they never had and substituting for the popular meaning, which reason no longer wished to tolerate, allegorical interpretations such as always appear when religions are fallen, promising them a deceptive support. Following Herodotus, Filangieri accepts that the Pelasgians, the first inhabitants of Greece, worshipped a multitude of divinities that they did not distinguish from one another and to which they did not give any name. However, he asks if several indistinguishable gods who are not designated by any particular

3. Very minor and perhaps fictional Roman gods known chiefly from a mocking reference by the Christian polemicist and Church Father Tertullian.—Trans.

4. Another possibly fictional Roman god of flatulence known only from Christian satire.—Trans.

name can represent anything but the unknown force adored in principle, which Herodotus, imbued with the ideas of polytheism, was unable to divine. The gods of the Pelasgians unquestionably represented something other than that abstract unity of the unknown force. The Negroes also adore thousands of fetishes, and they too call them only by the generic name of fetishes: certainly the Negroes do not adore the unity of the unknown force, but rather a host of divine forces, enemies of each other, which they believe reside in the stone, piece of wood, or animal skin before which they prostrate themselves while offering sacrifices or murmuring prayers.

# CHAPTER FOUR ❧ On the Priesthood

> When public worship was established . . . various reasons obliged the fathers of families, at first the only priests . . . to give up their ministry of religion and choose a certain number of individuals in order to confide the sacred offices exclusively to them. The priesthood thus formed a separate order.
>
> BOOK V, CHAPTER 5, P. 95.

It was not always in the way Filangieri indicates—that is, as a delegation of political authority—that the priestly power was constituted as a separate order. Among several nations the path taken was just the opposite. It is the priesthood which, constituting itself before any other power, put the direction of the affairs of the visible world into subordinate hands while nevertheless reserving for itself, in the name of religion, a supreme inspection over their agents. This difference relates to a distinction that all writers to this day have misunderstood. Depending on the climate and local or accidental circumstances, the priestly power either follows or precedes the temporal power.

When clans abandon fetishism by the progress of intelligence alone, then the priests, who have little authority in fetishism, remain in a secondary position for a long time. Thus among the Greeks of the heroic period the entire army allowed Agamemnon to insult and chase away Chryseis's father. It was only when the plague made frightened souls unusually superstitious that the son of Atreus saw himself forced to return his captive daughter to the priest. Even then, Calchas was fearful of putting his case and incurring a king's anger, and in the *Odyssey,* Ulysses kills without scruple the priest who was present at the festival of the claimants.[1]

1. The claimants for his wife Penelope's hand.—Trans.

It is not within our subject to inquire if, before the heroic period, the Greeks had not been subject to priestly guilds like the Egyptians and almost all the peoples of antiquity. Even after this fact, plausible enough, was proved, it would remain nonetheless certain that a revolution whose details are unknown and traces hidden delivered the Greeks from this yoke, and in breaking it they fell back into fetishism. Progress was afterwards what it would have been if they had never had any great body of priests.

When, on the contrary, either by an effect of the climate, of the difficulty of procuring physical subsistence, of the need to repulse the attacks of an ever-threatening nature with the aid of works which suppose more or less scientific calculation and which require assiduous and painful effort, or above all by the kind of religion which circumstances favor—I mean the adoration of the stars and the elements—priestly guilds form alongside the cradle of the nascent society. The priests, at first the sole kings, sole judges and sole legislators, delegate the temporal power, the administration of the state, and the conduct of war to subordinates whom they have chosen. This is what happened in Egypt, where the reign of the gods preceded that of the kings and lasted eighteen thousand years, if we are to believe that country's annals.[2] This is what happened in Ethiopia, where the priests sent the ruler the order to kill himself, and what probably happened in the Indies, which all religious traditions describe to us as long governed by the Brahmins. When the temporal power is thus constituted, the priesthood which created it still supervises it and briefly succeeds in keeping it in a dependent position. But sooner or later rivalries break out, and the delegates become the rivals and soon the enemies of their teachers. Everywhere history presents us with the spectacle of this ferocious struggle.

The Hindu books tell us that the Kshatriya or warriors, the children of the sun, became arrogant, threw off the yoke of the Brahmins, and cruelly persecuted them. Parasurama, the sixth incarnation of the race of the moon[3] and a Brahmin himself, but courageous as a Kshatriya, avenged his oppressed caste. He defeated his enemies in twenty-one pitched battles, filled entire lakes with their blood, shared out their goods, and pushed severity so far that the Brahmins themselves, whose empire he reestablished, were afflicted by the

2. Diodorus, bk. I, 2, 3.
3. Schlegel, *Sagesse des Indiens*, p. 184.

destruction he had caused.[4] These books also report that Bein or Vena, the son of Ruchnan, who succeeded to the throne after his father's flight, forbade all worship of the gods and all justice among men. He imposed silence on the Brahmins and drove them away. He then contracted a sacrilegious marriage with a woman of their caste. He allowed others to follow this example so that the children of the gods would be mingled with the children of men. Forty-two half-castes were born of these guilty unions. Then the Brahmins cursed him, and took his life. As he was without descendants, they rubbed his hands against each another, and from his blood there was born a son fully armed, learned in the holy sciences, and handsome as a god; from his left hand the Brahmins extracted a daughter, whom they gave to him in marriage. He ruled with justice, protecting his subjects, maintaining peace, punishing disorders, and honoring the Brahmins.[5] In these traditions one cannot fail to recognize the memory of the combats which the two powers waged in the Indies.[6]

The impiety of the kings of Egypt toward the gods of the country, says Diodorus, led to frequent revolts.[7] Two kings whom the annals written by the priests treat as tyrants and rebels, Cheops and Chephren, closed the temples for thirty years.[8] In turn the priest Sethos, having taken the throne, took away from the soldiers the lands they possessed,[9] but after his death there was a new revolution against the priests. Twelve kings were appointed. One

4. *Mythologie des Hindoux*, I, pp. 280–90.

5. *Rech. Asiat.* V, p. 252.

6. We could multiply the quotations. Often the Indian books attribute the destruction of the world to the decline of respect for the priestly order. In the second age, they say, during this catastrophe there were a small number of individuals from the Brahmin caste, from that of the merchants, and from that of the artisans who were spared. But there were none from the caste of the warriors or rulers because they had all abused their power and their authority. At the renewal of the world, a new caste of governors was created, but so that it was not so disposed to go astray, it was taken from the caste of the Brahmins; Rama, the first of this new caste, was the protector of the priests, and only acted with their advice. See Mayer, *Dictionnaire mythologique*, art. "Yog," pp. 482–84; *Lois de Menou*, bk. X, pp. 43–45. The Hindu books speak also of a Brahmin of Magadha who killed Nanda, the king of the country, and put a new dynasty on the throne. *As. Red.*, bk. II, p. 139.

7. Diodorus, bk. I, 2, 3.

8. Herodotus, bk. II, pp. 124–27. M. Denon notes that it was during this religious struggle that the only palace which belonged to the kings of Egypt was constructed.

9. Herodotus, bk. II, p. 115.

of them put himself back under priestly authority or protection in order to supplant his colleagues, and with the help of oracles secured the rule of all Egypt.[10] It is even probable that as early as the times of the theocracy and before the establishment of temporal kings, similar revolutions had troubled Egypt, and that these revolutions had taken place among the priests, and sometimes against them.[11]

Ethiopia, which should hardly be distinguished from Egypt with regard to religion, was the scene of still more murderous discord. The priests of Meroe condemned kings to death, and one of the latter, Ergamenes, a contemporary of the second Ptolemy, even had all the priests of Meroe massacred in their temples.[12]

We know of the annual festival celebrated in Persia commemorating the overthrow of the Magi, during which the members of that caste, even though it had reconquered great power, were forced to hide from the people's sight.[13] The same struggle is more obscurely visible in Etruria because its history is less known to us, but the order given to the Rutuli by their king Mezentius to present him with the first fruits which they customarily dedicated to

10. Herodotus, bk. II, pp. 141–52. *Heeren Africa*, p. 687.

11. Such is the most natural meaning of Herodotus's account of the reign of the eight old gods, the twelve later gods, and the divinities who were subsequently born of these twelve gods. "In ancient times," he says, "the gods reigned in Egypt. They had lived with men, and there had always been one of them who exercised sovereignty;" that is to say that in those times Egypt was governed by the priests, and this theocratic government was called by the name of the god to whom the grand priest who enjoyed sovereign authority was attached (Larcher, *Essai de chronol*, chap. 1, para. 10). Probably these grand priests quarreled among themselves and tore the supreme authority from one another. The caste of warriors, the second caste in the state, also seems to have risen up against the first, but the latter was victorious (Herodotus, bk. II, p. 41). See Larcher, *Notes*, bk. II, p. 460, which mentions an inscription intended to preserve the memory of this event. Despite the poor success of this attempt, with priestly government becoming daily more oppressive, the people sought refuge in royal authority. The first king of Egypt was Menes. His laws on religion limited the dominion of the priesthood (Diodorus, bk. I). They brought the anger of that order upon him, which, having regained its influence under his successors, authorized or forced Technatis to engrave curses against Menes on a column (Plutarch, *De Is. et Osir*; Larcher, *Chronol. d'Hérod.*, bk. VI, pp. 180–207). From that time on, the struggle between the two powers was constant and ferocious.

12. Diodorus, bk. III, p. 1.

13. Herodotus, bk. III, p. 79.

the gods could well have been just an attempt by the monarchy against the priesthood.[14]

If we care to pass from the peoples of antiquity to modern nations or, to speak more precisely, to nations discovered in modern times, we will recall that the Mexicans, after their migrations—during which they had, like the Jews, been led by priests—chose, some sooner, others later, temporal leaders.[15] In Japan, the dairi or mikado used to combine spiritual power with the most absolute political authority. He delegated the administration of terrestrial interests to a minister who, initially a despot in his master's name, soon became a despot in his own name. A guard, placed close to the supreme ruler under the pretext of rendering him homage, put him in no position to undertake anything,[16] and for the last three centuries, reduced to illusory titles and deprived of all real influence, he has retained only the privilege of creating gods whom he charges with the government of the universe and who submit accounts of their administration to him in secret meetings. On earth, he confers priestly dignities on those whom the koubo (this is the temporal ruler's name) designates, and he performs the apotheosis of the latter when he is struck down by death.[17] The Grand Lama experienced the same fate in Tibet, and such has also been that of the Caliphs dispossessed by the Emirs-al-omra.

We see how the progression of priestly power is far from being as regular in all cases as Filangieri claims it is. In his observations on this matter he was directed only by a fairly superficial study of Greek and Roman polytheism, other polytheisms being very poorly known at the time he wrote. Moreover, in discussing Roman religion, he completely misunderstood the meaning of the priesthood, to the extent that in Rome it was the result of the combination of two opposed forms of worship. It would require details which would lead

14. Macrobius, *Saturn*, bk. III, p. 5.

15. It is thus that Acamapitzin was chosen by the Tenochkan, in 1352 A.D.

16. Mayer, *Dictionn. Mythol.*, art. *Dairi* or *Coube*.

17. The chronology of this revolution is very clearly explained in the *Dictionnaire mythologique*, in the article *Japon*. The power of the dairi began to decline under the 73rd dairi, named Koujac in the annals of this empire. He reigned in the year 1142 A.D. The 81st dairi named a koubo or temporal general, and the 107th, in the year 1585 of our era, ceded power to one of the successors of this koubo. The new monarch had himself called *absolute master*, reigned despotically, subjected even the clergy to priests named by him, and united all the previously independent principalities.

us too far from our subject to explain the consequences of this combination (which has not yet been done anywhere). The Roman priesthood was an expression of the influence of constitutive elements of a religion which simultaneously combined Greek fables and Etruscan institutions.

As I said above, in Greece the priesthood did not exist as a body and had no political influence. In Etruria, as in Egypt, the priesthood was the leading group in the state, and political power was to a very large extent in its hands. Numa brought the Etruscan priesthood to Rome. The Tarquins made the legends and above all the spirit of Greek religion triumph at Rome. The priesthood survived this revolution, but was changed by it. The result was that without being as foreign to the constitution of the social body as in Greece, nor as identified with that constitution as in Etruria, the priesthood remained a regular power, which marched in the direction circumstances dictated to all powers.

Filangieri attributes the warlike disposition of the Roman people to the priesthood, given the interest he says the priesthood had in war, because the gods of the defeated peoples were worshipped on the Capitol. Since the Romans thought they compensated for the damage done other nations by adopting the worship of their tutelary divinities, the priesthood saw conquest as a way of multiplying gods, temples, and offerings—a fertile source of wealth.[18] But Filangieri takes an effect for a cause. The priesthood obeyed the warlike tendency; it did not create it. Constant warfare dominated the priesthood as it did the other powers of the state. Not by law but in fact, the high dignities of the priesthood belonged to men eminent in the army, and as these men were at the same time entrusted with high civil functions, religion became an instrument of the policy of conquest.

The reason put forward by Filangieri entered so little into determining the attitude of the priesthood that nowhere were foreign gods more constantly and more violently rejected than in Rome. The ordinances of the Senate in this regard are known, and they are innumerable. The divinities of the defeated peoples overcame the obstacles posed by the ordinances only in two ways. Sometimes they were introduced publicly, as in times of great calamities, because then it is in line with polytheism to look for help from everywhere, and it was thus, for example, that Cybele of Pessinus was brought to Rome.

18. See bk. 1, chap. 7, p. 78.

At other times they were introduced secretly, like smuggled goods, because despite the priesthood's desire for a monopoly, it is in accord with polytheism to persuade its devotees that one more god is one more protector. It is in this way that the Egyptian gods stole into the empire. But the Roman priesthood believed so little that its means of influence and wealth were increased by the introduction of foreign gods that these gods always arrived despite it, with their own priests, as the rivals and enemies of the old ones. All that is left to note is how frequently the gods and priests of Egypt were expelled. For the Roman priests the worship of foreign divinities meant a decrease in their profits and power.

This, I have already noted, is only indirectly related to Filangieri's work, and I thought that I might allow myself these brief reflections in order to prove how numerous are his mistakes. If any of my assertions shocks the opinion of my readers on certain points—if, for example, they are surprised that I deny that the Greek priesthood participated in political power, and the death of Socrates is raised as an objection—I would respond that it is not my fault if most of the time our philosophers have wanted to assign the remarkable facts of ancient history to causes which did not exist, and thus give credence to obvious mistakes. Socrates' death was not the work of priests, but of a political faction: the priests served it as tools serve the faction that bribes them, in the same way that the courts in this or that country serve the government. Religion was indeed the pretext for Socrates' death, but the priesthood as a body was not involved in it. They could not have been involved: even religious cases were decided by civil judges. But I must stop. To create an error, only a line is needed; to refute it takes volumes.

# CHAPTER FIVE ❧ On the Mysteries

> This was . . . a result of the intent to make people believe . . . that the mysteries contained religious truths, unknown to the multitude. This intention, combined with the knowledge of nascent civilization, led people to conceive that there were theological principles . . . fruits of the speculation of adepts who were already enlightened and civilized, and these principles . . . in fact ended up converting the mysteries into a school, a temple, where one taught and professed a different religion from that of the vulgar uninitiated.
>
> BOOK V, CHAPTER 6, P. 139.

The point of view from which Filangieri considers the mysteries—that important yet so badly known and so chimerically explained part of almost all the religions of antiquity—is much more just than one might have expected from a writer whose chief flaw was contemplating the doctrines and the institutions, in a word, the wisdom of the ancient peoples with superstitious respect. It is surprising that being so disposed he did not bow down before the hypotheses which make the mysteries a depository of a purified and sublime religion, professed since the beginning of the world, unknown to the peoples fallen somehow into ignorance, and preserved in a sanctuary—despite the folly of the uninitiated and the revolutions of the centuries—by philosophers who possessed, we cannot guess how, superior and privileged knowledge. But if the Italian author came close to the truth in this respect, he amply compensated for it in the account he was pleased to sketch two pages further on, about the cooperation between legislation and the priesthood to use the mysteries to destroy the old religion and replace it with a new one. In this account all kinds of impossibilities are found.

In the first place, the alliance between the political power and the priesthood to abolish the existing religion could never have happened. From the perspective of the political power, it could not happen because it saw in that religion both its sanction and its tool; nor could it happen from the priesthood's side, because religion was the guarantee of its influence. If the priests of antiquity introduced doctrines or rites into the mysteries which were different from the public religion, this was certainly not to prepare in secret, far from prying and curious eyes, its abandonment. On the contrary, it was in order to have one more means of maintaining religion in its imperfection and vulgarity, while depositing in a safe place scientific discoveries, metaphysical subtleties, and reasonings and facts which, although useful to preserve as a part of the priesthood's monopoly, would have shaken the belief which was the base of their power. All progressive ideas of the human mind are the priesthood's enemy, but it disarms these enemies by adopting them, because it adopts them on the express condition that they do not climb over the impenetrable wall with which it surrounds them. Also, it adopts them without distinction of origin and tendency. However contradictory they are, it makes all systems and all tales coexist, and their contradictions embarrass it little, because they are deposited in the sanctuary alongside one another, without touching each other, and consequently without fighting each other.

It is for this reason that all those who have wanted to discover a single and unchanging doctrine in the mysteries have always been mistaken. The mysteries were in a way a priestly encyclopedia, ever growing with everything the priests successively inserted into it. Thus when the Greek priesthood, always without any legal influence and limited by the political power, found in Greece's ancient traditions memories which presented the priests as more powerful and which attributed to the priesthood the rise from savagery and the first establishment of civilization, the priests introduced into the mysteries commemoration of the savage state, the discovery of food healthier and more pleasant than raw meat, the cultivation of land and the vine, and the softening of mores. When, as a natural and progressive result of the communication of peoples with one another, foreign priests—members of guilds much more powerful than the Greek priesthood—brought cosmological and theogonic hypotheses to that country, the Greek priesthood enriched the mysteries with these obscure theogonies and cosmologies. Later, when philosophy, also borrowed from the barbarians by the first Greek philosophers, gave birth to systems of theism, pantheism, and even atheism, these systems were also welcomed into the mysteries.

From this there arose a chaos whose confusion was nevertheless overlooked by the initiates, because they were told only partially and in isolation what was best adapted to their previous ideas. The priests thus always appeared to have been in advance of intellect, and to be the depositories of all that intelligence had conceived of the most sublime and the most abstract. In confiding the results of their meditations and even their dreams to the accepted neophytes as religious secrets, they separated these neophytes from the rest of the human species. From then on, far from having them for enemies, they possessed them as auxiliaries. But it is clear that the priesthood's work had no other purpose than its own power. For at the same time that the priests followed the progress of thought and science, in order to control them and cover them with a veil, they maintained externally, insofar as individual credulity and the institutions which existed alongside them made possible, the accepted belief in all its integrity.[1]

By supposing that the legislator allied with the priesthood in order to destroy a vulgar religion and establish a purer one, Filangieri thus begins from a false assumption, but he goes astray no less by lending such an intention to the legislator himself. During the rather long period of time during which the mysteries subsisted, we do not encounter a single example of an attempt by legislators to purify religion.[2] It purifies itself, and legislation, like society as a whole, yields to the inevitable effect of reason which becomes enlightened and morality which improves. But legislation yields while resisting, and as soon as it discovers the end toward which it is being led, its resistance becomes violent and often furious. Observe the efforts of the emperors to

1. I have only been able to describe here very briefly, and even then imperfectly, the perspective from which the mysteries of antiquity ought to be studied. I will examine the facts, and I will give an account of the proofs which seem to me to support this manner of understanding them, when I discuss the decline of polytheism in my work on religion.

2. One will wrongly raise as an objection Julian and the philosophers of the School of Alexandria who, being on the defensive, did their best to explain fallen polytheism by subtleties and allegories. Christianity, appearing in all its purity, forced its enemies into this fruitless and difficult task. It is very simple, for a rising religion forces an old cult to change, but this kind of involuntary and forced reform does not resemble at all the project that Filangieri, in his utopia, attributes to the government and the priesthood.

maintain polytheism, even though all the speculative ideas which Christianity revealed to men were taught in the mysteries.[3]

Finally, even if what we have demonstrated to be chimerical were true—even if the political power and the priesthood, surrendering their own interests and seized with philanthropic enthusiasm, wanted to give up the advantages of an already founded religion, one they had fashioned and tailored, in order to substitute for it dogmas more pure, and by that fact less subordinate, at least when new—it is not thus that a religion triumphs. Something other than invitations, be they sweet or threatening, from those who govern is required for men to believe. Filangieri falls back into his eternal mistake here. He always assumes that it is a fact that the government must want the good, and that it can do it. Unfortunately, it is not always certain that it wants the good, and when it does want it, it is through noninterference, through its inaction, and through its respect for the independence without which no improvement can take place that it has some chance of seeing its wishes fulfilled and its intentions realized.

3. In refuting Filangieri, I do not claim to deny that the mysteries contributed to the fall of the public religion in Greece and Rome, but this was against the government's and the priesthood's will. The people learned that in the mysteries one taught something other than what was ordained for them to believe. But as soon as the people doubt that their leaders have the same belief they do, they reject that belief as an absurdity and an insult.

## CHAPTER SIX AND LAST ❧ Conclusion

I here end this certainly imperfect *Commentary*, in which I have tried to establish one principal idea which seems to me to apply to everything, and without which we will not achieve anything useful or lasting. This idea is that the functions of government are negative: it should repress evil, and let the good take care of itself.

Filangieri's generally correct and just instincts sometimes led him to this conclusion, but the prejudices which still existed, and the imprudent appeal addressed by many of his contemporary philosophers to an authority which they thought themselves destined to take over, made him deviate constantly from the correct path. As a result, he continually passes from a truth to an error. Does he recognize that since the mores of one century are not those of the century which preceded it, nor of the century which follows it, the legislator should yield to these necessary changes? Then he immediately wants to put the legislator in charge of these changes, and it is Lycurgus or Solon that he cites to us.

Piercing through his vague expressions, I certainly find that he does not want any more than I to change the moderns into Athenians, nor above all into Spartans. Nonetheless, he falls into the grave mistake of describing peoples' mores as the effect of their legislators' will. To hear him, one would say that the only reason the Lacedaemonians rejected wealth was because Lycurgus detested it, that they only renounced trade because he had forbidden it, and that they were only warriors because he had dedicated them to a warlike leisure. In the same way, he attributes the industrious spirit of the Athenians to their legislator's call for industry, not reflecting that when industry is indispensable to a people's existence, or when a people has reached the industrial period of its social state, there is no need to call for industry by authority and laws. Let authority remain neutral, let the laws be silent; necessity will do the rest. And in regard to institutions, there are none that are good and lasting except those that are necessary.

If we were to take Filangieri's system literally, it would follow that governments ought to apportion laws to the spirit of peoples in the same way tutors apportion their lessons to the intelligence of their students. Governments do not ask any better, and they draw from this principle two equally false and deadly consequences. Most often they perpetuate absurd laws, under the pretext that for their improvement one must wait for greater maturity in the nations, and since it is in the interest of the governments exercising power never to recognize that maturity in those over whom they exercise it, and to slow it down when they can, they surrender themselves with delight to this politics of immobility and delay. Look at France before 1789, with very few exceptions, which derived from inconsistency rather than system. In this way the former monarchy let the revolution prepare itself. Look at other empires, whose ministers are only concerned with smothering the smallest seed of progressive improvement inside the state and attacking it elsewhere, and those others who march from promise to promise and from retraction to retraction.

At other times, when startled out of immobility which as a general rule pleases them so much by an unforeseen commotion, or circumstantial or particular interests, the holders of power go beyond the goal instead of reaching it. They declare themselves competent judges of the degree of maturity the people have reached, and are mistaken: sometimes about the timing, judging the people ready for reforms when they are not, and sometimes about the principles, in adopting as a reform what proves to be the opposite.

Would you like an example of this truth in a despotic country? Consult the history of the Portuguese nation under the ministry of the marquis de Pombal:

> At the death of John V, you will see Portugal plunged in ignorance and bent beneath the priests' yoke. A man of genius arrived at the head of the state. He did not calculate that to break that yoke and dissipate that ignorance it was necessary to have a base of support in national feeling. He looked for this base of support in authority. By striking the boulder, he wanted to make the vital spring shoot

> forth. His imprudent haste aroused opposition from the men most worthy of helping him. The priests' influence grew with the persecution of which they were the victims. The nobility rose up. The minister was subject to the hatred of all classes. After twenty years of useless efforts, the king's death deprived him of his protector. He escaped the scaffold by exile, and the nation blessed the moment when, delivered from the government which claimed to enlighten it despite its wishes, it could once again rest in superstition and apathy.[1]

I have taken an example from an absolute government. I could take one no less striking from a government animated by a spirit of freedom which, even today, excuses the mistakes which it committed. Read again the history of the Constituent Assembly:

> Opinion had long seemed to demand several of the improvements which this assembly tried to make. Too anxious to please it, this assembly of enlightened but impatient men thought they could not go far or fast enough. Opinion became frightened at the haste of its interpreters. It recoiled, because they wanted to lead it on. Delicate to the point of capriciousness, opinion becomes irritated when one takes its whims for its orders.[2] From the fact that it is pleased to criticize, it does not always follow that it wants to destroy. Often, like kings who would be angry if every word they said was converted into acts by their followers' zeal, opinion likes to talk, without having its words carry too much importance, in order to be able to speak freely. The most popular decrees of the Constituent Assembly were sometimes disapproved of by some of the people, and among the voices which were raised against those decrees there were doubtless many who had formerly called for them.[3]

At the time of this writing, chance has brought into my hands a not unskillful plea against the independence in which I wish public opinion to be left, and in favor of the exclusive action of government. In responding to it, I will complete building a wall of evidence around my doctrine.

> When the public mind [says a modern writer] is perverted by vanity, egoism, and the mania for equality; when the dominant opinions reject the indispensable

1. *On the Spirit of Conquest*, 4th ed., p. 200.

2. When authority says to opinion, as Sayda said to Mohammed, "I anticipated your command," opinion responds the way Mohammed responded to Sayda: "You should have waited"; and if authority refuses this delay, opinion has its revenge.

3. *On the Spirit of Conquest*, p. 202.

> superiority of virtue and knowledge; when a student mob rejects all political and religious institutions; when the spirit of the day asks of the legislator only the consecration of systems of anarchy, what should the legislator do? Appeal from the mistaken nation to the nation that has returned to its senses, from the spirit of the day to the spirit of centuries, and far from flattering popular prejudices, reform them, repress them, eradicate them.

In order to judge the sophist, let us take up and weigh each of his words.

"The spirit of the day is perverted by vanity." It never is except when institutions favor vanity. Doubtless, when a system is based on the distinctions which vanity solicits and which power accords; when, in order to struggle against the good sense of the century which no longer wants to be vain and which rejects distinctions, distinctions are accompanied by preferences which make them into positive advantages; when one thus forces the man whose character would be superior to these puerilities to bring himself down to their level; when displays of vanity become a kind of homage to power, a means of success, a route to profit—then public spirit can be and above all can appear to be perverted by vanity. But the blame for this lies in the work the government has done to pervert it.

For the rest, it is possible that we do not agree upon the meanings of words. Are we by chance calling vanity contempt for the distinctions for which up to now vanity was avid? We will make certain of this, and we will see then that vanity does not reside in those who are accused of it, but in those who complain of it.

"The public spirit is perverted by egoism." Leave egoism alone. Private egoisms clash with each other; they neutralize one another. Like vanity, egoism is dangerous only when institutions encourage it. The public spirit is perverted by egoism only when a bad government forms all the egoisms into a pack against all ideas of justice. Nature, which has given man self-love for his personal preservation, also gave him sympathy, generosity, and pity so that he would not destroy his fellows. Egoism becomes harmful only when this counterweight is destroyed. It is destroyed when authority calls on egoism to rally around its banners, and promises it impunity provided it enrolls under its standards, thus transforming a necessary instinct into a ferocious and unrestrained passion.

"The public spirit is perverted by the mania for equality." This reproach is clearer than the preceding ones, and as I announced, we finally discover that what is being assaulted under the name of vanity and egoism is the love of equality. Now, I ask, is it to the love of equality that one can impute vanity? Would there not be more vanity in the contrary claim? You call vain and presumptuous those who want to be your equals, and you who want to be their superiors regard yourselves as being reasonable and modest!

What is equality? It is distributive justice. It is not the absence of all difference in social advantages. No one has demanded, no one demands that kind of equality. Equality is the aptitude to gain those advantages according to the means and the faculties with which one is endowed. This is taken to be the vanity which perverts the public spirit! This public spirit would be much more perverted rather by the mania for inequality—that mania which puts a handful of men in a necessarily hostile position, and which, condemning them to defend this position against the rights of the mass, falsifies the ideas of this ever militant minority, is harmful to its education, and stamps its judgments with partiality.

Let us also compare the excesses that are produced by the two "manias"; I use the chosen term. The mania for equality causes upsets, I admit. The man who trembles beneath an enormous burden cannot rise up with enough scruples and delicacy not to disturb the weight which oppresses him. But look at the people after these impetuous movements: it is surprised by its victory, it seeks justice, it asks for it, and it goes back to justice as soon as it is shown it. This is because its interest is in justice, because justice is the guarantee of the greatest number, and because its suspension profits only a minority who create privileges or exemptions at the people's expense.

The mania for inequality brings with it, I confess, much less violence. But this is because up to the present the flaws of our institutions and the imperfection of our knowledge have given inequality the advantage of possession. One makes less noise in maintaining that which exists than in establishing that which does not exist. In order to preserve, immobility suffices; in order to build, one must first destroy. Also, it is the oppressed who are always accused of every disorder: as long as the Negroes remain tied up in the bottom of the hold, the slave ship and its crew enjoy an edifying peace. The Negroes suffocate, but order is not disturbed. When the Negroes want to breathe, disorder begins, and they are reproached for the mania which arises from the fact that they cannot breathe when deprived of air.

It is so true that the apparent moderation of the supporters of inequality derives from the fact that up to now they have been in almost uncontested possession, and that when that possession is momentarily interrupted, they throw themselves with as much fury and much more tenacity into all the excesses and all the murders that are called popular. The patricians of Rome striking down the tribunes were the worthy rivals of Masaniello and Wat Tyler; and the Des Adrets and Tavannes of the St. Bartholomew's Day Massacre, which was nothing but the action of privilege against religious equality, were in all respects worthy of the murderers of 2 September 1792.[4]

It is thus not the mania for equality which perverts the public spirit. But see the system of inequality working to win supporters, paying for fallacies, and sowing corruption; creating for each turncoat a private interest which isolates him from the general interest; dividing the human species into groups who are each other's enemies in order to govern it; confining the human species, so to speak, in an innumerable mass of corporations each invested with a privilege, that is to say, enriched with spoils and bribed with an iniquity; exciting the vile passions, developing the insolent passions, rewarding base actions. It is in this atmosphere that the public spirit becomes corrupt, and that we see all that is ignoble in the human heart bloom.

"The opinions which are dominant today reject the superiority of the virtues and of knowledge." Never has opinion rejected the superiority of the virtues. In times of the most revolting immorality, virtue is always respected in theory. As for the superiority of knowledge, where is knowledge? That is the question. Opinion is nothing but assent given to the principles that one thinks true. Knowledge is nothing but knowledge of the truth. Opinion must therefore believe itself to be in possession of knowledge. You come to say to opinion that you are the sole owners of truth: persuade it, and it will no longer reject your superiority. Opinion rejects your truth, because it does not recognize it for superior knowledge. To decide the question is not to resolve it. To decide it yourself in your own favor is not reasoning; it is impertinence.

"Political and religious institutions are rejected." Would one not say that

4. Masaniello was a seventeenth-century Neapolitan fisherman who led a bloody uprising against Spanish rule and aristocratic oppression in 1647. Wat Tyler was the leader of the English Peasants' Revolt of 1381. Des Adrets and Tavannes were figures from the sixteenth-century French Wars of Religion, des Adrets a murderous Protestant and Tavannes a murderous Catholic.—Trans.

all political institutions and all religious institutions are rejected? In government, as in religion, are there not institutions of different kinds? Can one not reject some and want others? The supporters of the government's intellectual supremacy and exclusive action—do they not also reject institutions which are opposed to this monopoly? The question thus always remains the same. The two parties have some institutions which they reject, and some institutions which they adopt; which one is right remains to be discovered. But to accuse men who want the government of opinion or to accuse opinion itself of rejecting all political and religious institutions is to suggest precisely the opposite of the truth.

What characterizes the friends of the government? It is their confidence in certain classes and certain men. They attribute to them innate rights and privileged knowledge. Consequently they ask little from institutions, and at most they invoke them as a defense only when they fear that the power concentrated in a few hands will be taken from them. On the contrary, those who think that opinion should be obeyed, that governments should be nothing but its interpreters, and that the mission of governments is to march with public opinion from improvement to improvement ask that one put behind each improvement an institution which guarantees it, preventing governments from once again taking away from the human species what it has conquered. In truth they do not wish these institutions to be unchangeable. They want opinion, thanks to whose progressive strength those institutions were established, to be able to improve them further after later progress. But in the meantime, precisely because they do not recognize an innate science and superior knowledge in the government, they have no trust in government at all, and they have recourse to institutions in order to register and protect the progress made, almost always in spite of the government's efforts to delay it.

"Perverted opinion wishes to substitute theories of anarchy for these institutions." What is anarchy? It is a state of affairs during which society is delivered up to the irregular action of opposing enemy powers. But equality subjects all classes and all individuals to a state of uniform laws, and by that very fact it sets aside all permanent cause of struggle and hostility between individuals and classes. Is not equality thus better able to repress anarchy than inequality can? That inequality which arms minorities, sometimes against one another, sometimes against the majority?

The government of opinion is of all governments the one which most completely shelters people from anarchy. Since opinion advances only by degrees, everything that the government does under its influence is well prepared, comes at the right time, finds a foundation in attitudes, is connected to the past, is linked with the future, corrects what is defective, and grafts itself onto what is good. When, on the contrary, you abandon yourself to the government, which is itself declared independent of and above opinion, you are at the mercy of private interests and unpredictable ideas. The system of the supremacy of the government, deciding by itself according to its so-called knowledge, is nothing but a sort of consecration of the anarchy of chance.

"The legislator should appeal from the mistaken nation to the nation once again become master of its senses." But is the legislator an abstract, impassive being? Does he not have an interest in arrogating to himself the largest sum of power that circumstances make available? Every time the nation questions some part of his power, will he not say that it is mistaken and that it has been led astray? I have already discussed this subject (pt. 1, chap. 8, p. 33). I have shown that governments—and by the word *legislator* here it is always of the government that one speaks—are more likely to be wrong than individuals, and above all more likely to be wrong than peoples.

The opinion of a people is the result of each individual opinion, separated from the private interests which falsify it in the case of each individual, and which, meeting in this common center, struggle against and mutually cancel each other out. The government or the legislator has, by contrast, these private interests in all their intensity within itself. Nothing protects it against them, nothing extracts from this harmful alloy the general ideas it may have conceived. You entrust the government with declaring when the nation is mistaken, but who will respond to you that it is not the nation which is mistaken? The government will declare the nation mistaken every time this nation's knowledge surpasses its own, every time this nation does not want to submit itself to its fantasies and its caprices. Surely Albert of Austria said that the Swiss nation was mistaken when it did not bend the knee before Gessler's hat.[5] Today the sultan probably says that the Greeks are mistaken, because

5. Habsburg official in Switzerland who made people bow before his hat on a pole, thus sparking the William Tell revolt in the fourteenth century.—Trans.

they resist the whip, rape, and the strangling cord. Throughout the ages we have seen people in France who, when the nation complained about one of our innumerable tyrannies, said that the nation was mistaken.

"The legislator should oppose the spirit of the day with the spirit of centuries." If the legislator opposes the spirit of the day with the spirit of past centuries, we are thrown back into that stationary politics which paralyzes all man's faculties, rejects all improvements, and eternalizes all errors. If the legislator opposes to the spirit of the day the spirit of future centuries, we are exposed to all the hasty, premature, fanciful innovations whose danger I depicted at the beginning of this chapter. Therefore, why object to leaving to the spirit of the day its realm? The spirit of the day is composed of the opinions of the day, such as they have been formed by the action of circumstances, and with the help of precedent, for they are not born spontaneously and in isolation in the minds of men. The spirit of the day is born from the interests of the day, such as the habits, the speculations, and the progress of industry have made them. The spirit of the day is the expression of the needs of the day. Therefore do not try either to painfully evoke the spirit of the previous day or appeal too quickly and imprudently to that of the day to come.

"Far from flattering popular prejudices, the legislator should reform them, repress them, eradicate them." Here, two questions present themselves. Does the legislator have a certainty or even a probability of success when he wants to eradicate dominant opinions? And if success is certain, would it be of a kind that societies should congratulate themselves on?

I prefer to respond to dogmatic assertions with facts. I am therefore going to take from history the most memorable example that it has transmitted to us of the struggle of government against opinion. I choose it all the more willingly because, in this particular case, the government was correct in many respects. I wish to speak of the severe measures adopted by the Roman Senate against the introduction of Greek philosophy.

Certainly, there were many truths, but there were also serious mistakes in the philosophy brought to Rome by the Athenian embassy to which Carneades belonged. On the one hand, the progress of knowledge had led the Greek philosophers to reject some absurd fables, to raise themselves to purer notions of religion, to separate morality from vulgar polytheism, and to place its basis and its guarantee in the heart and intelligence of man. On the other hand, the abuse of a subtle dialectic in the schools of several philosophers had shaken the natural and incontestable principles of justice and subjected everything to self-interest, and in that way blighted the motivations behind all actions and deprived virtue itself of what was most noble and pure in it.

Thus the Roman Senate had just motives for wishing that a doctrine mingled with so many impure additions should not seize hold of the mind of Roman youth without discernment and without restriction. What did it do? The Senate began by confusing the true with the false, the good with the bad. It was an initial error that the government could not avoid, because it is neither part of its mission nor of its power to devote itself to the in-depth examination of any opinion. It can only understand the external side of things. The Senate, having looked at philosophy as a whole, was much more struck by its inconveniences than by its advantages: this had to be the case. The sophisms of Carneades, who gloried in the contemptible talent of indiscriminately attacking the most opposite opinions, and spoke in public sometimes for and sometimes against justice, had to produce a very unfavorable impression of a hitherto unknown science. Accordingly, the Senate proscribed all Greek philosophy.

Thus in the first place, based on misleading appearances, the Senate rejected the only thing which, especially during a period when mores were being corrupted, could recall Romans to the love of freedom, truth, and virtue. Cato the Elder, who decided on the proscription of Greek philosophy, did not imagine that a century after him that same philosophy, better examined and better known, would be the sole shelter of his grandson against the betrayals of fortune and the haughty clemency of Caesar.

In the second place, the rigorous measures against Greek philosophy taken by the Senate did nothing but prepare a triumph for it, which became all the more complete for all that it had been delayed. The delegates of Athens were hastily sent back to their country. Harsh edicts against all foreign doctrines were frequently renewed. All these were useless efforts, as the impetus had been given and the government's means could not stop it.

Let us now suppose that the Roman Senate had wanted neither to reform, nor repress, nor eradicate by force, and that it had intervened neither for nor against philosophy. What would have happened? The enlightened men of the capital of the world would have examined the new doctrine impartially. They would have separated the truths which it contained from the sophisms which had been introduced into it, and they would have decided in favor of those truths. Certainly, it was not difficult to show that the arguments of Carneades against justice were nothing but miserable quibbles. It was not difficult to awaken in the hearts of Roman youth the indelible feelings which are in the hearts of all men, and to raise indignation from these still fresh souls against a theory which, entirely consisting of ambiguities and chicaneries, the most simple analysis ought soon to have covered with ridicule and contempt. But this analysis could not be the government's work. The government should only make it possible by allowing free examination, because when free examination is prohibited, it nonetheless occurs, but it is carried out badly, with confusion, passion, resentment, and violence. People want to substitute edicts and soldiers for this examination. These means are convenient and seem infallible. They seem to combine everything—rapidity, facility, and dignity—and they have only a single flaw: that of never succeeding.

The young Romans preserved the sophists' speeches all the more stubbornly in their memory, as their persons seemed to have been taken away unjustly. They regarded Carneades' dialectic less as an opinion that needed to be examined than as property which needed to be defended, because they were threatened with having it taken away. The study of Greek philosophy was no longer a matter of simple speculation but, what seems much more precious at a stage of life when the soul is endowed with all the forces of resistance, a triumph over the government. Enlightened men of a more mature age, reduced to choosing between the abandonment of all philosophical studies or disobedience to the government, were forced into the latter party by the taste for literature, a passion which grows daily, because its pleasure is intrinsic to itself. Some followed philosophy into exile in Athens, others sent their children there, and philosophy, returning later from its banishment, had all the more influence because it came from further away and had been acquired with more effort.

Modern history furnishes an example which supports the lessons we draw from ancient history. I borrow the reflections of an impartial and moderate writer:

> The metaphysics of Aristotle was struck with anathema by that redoubtable power which bent passions and ideas, sovereigns and subjects under its yoke. It was against the unfeeling ashes of a philosopher dead for twenty centuries

> that the Council of Paris, under Philip the Fair, directed its thunderbolts, and this inert dust emerged victorious from the fight. The metaphysics of Alexander's tutor was more than ever adopted in the schools. It became the object of a religious veneration. It had its apostles, its martyrs, its missionaries, and the theologians themselves bent the dogmas of Christianity in order to reconcile them with the maxims of the Peripaticians. So irresistible is opinion's progressive march, that the civil, religious and political power is forced despite itself to follow, happy, in order to save appearances, to sanction what it sought to forbid and to put itself at the head of a movement that at first it tried to stop.[6]

Let us now abandon this question. Let us renounce the victory we think we have won. Let us suppose the success of the government against opinion probable or possible. Let us further suppose that the government is right, that opinion is wrong, that the former in fact was fighting for the truth, and that the latter was the party of error; and let us see, in this hypothesis, what would be the consequences of the triumph even of truth when imposed by power.

Truth's natural support is evidence. The natural route toward truth is reasoning, comparison, examination. To persuade a man that the evidence, or what appears to him to be the evidence, is not the only motive which should decide his opinions, and that reasoning is not the only road he ought to follow, is to falsify his intellectual faculties. It is to establish an artificial relationship between the opinion one presents him with and the instrument with which he should judge it. It is no longer according to the intrinsic nature of this opinion that he expresses his view, but according to extraneous considerations, and his intelligence is perverted as soon as it takes this direction. Suppose that the power which arrogates to itself the right of teaching the truth is infallible. It nonetheless uses means which are not consistent; it nonetheless denatures both the truth it proclaims and the intelligence to which it ordains its own renunciation.

M. de Montesquieu rightly said[7] that a man condemned to death by laws to which he has consented is freer politically than one who lives peacefully under laws instituted without the consent of his will. One can say with equal justice that the adoption of an error on our own, and because it seems to us

6. The text does not identify the author.—Trans.

7. *Spirit of the Laws*, bk. 12, chap. 12.

to be the truth, is an operation more favorable to the perfection of our mind than the adoption of a truth on the word of any authority whatsoever.[8] In the first case, we teach ourselves to examine. If this examination does not lead us to good results in a given set of circumstances, we are, however, going in the right direction. In persevering in our scrupulous and independent examination, we will sooner or later get there. But in the second supposition, we are no more than the toy of the authority before which we have subordinated our own judgment. Should the dominant authority make a mistake or find it useful to be mistaken, not only will we adopt its errors in the future, but we will not even know how to draw from the truths with which this authority has acquainted us the conclusions which ought to result from them. The surrender of our intelligence will have turned us into miserable, passive beings. The springs of our mind will have been broken. What strength remains to us will serve only to lead us astray.

A writer, gifted with remarkable penetration, observes on this subject that a miracle performed to demonstrate a truth will not produce any real conviction in the spectators, but will damage their judgment,[9] for no natural connection exists between a miracle and a truth. A miracle is not in any way the proof of an assertion, but a proof of strength. To ask for assent to an opinion by a miracle is to require that one accord to force what one should accord only to the evidence. It is to reverse the order of ideas, and want an effect to be produced by what cannot be its cause. I only apply this reasoning to political and moral ideas, but in this sphere it cannot be contested.

Morality is only composed of the connection between causes and effects. In the same way, knowledge of the truth is only composed of the chain of principles and consequences. Every time you break this chain, you destroy morality and falsify the truth. Everything which is imposed on opinion by authority cannot be useful and becomes harmful, truth as well as error. The truth is harmful then not as truth; it is harmful because it has not penetrated the human mind by the natural route.

People object that there is a class whose opinions can be nothing but prejudices, a class which, not having the time to think, can learn only what it

8. It is in this sense that I once said at the tribune: *Free error* is worth more than imposed truth. Those who complained about this phrase did not understand me; I would have been astonished if they had understood me.

9. Godwin, *Political Justice*.

is taught, a class which should believe what it is told, and which, unable to devote itself to examination, has no interest in intellectual independence. It is this ignorant class, it is said, whose opinion should be directed by the government while leaving complete freedom to the educated class.

But a government which arrogates to itself this exclusive right will necessarily demand to have its privilege respected. It will not want individuals, whoever they are, to act in a way different from its own. I concede that at first it hides this wish behind tolerant forms. Nevertheless, there will result some restraints from this: these restraints will be ever increasing. From preference for one opinion to disapproval for the opposite opinion is a gap that it is impossible not to cross.

This first disadvantage is the cause of a second. Educated men will not be slow to separate themselves from a government which harms them. This is in the nature of the human mind, especially when it is strengthened by meditation and cultivated by study. The action of even the best-intentioned government has something brutal and coarse about it, and it irritates a thousand delicate fibers which suffer and revolt.

It is therefore to be feared that if one gives the government the right to direct the opinion of the ignorant classes, even toward the truth, while separating this direction from all influence on the educated class, the educated class, which feels that opinion is its domain, will begin to struggle against the government. A thousand evils result from this. Hatred of a government which intervenes in what is not its domain can grow so great that when the government acts in favor of enlightenment, the friends of enlightenment will line up on the side of prejudice. As I have already recalled, we saw this bizarre spectacle at several moments during our Revolution. A government founded on the clearest principles and professing the soundest theories, but which by the nature of the means it employs alienates the cultivated class, will infallibly become either the most discredited or the most oppressive government. Often it will even combine these two categories, which seem to exclude one another.

For everything which has nothing to do with actual crimes, let us therefore cross out the words *repress*, *eradicate*, and even *direct* from the government's dictionary. For thought, for education, for industry, the motto of governments ought to be: *Laissez-faire et laissez-passer.*

End of the Commentary

# Index

This book is set in 10.5 on 14 Minion Pro, a typeface
designed for Adobe in 1990 by Robert Slimbach.
Minion is inspired by the highly readable typefaces
of the late Renaissance.

This book is printed on paper that is acid-free and
meets the requirements of the American National Standard
for Permanence of Paper for Printed Library Materials,
z39.48-1992. ♾

Book design by Erin Kirk New
Typography by Graphic Composition, Inc., Bogart, Georgia
Printed and bound by Thomson-Shore, Inc., Dexter, Michigan